Truly the primer for and advanced placement of a new paradigm within an existing organization. Best practices, as well as worst potholes to avoid, are explicitly detailed in this all important work on innovation. America's—indeed, the world's—future is innovation, and Govindarajan and Trimble get one to think outside the box.

—ALAN G. HASSENFELD, Chairman, Hasbro, Inc.

As many of us know from experience, it is a daunting challenge for established companies to breathe life into an entirely new business. Govindarajan and Trimble do a terrific job of pinpointing key factors that can turn potential into meaningful, sustained results.

—ROBERT W. LANE, Chairman, CEO and President, John Deere Company

Driving innovation is one thing for a start-up company—but it poses entirely different challenges for a large, established corporation. Govindarajan and Trimble not only map the differences but also provide a guidebook for managing strategic innovation that leverages the benefits, while discarding the baggage of being large and established.

—RICHARD J. HARRINGTON, President & CEO, The Thomson Corporation

Drawing on a series of case studies, Govindarajan and Trimble's fascinating new book explores the challenges corporations face while pursuing strategic innovation. At the heart of *Ten Rules for Strategic Innovators* is an actionable, systematic approach to business innovation. The authors offer fresh, compelling insights into the opportunities and perils of the innovation process. This book is essential reading for corporations and entrepreneurs alike.

—N. R. NARAYANA MURTHY, Chairman of the Board and Chief Mentor, Infosys Technologies, Ltd.

Successfully building innovative new businesses is the critical challenge for established companies that want to thrive. *Ten Rules* clearly outlines many of the roadblocks to building breakthrough businesses and creates a strong, practical framework for success. Through the novel concepts of forgetting, borrowing, and learning, Govindarajan and Trimble have developed a compelling, hands-on guide for business leaders driving growth.

—CHRISTINA L. SHEA, Senior Vice President, External Relations, and former President, New Ventures Division, General Mills, Inc.

Ten Rules for Strategic Innovators is a fabulous contribution to the literature on innovation and organizational competitiveness. Govindarajan and Trimble's research and synthesis of the dynamic-capability literature provide breakthrough insights for managers interested in deeply understanding the roots of innova-

tion and organizational change. Better yet, they couple their fresh ideas with a diverse set of detailed cases in which managers put these ideas into practice. This book will be of great value to both scholars and practitioners.

—MICHAEL L. TUSHMAN, Paul R. Lawrence MBA Class of 1942 Professor of Business Administration, Harvard Business School

An original and powerful book! The authors demystify the process of how promising, new ventures can fail or bring about breakthrough growth. This is one of the best books, if not the best, on the management of innovation.

—WARREN BENNIS, Distinguished Professor of Business, USC, and coauthor, *Geeks and Geezers: How Era, Values and Defining Moments Shape Leaders*

The most difficult managerial challenge facing business leaders today is how to grow through innovation! This book offers us true thought leadership regarding this challenge, not the usual cookbook solutions! The authors emphasize the critical dilemmas at hand to achieving innovation-driven growth. The path-breaking research, so well reported, will provide guidance and inspiration to all those coping with the implementation of innovation and growth.

—PETER LORANGE, President and Nestlé Professor of Strategy, IMD International

Old dogs *can* learn new tricks. Govindarajan and Trimble tackle the toughest challenge in business: They show executives of established firms how to translate strategic dreams for growth into real business realities. A wise, insightful read.

—KATHLEEN M. EISENHARDT, S. W. Ascherman Professor of Strategy, Stanford University, and coauthor, *Competing on the Edge: Strategy as Structured Chaos*

TEN RULES FOR STRATEGIC INNOVATORS

Ten Rules for Strategic Innovators

From Idea to Execution

Vijay Govindarajan

Chris Trimble

Harvard Business School Press

Boston, Massachusetts

978-1-59139-758-8 (ISBN 13)

Library of Congress Cataloging-in-Publication Data
Govindarajan, Vijay.
    10 Rules for strategic innovators : from idea to execution / Vijay Govindarajan,
Chris Trimble.
       p. cm.
    ISBN 1-59139-758-8
    1. New business enterprises—Management. 2. Entrepreneurship. 3. Creative
ability in business. 4. Strategic planning. 5. New business enterprises—United
States—Case studies. I. Title: Breakthrough businesses within established
organizations. II. Trimble, Chris. III. Title.
    HD62.5.G68 2005
    658.4'06—dc22

                                                                    2005014230

The paper used in this publication meets the minimum requirements of the American National Standard for Information Sciences—Permanence of Paper for Printed
Library Materials, ANSI Z39.48-1992.

For six special women in my life: my mother, Padma;
my wife, Kirthi; my daughters, Tarunya and Pasy;
my sister, Bama; and my aunt, Raji.
— Vijay Govindarajan

For my parents, Henry and Sally; my sister, Leslie;
my wife, Lisa; and my son Roberto Henry.
— Chris Trimble

For Bill Achtmeyer, who so graciously and generously
supported this project in so many ways.
— VG and Chris

CONTENTS

PREFACE

IN JUNE 2000, the White House announced that the scientific community reached a momentous milestone—the complete mapping of the human genome. No other scientific field was growing as explosively as genomics. Researchers sought new knowledge about the genetic basis of life, particularly the genetic predictors of disease. They foresaw a revolution in medical therapies.

Even before this milestone, scientists experimented with partial strands of human DNA and with DNA of simpler organisms such as yeast. Because genomics research requires a staggering number of experiments, researchers wanted to automate and accelerate the process. A new industry sprouted in the 1990s to supply these scientists with DNA, reactants, sophisticated computational systems, and laboratory apparatus.

One critical apparatus was the DNA *microarray*, a small glass slide with thousands of microscopic DNA samples adhered to its surface. Unhappy with offerings from suppliers, many genomics researchers chose to "print" their own microarrays, but that introduced sources of error and wasted expensive senior researcher time.

Scientists at Corning saw an enticing business opportunity in offering genomics researchers a reliable, inexpensive supply of preprinted microarrays. Corning had accumulated great expertise in manufacturing sophisticated specialty glass products and could attach microscopic quantities of fluid to glass surfaces. From informal talks with others in the industry, the scientists at Corning believed that this step was the most difficult in producing DNA microarrays. Several Corning scientists encouraged the company's leaders to pursue this promising new market.

In 1998, during its annual strategic review process, Corning asked an outside consulting firm to evaluate several growth opportunities, including microarrays. The advisers encouraged investment because the market promised high growth and Corning was well positioned to capture it. Corning had a great idea and a great opportunity. It created a new division, Corning Microarray Technologies (CMT).

Where do such ideas originate? How can corporations generate more of them? Worthy questions, and ones well-studied. But generating a great idea is only the first step. Strategic innovators need more than a great idea. They need to move *from idea to execution*. Great idea in hand, those involved with CMT moved on to a quest that would bring both great expectations and excruciating frustrations.

This book is about adventure. We dedicate it to executives who take on what may well be the triple-flip-with-a-quadruple-twist of general management: leadership of a new high-growth-potential business inside an established organization. We also direct our message to CEOs and members of senior corporate staffs, who can greatly improve the odds of success.

For the past four years we have been on our own adventure, and the result is this book. We set out to learn how to design an organization that could build a breakthrough business while maintaining excellence in its existing one—an endeavor fraught with contradictions. We knew that we would not find any single company that did everything right, so we looked for best practices within each organization we studied. Drawing on in-depth interviews and archived documents, we compiled multiyear histories of innovative efforts at ten companies: Corning, The New York Times Company, Capston-White (not its real name), Analog Devices, Unilever, Cisco Systems, Hasbro, Nucor, Stora Enso, and the Thomson Corporation.[1] We supplemented our analysis with our previous research at Sun Microsystems, 3M, Wal-Mart, Southwest Airlines, and Encyclopedia Britannica; and we studied the case work of other scholars on such companies as Polaroid, General Motors, Intel, DuPont, R.R. Donnelly, Booz Allen Hamilton, and Lucent. Finally, we compiled examples from media accounts of Kodak, Microsoft, Disney, Oracle, Amazon.com, Philips, Porsche, Cargill, FedEx, Johnson & Johnson, Eli Lilly, Seagate, Procter & Gamble, and Visa.

With few exceptions, the endeavors of the dozens of executives we interviewed provided both the most exciting and the most anxiety-laden moments of their professional careers. In many interviews, executives conveyed powerful emotions: enthusiasm for new possibilities, disillusionment with needless barriers, satisfaction with ultimate fulfillment, or disappointment in defeat. No one—not even those executives who had failed and still struggled to comprehend what had happened and why—regretted his or her involvement. From their lasting energy, we drew our own.

We had a second motivation. Our research proceeded through a dark period for private enterprise. At the end of the dot-com era, seemingly overnight, media coverage of the business world went from glowing to glowering, from celebration of wild growth and unbridled innovation to castigation for poor governance and pervasive irresponsibility. So negative the coverage, it became all too easy to presume that the pursuit of profit and the pursuit of social good must be mutually exclusive.[2] Unfortunately, business leaders did little to reverse this misperception. They became so busy defending themselves or promoting their extracurricular community involvement that few articulated the primary mechanisms through which business improves society every day. Perhaps like you, surrounded by dim news, we needed to rediscover what is honorable and noble about business.

Companies simultaneously enhance society and increase profits in two ways, both involving innovation:

- They improve the productivity of existing work processes by increasing specialization, redesigning processes, investing in new equipment, and so on, and this enriches society as a whole in the long run. In total, society can consume no more than it produces. Therefore, the more we produce per person per day (the greater our productivity), the more we can consume per person per day— more health care, more education, more entertainment—our choice.

- They take risks to commercialize new products and services that meet previously unfulfilled needs. This also enhances society. Can you imagine your life without cellular telephones, ATMs, DVD players, personal computers, Internet search engines, and any number of sophisticated medical devices and noninvasive treatments?

Innovation is at the core of economic vitality.

It drives growth.

It creates jobs.

It builds wealth.

It gives employees new purpose.

It revitalizes organizations.

And, it enhances the lives of consumers through great new products and services.

Many grand stories of innovation showcase bold visionaries who launch their own companies from scratch to commercialize their inventions. But not all spectacular innovations can spring from garages or dorm rooms. Could a small start-up have assembled the requisite competence in specialty glass manufacturing to commercialize high-quality DNA microarrays? Probably not. This product, like many of the innovations studied here, could have come only from a large, resourceful organization.

We hope that this book improves your company's capacity to be a strategic innovator and to enhance society by commercializing valuable new products and services based on new business models.

Acknowledgments

THIS BOOK is an important personal milestone for both authors. We first met in 1994, when Chris was a student of VG's. We developed a strong mutual respect. Our paths diverged after Chris graduated, but fate brought us back together in 2000. Bill Achtmeyer, a special friend of Tuck's, generously provided the financial support needed to found the Center for Global Leadership. After being asked to direct the new research center, it did not take VG long to persuade Chris to join him.

Our collaboration has been strengthened by several shared beliefs, interests, and values. We believe that the best business school research has both rigor and relevance. We are inspired by ideas, but strive for ideas with impact. We want both to advance theory and to advance solutions to problems that real managers face in real companies. We believe that refining the art of management is important because companies are a powerful positive force for the greater good, and have potential to achieve much more. Finally, we are both passionate about the central research question addressed in this book: How can established companies convert breakthrough ideas into breakthrough growth?

At the time we initiated this research, we did not foresee the tremendous energy that our partnership would generate. We both worked long hours, pushed each other hard, and had many pointed, take-no-prisoners debates which forced us to refine, sharpen, and rethink, advancing far beyond what either of us could have achieved alone. Our mutual respect, mutual trust, and lasting friendship sustained us. Above all, we had a great deal of fun working on this project and writing this book.

That said, we could not have completed this book without numerous contributions from a great many people. To address the challenges of building breakthrough businesses within established organizations, we built on the intellectual heritage and scholarly contributions of researchers in strategy, leadership, organizational design, knowledge management, innovation, organizational learning, management control systems, technology, organizational change, entrepreneurship, and others.

In this constellation of academic fields, our work lies at the intersection of strategy, innovation, and execution. In strategy, we benefited from the pioneering work of Rich D'Aveni, Sumantra Ghoshal, Ranjay Gulati, Don Hambrick, Gary Hamel, Chan Kim, Costas Markides, Margie Peteraf, Henry Mintzberg, Mike Porter, C. K. Prahalad, Brian Quinn, Harbir Singh, and Ed Zajac. In innovation, we gratefully acknowledge such thought leaders as Gautam Ahuja, Phil Anderson, Bob Burgelman, Clay Christensen, Peter Drucker, Kathy Eisenhardt, Ian MacMillan, Mike Tushman, and Andy Van de Ven. Finally, in execution, we benefited greatly from the work of Bob Anthony, Chris Argyris, Warren Bennis, Syd Finkelstein, Jay Galbraith, Anil Gupta, Charles Handy, John Kotter, Paul Lawrence, Jim March, and Jeff Pfeffer.

We received funding for this project from the William F. Achtmeyer Center for Global Leadership. We wholeheartedly thank Bill Achtmeyer for his generous spirit and personal friendship. We also thank Dean Paul Danos of the Tuck School, whose intellectual and institutional support fueled our efforts.

Dozens of busy executives shared their thoughts and observations with us. We thank those who opened doors for us at their corporations: at Corning, Peter Volanakis and Tom Hinman; at New York Times Digital, Martin Nisenholtz; at Hasbro, Alan Hassenfeld and Al Verrecchia; at Analog Devices, Ray Stata and Jerry Fishman. We also thank Dave Shaffer and Bob Cullen at the Thomson Corporation, Amir Hartman and Craig Legrande at Cisco Systems, Bob Leach at Stora Enso, and M. S. Banga at Hindustan Lever for enabling us to complete additional case studies that informed our conclusions. We also thank the CEOs and senior executives who participated in the Center for Global Leadership's CEO leadership summits, an invaluable forum for exchanging ideas related to this book: Glenn Britt (CEO, Time Warner Cable), Eric Bourdais de Charbonnaire (chairman, Michelin), Robert Louis-Dreyfus (former chairman, adidas), Peter Dolan (CEO, Bristol-Myers Squibb), Michael Dolan (former CEO, Young & Rubicam), John Foster (Managing Director, HealthPoint LLC), Peter Francis (CEO, J.M.

Huber), Jukka Harmala (CEO, Stora Enso), Dick Harrington (CEO, Thomson Corporation), Russ Lewis (CEO, The New York Times Company), Narayana Murthy (chairman, Infosys), Dave Shaffer (CEO, Thomson Learning), and John Thornton (president and COO, Goldman Sachs). We also benefited greatly from several prominent speakers at the Tuck School who discussed the book's ideas with us: Meg Whitman (CEO, eBay), John Pepper (chairman, Procter & Gamble), Orit Gadeish (chairman, Bain & Company), Indra Nooyi (president, PepsiCo), and John Morgridge (chairman, Cisco Systems).

In addition, we received intelligent and inspirational feedback from our editors. Kirsten Sandberg at Harvard Business School Press contributed numerous outstanding insights. We also thank Lorraine Anderson, Jody Larson, and Susan Catterall Francis for their expertise in preparing this manuscript.

We would be lost without the administrative support of Kristy Snow, who anticipates our every need. Effective and efficient, she is everything we could possibly want in an assistant, and we thoroughly enjoy working with her.

We hope that you share our enthusiasm for building breakthrough businesses within established organizations, and we welcome your comments. You can reach us by e-mail. Vijay's address is vg@dartmouth.edu and Chris's is chris.trimble@dartmouth.edu.

INTRODUCTION

K NOWLEDGE of the genetic code is knowledge of the fundamental rules that guide human behavior. Geneticists now seek a new code for an organism immune from disease, even resistant to the aging process itself.

Similarly, management researchers seek an *organizational* code—a set of rules that can reduce dysfunctions, sustain growth, and lengthen the average corporate life span beyond that of a human being. The code will have to enable *strategic innovation*: a process of exploring experimental strategies.[1]

Strategic innovation involves testing new, unproven, and significantly different answers to at least one of the three fundamental questions of strategy: who is your customer? What is the value you offer to the customer? How do you deliver that value?[2] In this introduction, we describe and demystify strategic innovation and underscore its criticality in an organization's survival and success.

What Is Strategic Innovation?

Today's marketplace is characterized by rapid and nonlinear change.[3] New digital technologies are transforming the service sector. Nanotechnology and genetic engineering are revolutionizing the pharmaceutical and semiconductor industries. Formerly distinct industries such as mass media entertainment, telephony, and computing are converging. Globalization of commercial networks and infrastructures is turning emerging economies like those of India and China into powerhouses.

Customers everywhere are empowered, and their needs are changing rapidly as they live longer in the developed world and live better in the developing world. Such changes affect new industries and old, high-tech and low-tech, manufacturing and services.

As a result, executives find themselves continually reinventing their strategies; the underlying assumptions are no longer valid, and rivals have steadily copied away any competitive advantage. Consider how the following well-known companies have responded—by fundamentally redefining their customer, the value offered, and the delivery method—through strategic innovation:

- In the mid-1990s, General Motors formed a new business unit, OnStar, to commercialize an integrated information, safety, and communications system for some GM vehicles. The leaders visualized a wide range of functionality. In an accident, the system would automatically alert emergency services. At any time, drivers could make hands-free cellular calls, get directions from a built-in mapping and satellite positioning system, and contact an OnStar service center to request emergency assistance, track a stolen vehicle, remotely unlock doors, or access a variety of conveniences, such as making reservations or locating a nearby restaurant.[4]

- In 2001, Procter & Gamble launched Tremor, a new marketing service for other corporations. Seeking more effective marketing mechanisms for its own products, P&G had experimented with systematic approaches to generating word-of-mouth referrals. The company had invented methods for identifying talkative opinion leaders within groups of teenagers, based in part on how they used the Internet. P&G then encouraged these leaders to try products, discuss them with friends, and distribute coupons and samples to anyone interested. In two years, P&G had built a marketing army of more than two hundred thousand teens. When P&G recognized that it could provide other companies with access to this network for a fee, it launched Tremor.[5]

- In 2003, the Walt Disney Company introduced Moviebeam, a wireless set-top box that served as an automatic, no-hassle, in-home video rental store. The system allowed users to select from as many as a hundred movies on any given night; this selection was replenished at a rate of ten new movies per week. Subscribers paid a monthly fee plus a per-movie charge. The offering competed with traditional video stores, new on-demand services of cable companies, and DVD rental services through the mail.[6]

Strategic innovation can redefine potential customers; one example is Canon's pioneering focus in the 1970s on the development of photocopiers aimed at small businesses and home offices rather than large corporations. Strategic innovation also can reconceptualize delivered customer value, as in IBM's shift from selling hardware and software products to selling complete solutions in the 1990s. Or strategic innovation can redesign the end-to-end value chain architecture, as in Dell Computer's direct sales model, introduced in the 1980s.

Strategic innovation proceeds with *strategic experiments*—high-growth-potential new businesses such as OnStar, Tremor, and Moviebeam—that test the viability of unproven business models. Strategic experiments have ten common characteristics (see figure I-1):

- They have very high potential for revenue growth (e.g., 10× over three to five years).

- They target emerging or poorly defined industries created by nonlinear shifts in the industry environment.[7]

- They are launched before any competitor has proven itself and before any clear formula for making a profit has emerged.

- They depart from the corporation's proven business definition and its assumptions about how businesses succeed. GM moved from selling automobiles to offering services, a different value proposition requiring an unfamiliar set of business processes to deliver that value. Procter & Gamble shifted from consumer products to business services, a new customer base and unproven technology for delivering value. And Disney augmented its content production with new direct-to-consumer distribution, a change in all three elements of the business definition.

- They leverage some of the corporation's existing assets and capabilities in addition to capital; they are not simply financial investments.

- They require the corporation to develop some new knowledge and capabilities.[8]

FIGURE I-1

Ten characteristics of strategic experiments

1. High revenue growth potential
2. Focus on emerging or fuzzy industries
3. Test an unproven business model
4. Radical departure from existing business
5. Use of some existing assets and competencies
6. Development of new knowledge and capabilities
7. Discontinuous rather than incremental value creation
8. Great uncertainty across multiple functions
9. Unprofitable for several quarters or more
10. No clear picture of performance early on

- They revolutionize the definition of a business rather than enhance performance within the proven business definition through product line extensions, geographic expansions, or technological improvements.

- They involve multiple dimensions of uncertainty across multiple functions. Potential customers may be mere possibilities. Value propositions are often only guesses, because customers themselves have not figured out exactly what they want. And the processes and technologies for delivering products or services are often unproven. The unanswered questions in our examples included, for example, which of many possible services would OnStar's customers value most? How well would Tremor compete against traditional mediacentric approaches to marketing? How would movie-distribution technologies evolve and affect Moviebeam's viability? No amount of research could have resolved these mammoth uncertainties before launch.

- They remain unprofitable for several quarters or more and thus are too expensive to repeat. You get only one chance.

- They are difficult to evaluate. Feedback is delayed and ambiguous, and leaders may not know for several quarters whether they are succeeding or failing.

As you will see, strategic experiments benefit from being organized as separate business units within the corporation. Let us call the strategic experiment "NewCo" and the most closely related established business unit "CoreCo."[9]

Not All Innovations Are Equal

There is no shortage of published ideas on how best to manage innovation. Empower employees. Encourage initiative. Cultivate risk taking. Overcome mindlessness such as, "We do it this way because it has always been done this way." But managers need more than such generic advice because there are many different kinds of innovation, and each requires a profoundly different managerial approach.

This book focuses strictly on strategic innovation, which differs sharply from three other categories of innovation:[10]

- *Continuous process improvement* involves countless small investments in incremental process innovations. General Electric excelled at this pattern of innovation through its well-known six sigma program.

- *Process revolutions* also improve existing business processes, but in major leaps—say, a 30 percent increase in productivity—through the implementation of major new technologies. For example, Wal-Mart is investing heavily in "smart tags" (radio frequency identification, or RFID, tags), which identify what a product is, where it is, where it has been, how it has been handled, and so on. The technology may revolutionize processes for tracking consumer products from production to consumption and yield dramatic new supply chain efficiencies.

- *Product* or *service innovations* are creative new ideas that do not alter established business models. Consumer products companies such as toy and game manufacturers excel in this type of innovation and are constantly priming developers for the next Cabbage Patch doll, Tickle Me Elmo, or Razor scooter.

- *Strategic innovations*, such as OnStar, Tremor, and Moviebeam, are the subject of this book. They may include innovations in process or product but always involve unproven business models.

Innovative strategies alone—without changes to either the underlying technologies or the products and services sold to customers—drive the success of many companies, such as IKEA and Southwest Airlines.

The four types of innovation require different managerial approaches, because they differ along three important dimensions: the expense of a single experiment, the time frame over which results become apparent, and the ambiguity of results (see table I-1).[11] For example, a single process improvement is inexpensive, and its effects are quickly evident and measurable against past operational performance. Process revolutions cost more and take longer. Major product or service innovations, even those that retain the proven business model, generally involve more capital still—enough that a string of failures could sink a corporation—and results may remain uncertain for several quarters. Strategic innovations generally require the greatest investments over the longest time periods, and results can remain indecipherable for years.

These differences in expense, time frame, and uncertainty factor in to such decisions as who should lead and participate in an innovation initiative, how resources should be allocated, how progress should be assessed, when the plug should be pulled, and so on.

TABLE I-1

Defining characteristics of four different types of innovation

Innovation type	Expense of single experiment	Length of each experiment	Ambiguity of results
Continuous process improvement	Smallest	Shortest (could be days)	Clearest
Process revolution			
Product/service innovation			
Strategic innovation	Largest	Longest (could be years)	Most ambiguous

By choosing to focus on strategic innovation, we are not implying that other forms of innovation must stop. Leaders cannot allow New-Co's youthful quest for an entirely new future to cast CoreCo as an aging dinosaur. NewCo's future is uncertain, and CoreCo is the foundation. CoreCo must always strive to reinvigorate itself through continuous process improvements, process revolutions, and new product and service launches. For example, the remarkable turnaround of McDonald's resulted from new CEO James Cantalupo's emphasis on refreshing its core business. By March 2004, the stock price had more than doubled from its nadir in March 2003, two months after Cantalupo's arrival.[12]

We choose to focus on strategic innovation because the long-term survival of a company depends on it more than ever before, and because it is perhaps the most devilishly difficult and most enigmatic management challenge.

The Strategic Innovation Imperative

Given the list presented earlier of characteristics of strategic experiments, why would a company try something so risky, demanding, and complex?[13] As a business ripens, growth inevitably becomes more difficult.[14] The growth potential of any business model eventually decays.

Of course, Wall Street investors and analysts still demand double-digit growth rates from almost every company. Without growth, stocks perform dismally and CEOs lose their jobs. Without growth, employees stagnate and careers stall. Organizations themselves grow stale, and their competitiveness suffers.

What can managers do? They can buy their way to growth through bold acquisitions, but that strategy rarely benefits investors, customers, or employees in the long run.[15] Generating growth from within—organic growth—is the more robust and more difficult strategy. As companies age and industries mature, growth within established markets comes only at the expense of other entrenched competitors, and it is never easy to buy market share. Therefore, strategic innovation soon becomes the most attractive option (see figure I-2). Developing this competence is critical. Companies that successfully execute strategic innovation can deliver breakthrough growth and generate entirely new life-cycle curves (see figure I-3).

FIGURE I-2

Options for growth

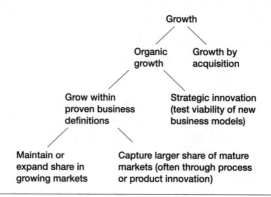

Companies that develop their capability for strategic innovation early in life delight investors with sustained growth and surprise competitors by changing the rules of the game. Most companies, however, are satisfied with their existing business models until they hit the growth wall and performance begins to suffer noticeably. Eventually, strategic innovation becomes a matter of life and death. After all, the same forces that create opportunities for breakthrough growth—nonlinear change in the economic environment—can also shake the foun-

FIGURE I-3

Strategic innovation can deliver breakthrough growth

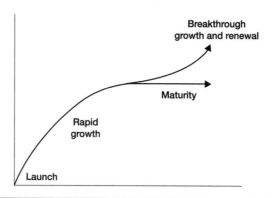

dations of an industry (see figure I-4). In such an unpredictable environment, all glory is fleeting.

To be sure, nonlinear change affects each industry differently. Jukka Harmala, CEO of Stora Enso, an international paper corporation, told us, "People have been predicting the end of the paper industry for decades. You've heard of the 'paperless office,' but have you seen one?" Fair enough. But the chief executive who dismisses the threat of a revolution walks a perilous path. Even two years after the dot-com bubble burst, Kodak announced what it termed a "historic shift" in strategy that boosted investment in internal ventures in digital photography while increasing the rate at which it phased out its traditional film business. A faster-than-anticipated acceleration in consumers' transition from film to digital photographs motivated this decision.[16] Sun Microsystems, once a high-flying technology company with a well-performing high-end hardware business, now looks nervously in several directions, particularly software, for its next source of high growth.

Through cycles of boom and bust, a fundamental truth endures: change is constant—and often nonlinear. Financial markets are misleading, because change does not alternate between periods of hyperactivity and inertness. Through strategic innovation, corporations can not only stay ahead of change, they can create change. They can pile new successes on existing ones. They can consistently create, grow, and profit from new business models.

FIGURE I-4

Nonlinear change creates high-growth opportunities but also can threaten established business

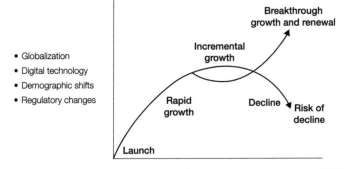

A New Frontier in the Science of Management

As essential as it is to the long-term health of organizations, knowledge about best practices for managing strategic innovation is scarce. For every strategic experiment studied, we observed a unique approach to management. There is no commonly accepted principle or standard.

Management theory has evolved rapidly over the past few decades. For example, the once-popular notion that the essence of strategy is to maintain stability has given way to acceptance that stability is illusory. Modern strategists do not seek to build and defend a competitive advantage from change by, say, erecting barriers to entry. Instead, they recognize that to stay ahead, corporations must always look for new markets and new sources of competitive advantage.[17]

This shift in emphasis in strategy formulation demands a similar shift in the field of strategy execution, but the latter field lags. Although the *what* of strategy now focuses on innovation and change, knowledge of the *how* is still nascent.[18]

In part, the reason for the slow accumulation of knowledge in this area is that it requires difficult and expensive research. Study of *which* strategies to choose can proceed with largely quantitative and statistical techniques, but the utility of using such methods to approach the *how* of strategy is limited. The management of innovation is a rich and complex problem. Statistical studies can point in only a few broad directions. They can tell us something about which management decisions correlate with success, but little about why.

Truly understanding what works and why requires multiyear, qualitative, interpretive study. The study of strategic innovation resembles history or psychology more than finance or economics. Furthermore, the little existing research-based knowledge emphasizes the very early stages of managing strategic innovation, particularly the generation of and evaluation of creative ideas. That leaves much terrain uncharted.

If research-based knowledge about managing strategic innovation is limited, then how much can actual managers know? Practitioners will always have better understanding of certain areas of human endeavor than researchers will, especially when practitioners develop a deep, intuitive understanding through repetition. What scientist understands how to hit a baseball better than Alex Rodriguez?

But practitioners of strategic innovation have few opportunities for repetition because each attempt takes at least a few years. Only a handful of the people in our study had participated in a strategic experiment even once before, in part because many corporations bet on them only sporadically. Early in life, many companies conclude that all their resources must support the growth and expansion of the existing business. Senior executives defer strategic experiments until growth declines. When times are better than expected, executives ask, "Why take the risk?" When times are tough, they say, "We must focus all our energies on restoring our core business to good performance." With such inconsistent investment, deep knowledge about the management of strategic innovation cannot accumulate in any one organization.

Further, rarely do managers of strategic experiments return for an encore. Those who succeed ascend internally to bigger responsibilities (as measured by current revenues or employees under supervision), and those who fail often leave for opportunities elsewhere. Corporations large enough to fund entire divisions dedicated to supporting multiple strategic experiments would seem to be likely centers for the accumulation of experience on this topic, but these divisions are highly vulnerable to funding cuts during recessions.

If you are preparing to initiate, lead, or support a strategic experiment, consider the following:

- You may face this particular challenge only once in your career.

- Limits to innovation have less to do with technology or creativity than with management skill.

- Few people, if any, within your organization can guide you from their direct experience.

You can, however, learn from the wrenching experiences of many others in various organizations and industries. That is what this book offers.

Chapter One

WHY STRATEGIC INNOVATORS NEED A DIFFERENT APPROACH TO EXECUTION

HERE IS A SEQUENCE of events that is familiar to us from our research and may be familiar to you as well: a CEO announces that the strategic imperative for next year is breakthrough growth. Incremental growth from incremental initiatives is no longer enough. To continue to thrive, the company must do new things. It must break all the rules. It must redefine the industry.

The CEO brings in motivational speakers and experts on innovation to inspire the troops, create the right conversations, and get the creative juices flowing. The company establishes a committee to review preliminary ideas for new growth opportunities. Dozens are submitted, and a handful are selected for further research. Business plans are written. One plan in particular looks most promising.

The CEO examines the chosen project from every angle. Many reasonable proposals are competing for the firm's capital, but none has the chance to reinvigorate growth like this one. The CEO hires an outside expert and receives confirmation that the high-growth-potential business looks like a winner. Now it's a done deal. The CEO commits to the plan, assigns the best available general manager to lead the strategic experiment, and asks a member of the senior corporate staff to shepherd it.

Then the CEO makes a big mistake.

The CEO moves on to other matters. The new business, after all, is only a tiny fraction of a multibillion-dollar organization.

How to Fail at Strategic Innovation

Asked to think about the challenges of *innovation*, most managers think first of the creative, brilliant, and inspired soul who sees the future in a different way—a rebel on a mission. This romance is deeply embedded in our business culture.

The CEO's mistake lies in buying in to the romance. The error is in assuming that the company has already hurdled the most difficult barriers to innovation: finding a great idea and a great leader. In fact, the biggest challenges are still to come.[1] Our research has shown that strategic experiments face their stiffest resistance once they are showing signs of success, consuming more resources, and clashing with CoreCo at multiple levels.

Ideas get you only so far. Consider companies that have struggled when their competitors have redefined the industry. Why did Xerox and Sears continue to struggle even after the genius behind Canon's personal copiers and Wal-Mart's new everyday-low-price discount retailing format was apparent to everyone? It's because the leaders of any groundbreaking new business must not only identify the big idea but also (1) attract funding, (2) learn quickly from success and failure, (3) rally people around a fuzzy view of the future, (4) reorganize to leverage the lessons learned, and (5) manage expectations of performance amid chaos.

Tendencies within established organizations present additional barriers. In addition to the five challenges just mentioned, the leader must also (1) protect funding for NewCo regardless of the performance of CoreCo, (2) establish new organizational norms and policies that make sense for NewCo, (3) overcome tensions between NewCo and CoreCo when those norms and policies conflict, (4) effect changes in the existing power structure required to support NewCo, (5) engage CoreCo employees in supporting NewCo, and (6) recruit talented CoreCo managers to work within NewCo.[2] The degree of managerial difficulty is very high.[3]

Hoping to shed some light on these challenges, researchers have studied the role of the leader of NewCo. The tenor of Gifford Pinchot's book *Intrapreneuring: Why You Don't Have to Leave the Corporation to*

Become an Entrepreneur typifies their findings. The author lists the following "Intrapreneur's Ten Commandments":

1. Come to work each day willing to be fired.

2. Circumvent any orders aimed at stopping your dream.

3. Do any job needed to make your project work, regardless of your job description.

4. Find people to help you.

5. Follow your intuition about the people you choose, and work only with the best.

6. Work underground as long as you can—publicity triggers the corporate immune mechanism.

7. Never bet on a race unless you are running in it.

8. Remember it is easier to ask for forgiveness than for permission.

9. Be true to your goals, but be realistic about the ways to achieve them.

10. Honor your sponsors.[4]

Certain ingenious, creative, and highly determined souls can doubtless overcome both the long odds facing any strategic experiment *and* the organization fighting them at every turn, but these people are rare. Organizations are almost always more powerful than individuals. Corporations that truly want to build the capacity for strategic innovation cannot simply hope for a few good "intrapreneurs" to save the day on their own initiative.[5]

Research has also called for leaders of strategic experiments to appoint a senior executive *champion*—someone who actively musters support for NewCo and breaks down barriers in CoreCo. Such an effective champion can surely help, but the odds of success are still low. For example, Polaroid created a business that focused on commercializing services that enhanced vacation experiences with photography.[6] The leader of NewCo had all the right stuff: boundless energy, an ability to excite others enough to contribute after hours, an attitude in sync with Pinchot's "Ten Commandments," and an especially dedicated senior executive champion. Nonetheless, she could neither secure an unflinching commitment from the top nor uproot the belief that the company should co-opt and reconstitute NewCo as a new marketing mechanism for CoreCo. We cannot know whether that strategic experiment would have succeeded even in the best possible organizational setting—but CoreCo never gave it a realistic chance.

Simply put, strategic experiments are likely to fail if the company relies solely on the heroism of a hypertalented individual, even one who has a great idea, is backed by a gifted senior executive champion, and faithfully follows ten commandments of intrapreneurship. Instead, companies need to build organizations based on the ten rules we develop in this book.

Creativity and Execution

Many companies have attempted to alter their organizational codes to accelerate innovation. But in doing so, they have focused mostly on creativity—generating ideas—and little on execution—converting ideas to results. In fact, we asked hundreds of executives in *Fortune* 500 companies to rate their companies' innovation skills on a scale of 1 to 10, where 1 represents minimal skill and 10 represents mastery. Survey participants overwhelmingly believe that their companies are far better at generating good ideas (giving this skill a score of at least 5 or 6) than they are at determining what to do with them (giving scores as low as 1 or 2).

We think of an organization's capacity for innovation as the product of creativity and execution. We say "product" and not "sum," because if either creativity or execution is zero, then capacity for innovation is also zero.

Some quick math: which is more effective—lifting your creativity score from 6 to 7, or doubling your execution score from 1 to 2? Nonetheless, most companies, when hoping to improve innovation, focus on generating ideas. Managers obsess over the front end of the innovation process. But the real leverage is in the back end—in execution.

Interestingly, we are touching on an age-old question: which matters more—a great strategy or great execution? In the context of innovation, the case for execution is strong.[7] The value of the strategy (the value of the innovative idea) is limited, simply because it is speculative and uncertain. Even a well-researched business plan includes a great deal of guesswork. It is not the idea that counts; it is what you do with it.

The Mystery of the Middle

If ideas are only a beginning and if organizations are more powerful than people, then what is the *organizational code* that enables a company to excel at turning breakthrough ideas into breakthrough growth?

Companies that focus on creativity often adopt an *anticode*: they break all the rules in the belief that creative organizations have little in common with disciplined, efficient ones. There is some validity to this notion.

To be efficient (code A)	*To be creative (code B)*
• You stick to your knitting.	• You think outside the box.
• You exploit what you know.	• You explore what you don't know.
• You meet current customer needs.	• You anticipate future customer needs.
• You plan.	• You let things emerge.
• You demand accountability.	• You allow freedom and flexibility.
• You impose process and structure.	• You avoid process and encourage unstructured interaction.

Code A encourages discipline. Code B encourages creativity. In most companies, code A is mainstream, and code B is counterculture. In our observations of breakthrough new businesses, clashes between the two were pervasive. Inevitably, CoreCo believes that code A delivers results and that NewCo must soon deliver results, too. NewCo, on the other hand, sees that it needed code B to get started and wants to stick with it. Both sides are passionate. The debate dominates meetings and defines the agenda.

Such struggles are unproductive. To see why, consider that every innovation story has a beginning, a middle, and an end. Great companies are masters of efficiency—code A. That helps, but efficiency is not needed until the *end* of the innovation process. Most companies also understand that creativity is in many ways the opposite of efficiency. That is also good, but creativity is the dominant priority only at the *beginning* of the innovation process.

In the middle, most companies are lost. They do not understand the code for turning breakthrough ideas into breakthrough growth. Because they are lost, they gnash their teeth over the stark contrasts of the two organizational codes that they understand: A and B, code and anticode. But during NewCo's awkward adolescence, neither creativity nor efficiency is the dominant priority. The need for creativity declines after you have a business plan, and focusing on efficiency is premature until the business is proven and stable.

So the question is, what is the nature of the journey from business plan to profitability? From creativity to efficiency? What kind of organization can excel in the *middle* of the innovation process?

Let's call it code X. We dedicate the rest of this book to revealing the ten rules of code X that will help you turn mere concepts into breakthrough growth. First, recognize that code X is not simply a mix of A and B; code A may be black, and code B white, but code X is *not* gray.

Code X must address the three unique challenges that arise from the unnatural coexistence of a new and a mature business within the same corporation: a forgetting challenge, a borrowing challenge, and a learning challenge (see figure 1-1). NewCo must *forget* some of what made CoreCo successful. It must *borrow* some of CoreCo's assets— the greatest advantage NewCo has over independent start-ups. And it must be prepared to *learn* how to succeed in an emerging and uncertain market.

FIGURE 1-1

What is the nature of the transition between creativity and efficiency?

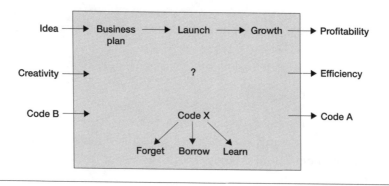

The Forgetting Challenge

Why must NewCo forget?[8] Executives usually repeat actions that they believe have produced success. If success continues, then not only individual executives but also entire organizations shift from consciously repeating these actions to unconsciously accepting them as correct. Soon, these assumptions are embedded not only in managers' minds but also in the relationships, processes, and communication patterns that make the organization tick. Even when organizations face failure, it is a struggle for them to reassess these deeply entrenched assumptions. They become orthodoxy.[9]

NewCo must forget three things. First, it must forget CoreCo's business definition. Strategy itself can become an orthodoxy, as answers to the basic questions that define a business—Who are our customers? What value do we provide? How do we deliver that value?—become second nature.[10] NewCo must have the freedom to answer these questions differently and even to pursue options that may cannibalize CoreCo revenues. Second, NewCo must recognize that a different business model requires different competencies. CoreCo's areas of expertise will not matter as much to NewCo as will the new competencies it must develop. Third, NewCo must forget CoreCo's focus on *exploitation* of a proven business model and shift to *exploration* of new possibilities.

For example, when GM created OnStar—its integrated automobile information, safety, and communications system—it had to forget all three. It had to adapt to a new business model; the communications services market demanded a much different value proposition and a much shorter product development process than did automaking. It had to build a new competency in information technology and make it preeminent within OnStar. And it had to systematically identify and eliminate unknowns rather than exploit a proven business.

The Borrowing Challenge

Consider the advantages that independent start-ups have over existing corporations. They can offer the possibility of tremendous wealth to the management team. They can move quickly, unhindered by the bureaucratic decision-making processes that sometimes debilitate large corporations. They also benefit from the advice of professional investors who understand the needs of new ventures. Further, they have no entrenched mind-sets to overcome. Independent start-ups have nothing to forget.

NewCo can compete effectively against start-ups only by *borrowing* CoreCo's assets: existing customer relationships, distribution channels, supply networks, brands, credibility, manufacturing capacity, and expertise in a variety of technologies—resources that start-up ventures can only dream of.[11]

In every strategic experiment we studied, part of the justification for making a risky investment was that there was some unique asset or capability that CoreCo could offer NewCo. Corning could help Corning Microarray Technologies (CMT) by sharing its existing facilities and its expertise in manufacturing processes that required precise control of tiny quantities of fluids. The New York Times Company offered New York Times Digital (NYTD), its Internet division, a well-respected brand in addition to the journalistic content it produced for the newspaper. Analog Devices lent its expertise in semiconductor manufacturing methods to its strategic experiment to commercialize a new technology for automotive crash sensors. In each case, NewCo had little chance if it failed to borrow.

Note that there is an important distinction between forgetting and borrowing. NewCo must forget *assumptions*, *mind-set*s, and *biases*. New-Co must borrow *assets*. That is, forgetting is about what goes on in your head. Borrowing is gaining access to resources with concrete value.

The Learning Challenge

In addition to forgetting and borrowing, NewCo must learn. The notion of organizational learning is a broad one, but in the context of strategic innovation its meaning is specific.[12] One learning curve matters more than any other for NewCo: improvement in its predictions of its business performance.

At the outset, such predictions are always wild guesses. For example, revenue forecasts for three years out are commonly off by a factor of 10. But as the management team learns, wild guesses become informed estimates and informed estimates become reliable forecasts (see figure 1-2).

FIGURE 1-2

The best indicator that learning is taking place is that predictions improve

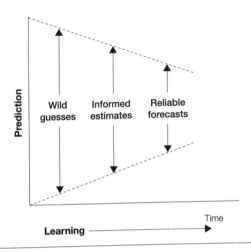

   This learning is crucial. The faster predictions improve, the faster NewCo will zero in on a working business model—or abandon a failed experiment. Fast learning minimizes time to profitability, lowers risk exposure, and maximizes the probability of a major victory over the competition.

   In learning to predict performance, NewCo proves or disproves theories about what can work. Initial theories are usually wrong. For example, Corning anticipated that mastering the steps in specialty glass manufacturing would be the most challenging part of manufacturing DNA microarrays, but it found much bigger challenges elsewhere. New York Times Digital initially expected to build a separate and independent newsroom for the new online medium but eventually found it unnecessary. Analog Devices anticipated that its new semiconductor technology would lead to the development of new markets in addition to automotive crash sensors, but only the automotive market proved economically viable. The faster these kinds of uncertainties are resolved, the sooner NewCo can put itself on a clear path to success.

   Note that a failure to forget cripples the learning effort. If NewCo cannot let go of CoreCo's success formula, it cannot discover its own.

An Organization's Inner Logic

Successful execution of strategic experiments requires more than a great leader. No single person is strong enough to address the real sources of the forgetting, borrowing, and learning challenges. The roots of these challenges lie deep within an organization's inner logic.

Every biological organism also has an inner logic that shapes its skills, abilities, and behaviors. That logic is written in its DNA, and it guides the organism in pursuing growth, in dealing with environmental stresses, and in overcoming diseases. For most people—molecular biologists excepted—DNA is invisible and mysterious, but our genetic inheritance has an enormous impact on who we are and what we do.

Organizational DNA is similar. It is not easily observable, and it determines the organization's collective skills, abilities, and behaviors. The difference between biological DNA and organizational DNA is that the latter can be manipulated by senior executives. Organizational DNA is not simply inherited at birth. Consciously or unconsciously, leaders select the rules embedded in organizational DNA. It can be changed, though not easily. It becomes entrenched early in an organization's life, and it can be changed only through a diligent and time-consuming effort by the senior team.

At the launch of a strategic experiment, however, senior executives have the unusual opportunity to create new organizational DNA from scratch. They can establish a unique set of rules for NewCo by copying most or none of CoreCo's DNA. This process demands careful consideration because DNA is extraordinarily powerful. In fact, it is the only force potent enough to overcome the challenges of forgetting, borrowing, and learning.

To be skilled at manipulating organizational DNA, senior executives must be aware of its elements. We find it helpful to separate these into four categories—staff, structure, systems, and culture—as summarized in figure 1-3.[13]

Executives should not underestimate the importance of organizational DNA. Consider these well-known companies, and the impact of just one element of organizational DNA:

- Staffing choices can create new areas of expertise. For example, Cisco acquires talented networking engineers by buying small technology companies.

FIGURE 1-3

The four elements of organizational DNA

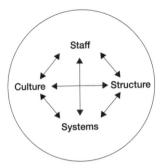

Staff	Leadership traits, staffing policies, competencies, promotion policies, career paths
Structure	Formal reporting structure, decision authority, information flows, task and process flows
Systems	Planning, budgeting, and control systems; business performance evaluation criteria, incentive and compensation systems
Culture	Notions about behaviors that are valued; embedded business assumptions; decision biases

- Structure shapes an organization's flexibility. For example, General Electric's decentralized structure enables it to serve markets as diverse as credit cards and nuclear reactors.

- Systems signal which dimensions of performance an organization values. For example, 3M's "30% rule" demands that 30 percent of revenues in any year come from new products.

- Culture establishes the values that employees aspire to. For example, "the credo" at Johnson & Johnson captures the central promise that the organization makes to each of its stakeholders.[14]

In the context of strategic innovation, organizational DNA matters because CEOs cannot be on call to solve every problem that NewCo faces. They cannot make every decision; instead, they must *shape* decisions by encoding assumptions, values, and decision biases into NewCo's DNA at the time it is created.

Staff includes attributes of leadership style along with policies for hiring, training, and promotion. When building NewCo, senior executives must decide who should lead. Entrepreneur or corporate executive? An insider who is politically connected within CoreCo, or an outsider who is more familiar with unique NewCo technologies? A general manager or a technical expert? A naive young executive who cannot imagine failure, or a seasoned executive who cannot risk failing and losing everything invested in reaching the top? Where should the remaining staff come from? It may be more convenient to transfer insiders, but only outsiders can bring in new expertise and new perspectives. Should outsiders fill NewCo's management posts, or only its operational jobs?

Structure includes the specification of formal reporting relationships, decision rights, information flows, and task flows. A key decision is whom the head of NewCo should report to. The functional manager within CoreCo who can help NewCo the most? The general manager of an existing business unit? Directly to the CEO? In any case, what roles should NewCo's boss be prepared to play? Should he simply set expectations and monitor results, or is the role more complex? What should the reporting structure within NewCo look like? Should it mimic the structure of other CoreCo business units? How and for what purpose should NewCo and CoreCo interact? Which should be the more powerful party in the interaction?

Systems include planning and budgeting processes, norms for evaluating business performance, selection of performance measures, and incentive systems. What expectations are reasonable for NewCo? To what extent can you hold NewCo's leader accountable for the results of an experiment? How often should you evaluate NewCo? On what basis? Which performance measures are most relevant? How similar are these measures to the ones used in CoreCo? How much should you invest in NewCo, and when? How often should you revisit NewCo's budget? What career and compensation incentives make sense for NewCo's leaders? If they are given the opportunity for large bonuses, what commensurate risks should they be exposed to?

Finally, *culture* includes shared notions about valued behaviors as well as embedded assumptions about what leads to success in business. Which assumptions that are deeply ingrained in CoreCo may not apply to NewCo? Which elements of CoreCo's culture might create barriers for NewCo, and how can you overcome this problem? How can you create a risk-taking, experimental culture within NewCo?

Organizational DNA and the Three Challenges

In analyzing each strategic experiment that we researched, we focused on the ability of NewCo to overcome the forgetting, borrowing, and learning challenges. Ultimate success for NewCo also depends on several other factors, but most of them are not controllable. For example, because strategy formulation in any nascent market involves a great deal of guesswork, luck plays a role. Among the controllable factors, however, we believe that organizational DNA is by far the most important.

When initiating a strategic experiment, executives must make difficult choices to give NewCo the DNA it needs. Because of everything that must be forgotten, NewCo's DNA must be very different from CoreCo's (see figure 1-4). For example, NewCo may need external hires to build new areas of expertise, whereas CoreCo emphasizes internal promotion. NewCo may use a flat organizational structure and encourage unstructured interaction, whereas CoreCo prefers more hierarchy and formal reporting. NewCo may emphasize experimenting and learning, while CoreCo demands accountability to plans. NewCo may encourage risk taking, whereas CoreCo seeks a more conservative culture.

But giving NewCo a unique DNA can lead to resistance. Corporate executives who have played by the rules to work their way up a career ladder in CoreCo will resent changes in routines for such things as establishing organizational hierarchy, assigning staff, granting promotions, allocating resources, providing incentive compensation, or evaluating

FIGURE 1-4

All four elements of NewCo's DNA must differ from CoreCo's

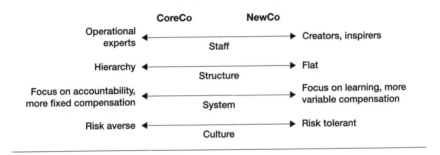

business performance. Therefore, in creating NewCo, CEOs must be prepared to make unpopular choices, and they must avoid making the choices that are easiest and most convenient.

CEOs who aren't willing to make difficult choices will simply replicate CoreCo's DNA for NewCo. This makes it hard for NewCo to surmount the forgetting challenge, because it remains immersed in CoreCo's assumptions, values, and decision biases. It also makes it difficult to learn, because CoreCo's culture and management systems are designed to exploit a proven business and not to experiment with a new one. When NewCo's DNA is the same as CoreCo's, NewCo is effective only at borrowing. It overcomes only one of the three challenges.

Other CEOs may be willing to create a unique DNA for NewCo but become preoccupied with the conflicts and tensions that result at points of interaction between NewCo and CoreCo. For example, CoreCo understands existing customers, but NewCo must be attentive to emerging customers. CoreCo is focused on efficiency, often through rigorous definition of processes, while NewCo must remain flexible and emphasize learning. And CoreCo is loath to prioritize the long-term needs of tiny NewCo over the immediate needs of its own, much bigger business. Not surprisingly, many of the executives we spoke to cited points of interaction between NewCo and CoreCo as critical trouble spots.

These conflicts lead to an urge to isolate NewCo from CoreCo, a step that some researchers have suggested.[15] But we maintain that this is an overreaction to legitimate concerns. An isolated NewCo may succeed at forgetting and learning but will not be able to borrow from CoreCo, because borrowing requires interaction. As mentioned earlier, an ability to borrow existing assets is the most important advantage that corporations have over independent start-ups.[16]

Neither replication nor isolation works. Replication facilitates borrowing, but not forgetting or learning. Isolation may allow forgetting and learning, but not borrowing.

Note that for other kinds of innovation initiatives (and not strategic experiments), replication or isolation can work. For example, a new product launch that does not alter the business model may succeed through replication; it need not forget. A strictly financial investment in a new business that is entirely unrelated to the core business may succeed through isolation; it need not borrow. But a strategic experiment must both forget and borrow (see figure 1-5).

FIGURE 1-5

Strategic experiments require a design that enables both borrowing and forgetting

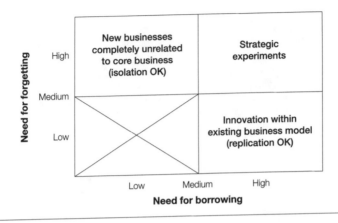

Indeed, strategic innovation demands a design that overcomes all three challenges. In the chapters that follow we will explore the specifics of such a design.[17]

In brief, you will see that NewCo can forget only by departing from CoreCo's organizational norms. NewCo must have its own DNA.[18] A common mistake is assuming that it's sufficient to have conversational awareness of the differences between NewCo's and CoreCo's business models. Forgetting, however, is about changing behavior. It is easy for NewCo to talk like NewCo but act like CoreCo. As you will see, there are powerful sources of organizational memory at work.

For NewCo to borrow, CEOs must establish a limited number of links between CoreCo and NewCo. They must then foster favorable conditions for cooperation between the two entities and carefully monitor their interactions. Figure 1-6 illustrates the tensions between forgetting and borrowing and shows how common design approaches fail to enable NewCo to meet both challenges.

Finally, for NewCo to learn, it needs unconventional planning systems tailored to the dynamic environment faced by strategic experiments. The planning approach must value learning over accountability, and it must ensure that disparities between predictions and outcomes

FIGURE 1-6

Common mistakes in designing NewCo

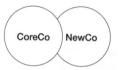

Design: Similar to CoreCo and closely integrated.

Problem: NewCo can borrow but cannot forget. NewCo inevitably tries to apply CoreCo's success formula in an environment where it is unlikely to work.

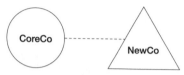

Design: Distinct from CoreCo and linked.

Problem: Senior management team not engaged in ensuring link is healthy. Cooperation disintegrates. Effort to borrow fails.

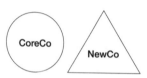

Design: NewCo is distinct from CoreCo and isolated from it.

Problem: NewCo can forget but cannot borrow. It cannot benefit from CoreCo's valuable assets.

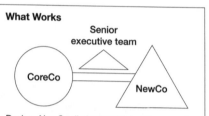

What Works

Design: NewCo distinct and linked in one or two high-leverage areas. Senior executives engaged in keeping links healthy and productive.

Result: NewCo forgets and borrows.

are analyzed quickly and dispassionately. Note that if NewCo struggles to forget, it will inevitably struggle to learn. It cannot find its own success formula if it remains bound to CoreCo's.

Table 1-1 briefly summarizes the three challenges and the methods for overcoming them.[19]

A Road Map for This Book

Later chapters analyze the stories of several strategic experiments. Although we write about U.S.-based corporations in this book, strategic innovation is relevant in all corners of the global economy. In fact, the forces of nonlinear change may be strongest in emerging economies. Because they are not tied to past investments, some industries in emerging economies can leapfrog directly from past to future. For example, several Latin American countries jumped straight to a cellular infrastructure rather than lay miles of wire in rural locations. And on-

TABLE 1-1

Overview of the three challenges

Challenge	Goal	Method
Forget	CoreCo has proven and stable answers to the questions of *what* its business is and *how* it wins. NewCo's answers are different. NewCo must *forget* CoreCo's success formula.	Conversational awareness of differences is not enough. Conversations are fleeting. To forget, the corporation must alter the established organizational design. NewCo must be distinct from CoreCo.
Borrow	NewCo has access to resources within CoreCo that independent start-ups can only dream of: manufacturing capacity, expertise, sales relationships, distribution channels, and much more. NewCo can gain critical competitive advantages if it can *borrow* these resources.	The senior management team must carefully select and closely supervise organizational links between NewCo and CoreCo. Careful: too much interaction between NewCo and CoreCo makes it extremely difficult to forget.
Learn	Whereas CoreCo's success formula is proven and stable, NewCo's is a guess. NewCo must *learn*. Specifically, NewCo must resolve the critical unknowns in its business plan and zero in on a working business model as quickly as possible.	NewCo needs a much different planning process than CoreCo—one that focuses on carefully resolving disparities between predictions and outcomes and emphasizes learning over accountability. Note that if NewCo cannot forget CoreCo's success formula, it will struggle to learn its own.

line education will likely take hold first in Asia, where escalating demand for higher education greatly outpaces the construction of new brick-and-mortar institutions.

We review high-growth-potential businesses that turned into financial successes and those that did not.[20] Venture capitalists expect only one breakthrough success for every ten investments in independent start-ups. Yet two of the five companies that we profile in this book overcame those long odds. Both are profitable, and both still have tremendous potential for growth.

Long before you can pronounce a strategic experiment a financial success or failure, you can observe how well it is succeeding in forgetting, borrowing, and learning. Our objective in reviewing each story is not only to tell what happened but also to explain why it happened and how each decision regarding organizational DNA either accelerated or constrained progress on the three challenges. Although we are sometimes critical, we were consistently impressed with the thoughtfulness and intelligence of the people we interviewed. We recognize that our interpretation benefits from both hindsight and the ability to compare experiences across multiple corporations.

We tackle each of the three challenges in two parts. First, we analyze the root causes that lead to problems associated with forgetting, borrowing, and learning. Second, we offer frameworks and specific recommendations for overcoming each challenge. In general, the chapters alternate between those devoted to understanding root causes and those that describe solutions.

There is one exception to this chapter layout. Our exploration of the root causes of problems associated with learning is more extensive than it is for forgetting or borrowing. Consequently, we dedicate three chapters to this task (see table 1-2).

We conclude by reducing the frameworks and recommendations throughout the book to ten rules for strategic innovators.

Here is a detailed summary of each chapter:

- Chapter 2, "Why Organizations, Like Elephants, Never Forget," continues the story of Corning Microarray Technologies and demonstrates how Corning's initial choice to replicate its existing DNA for CMT made it difficult for CMT to overcome the forgetting challenge.

- Chapter 3, "Taming the Elephant," describes how Corning subsequently changed CMT's organizational design. We explain why the revised approach was more successful, and we develop a framework that guides organizational choices so that NewCo effectively copes with the forgetting challenge.

TABLE 1-2

Road map for this book

	Forgetting	Borrowing	Learning
Understanding root causes	Chapter 2	Chapter 4	Chapters 6, 7, and 8
Developing solutions	Chapter 3	Chapter 5	Chapter 9

- Chapter 4, "Why Tensions Rise When NewCo Borrows from CoreCo," summarizes the development of New York Times Digital (NYTD), a business unit of The New York Times Company that provides online news and information services in multimedia format. We describe the difficult stresses that arose as NYTD discovered that it needed to assert its distinctiveness and independence while continuing to benefit from access to the resources of the *New York Times* newspaper.

- Chapter 5, "Turning Tension into a Productive Force," offers specific roles and responsibilities for a senior executive responsible for ensuring the effectiveness of six types of operational links between NewCo and CoreCo. NYTD is profitable and continues to grow because its organizational design allows forgetting and borrowing at the same time.

- Chapters 6–8 explore the root causes of learning difficulties. Chapter 6, "Why Learning from Experience Is an Unnatural Act," introduces key concepts and explains why learning is challenging. Chapters 7 and 8, "How Being Bold, Competitive, or Demanding Can Inhibit Learning," and "How Being Reasonable, Inspiring, or Diligent Can Inhibit Learning," show how the inevitable pressures associated with strategic experiments lead to well intentioned actions that disable the learning process by altering aspirations, expectations, and judgments about performance. Chapter 7 reviews the history of Hasbro Interactive, an ambitious initiative that targeted the video games market. Chapter 8 analyzes the development of a new services business at Capston-White (not its real name), a large information technology company.

- Chapter 9, "Finding Gold with Theory-Focused Planning," describes a solution for overcoming the barriers to learning described in chapters 7 and 8. TFP is an entirely different approach to planning and is much better suited than conventional planning approaches to the dynamic and uncertain environments faced by strategic experiments. This chapter describes six alterations executives should make to the planning process.

- Chapter 10, "The Ten Rules Explained," summarizes our advice as ten rules for strategic innovators. We introduce no new analysis or recommendations in this final chapter. Our vehicle for describing the ten rules is the story of Analog Devices and its effort to develop a new technology for automotive crash sensors. To commercialize the revolutionary crash sensors, the company's leadership team succeeded in overcoming all three challenges: forgetting, borrowing, and learning. As a result, the business is profitable and still has tremendous growth potential.

Chapter Two

WHY ORGANIZATIONS, LIKE ELEPHANTS, NEVER FORGET

A S SUGGESTED in chapter 1, NewCo can fail because it adopts the very habits that have made CoreCo successful. Ensuring that this does not happen is the essence of the forgetting challenge. This chapter explores the root causes of the forgetting problem by continuing the story of Corning Microarray Technologies (CMT).

Corning has a long history of successful innovation. One testament to this success is simply its age. In 2001 Corning celebrated its 150th birthday, having enjoyed a much longer life than the average corporation. Building on a number of breakthrough advances in scientific research, the company had reinvented itself many times. Nonetheless, Corning's revenues were only $6.2 billion in 2001.

One reason the company had not grown much larger was that it had divested mature divisions. It no longer produced, for example, lightbulbs or cookware, important products from earlier in its history. In this way, Corning remained focused on high-margin, technologically advanced products. By the 1990s Corning produced a wide range of specialty glass and ceramics products, including display glass for computers and televisions, ceramic substrates for automotive emissions control, and optical fiber for telecommunications networks.

Despite this history of success, Corning initially stumbled with CMT. It was unable to surmount the forgetting challenge because the senior management team replicated Corning's organizational DNA when it created CMT.

Corning's Stretch to Biotechnology

The need to forget arises because there is a mismatch between an opportunity and the organization that pursues it. Senior executives at Corning did not initially consider the forgetting challenge in these terms. If they had, what would they have seen? What would you have seen?

The Opportunity

Throughout the 1990s, researchers in the field of biotechnology focused on a mission: to understand much more about the meaning of the genetic code and to apply it in medicine. The apparent path to discovery could be described as brute force. Literally millions of experiments were needed, so automation was crucial. If machines could accelerate the rate of experimentation and computers could sift through the results, the time to new revolutions in medical therapies could be reduced.

Thus, rapid growth in experimentation created equally rapid growth in the markets for researchers' supplies and equipment, including DNA, reactants, laboratory apparatus, and specialized computers. One critical piece of experimental apparatus was the *DNA microarray*: a rectangular glass slide, a few inches long, on which hundreds of microscopic samples of DNA are adhered. With microarrays, along with several other exotic pieces of equipment, researchers could conduct hundreds of experiments at once.

The market opportunity appealed to many corporations. Genomics researchers needed a better solution, particularly, better choices for microarrays. Many researchers "printed" their own microarrays, a time-consuming process for senior researchers and one that inevitably introduced sources of error into experiments. Other researchers chose to purchase microarrays from a certain small biotechnology company. However, these were compatible only with that company's entire experimentation system, a system that, according to many researchers, left much to be desired.

Senior leaders at major biotechnology research facilities weighed investment decisions in equipment to automate experimentation. The choices were tricky. It was not clear how soon suppliers would be able to offer vastly improved equipment, nor was there any guarantee that new equipment would be compatible with existing equipment. Even the extent to which experimentation could be automated was uncertain; clearly, human judgment would play a role in interpreting experimental results, but how much of a role?

The Organization

Corning's business model was consistent across almost all its markets. The company excelled in the science and manufacture of glass and ceramics. It held strong intellectual property rights on its products and therefore faced limited competition. It sold components to industrial manufacturers and almost always emphasized high quality and high reliability more than other product attributes.

Corning was a disciplined organization. Its executives planned rigorously. Managers were held accountable to plans in performance reviews and promotions. Although some might view the process of innovation as organic and unstructured, Corning also applied its practice of disciplined accountability there. A detailed five-stage process guided product development. In fact, innovation was the centerpiece of Corning's culture, and newly hired managers studied the innovation process thoroughly. With experience, the company became adept at setting challenging but achievable expectations for its product development teams to complete each stage.

The innovation process was embedded in Corning's organizational structure, which included a single centralized research group and a single centralized development group. In simple terms, the innovation process dictated that the research group prove the basic science and develop a prototype, the development group design the product, and the business unit establish manufacturability and launch the product. The process included specific milestones that marked transfers of certain responsibilities from one group to the next.

Corning launched its Life Sciences business in the 1920s when it developed a specialty glass it called Pyrex. Soon Corning Life Sciences was selling a wide range of glass laboratory products such as beakers, bottles, test tubes, traps, and cylinders. Through the early 1990s, this product line changed only incrementally. By then, Corning Life Sciences represented only about 2 percent of Corning's total revenue.

The Life Sciences division departed from the typical Corning business model. Unlike most Corning businesses, it no longer relied on proprietary technology, and it sold its products to administrative purchasing agents in academic or industrial research laboratories rather than to industrial manufacturers. Corning allocated its R&D budget to other technologies and other markets where there appeared to be greater opportunity. Life Sciences became a reliable, if relatively stagnant, business.

In the 1990s, advances in biotechnology gave the Life Sciences division ambitions for dramatic growth for the first time in decades. Its research into this market, which seemed poised to explode, revealed that the manufacture of DNA microarrays would allow Corning to leverage three specific and relevant areas of expertise: applying unusual coatings to glass, controlling liquid flows on microscopic scales, and continuously improving microscopic manufacturing processes.

Key Elements of the Forgetting Challenge

It was these opportunities to borrow that Corning found alluring. The need to forget was less obvious.

Based on our research, there are three generic questions that executives should ask before embarking on any strategic experiment so that they can fully understand the forgetting challenge and the organizational implications for NewCo. These questions, summarized in table 2-1, are discussed in the following paragraphs.

TABLE 2-1

Questions about key elements of the forgetting challenge

Business model	How does NewCo's business model differ from CoreCo's? • Who are our customers? • What value do we provide them? • How do we deliver that value?
Competencies	How does NewCo's desired competency set differ from CoreCo's? • What areas of expertise does NewCo need? • What is the relative importance of each? • How does this differ from CoreCo?
Uncertainty	How uncertain is NewCo's business model relative to CoreCo's? • How should predictions and forecasts be used? • On what basis can managers be held accountable?

How Does NewCo's Business Model Differ from CoreCo's?

Strategic experiments are unproven, while CoreCo is established and profitable. Therefore, there must be distinct differences between New-Co's business definition and CoreCo's. All three of the basic components of a business model must be considered in this light.

- NewCo may need to target a different customer from CoreCo's.[1]

- NewCo may need to emphasize different attributes in its value proposition.

- NewCo may require an entirely different set of business processes in order to deliver that value.

It is difficult to leave behind elements of the established business model. In our research, we repeatedly observed strategic experiments behaving as though they still served the same customer, still offered the same value proposition, or still could rely on the same business processes.

How Do NewCo's Desired Competencies Differ?

A different business model often implies a different set of underlying competencies. In most organizations, power is centered on the group of people who have the core skill that creates a competitive advantage. For example, in a consumer products company such as Procter & Gamble it may be the marketing group; in a logistics company such as UPS it may be the operations group. Typically, NewCo needs to emphasize a different competency than CoreCo.

How Uncertain Is NewCo's Business Model?

Again, by definition, strategic experiments are attempts to prove the viability of new business models. This means that there is much greater uncertainty than there is within CoreCo. NewCo's future is unknowable. Therefore, NewCo's mission must be recognized as one of exploration of an unproven opportunity, and not exploitation of a proven one. This means that NewCo must abandon a deeply embedded assumption of *reliable predictability*.

Such an assumption is common in many successful corporations. Managers make confident predictions based on many years of past data.

CEOs then report aggregate predictions to investors, and the CEOs' success depends on their ability to deliver the results they promise. To get these results, they hold managers accountable for their planned contributions by making results versus plan the primary basis for judging managerial performance. Belief in this approach to accountability is strong. In fact, a performance-oriented culture—one that holds managers accountable for the numbers in their plans—is often cited as a hallmark of successful companies.[2] Escaping such a culture can be difficult. But strategic experiments *are just that*—experiments. If anything, they are *reliably unpredictable*.

Root Causes of the Forgetting Problem

The forgetting challenge is much more difficult than it may at first appear. That is because it takes minimal effort to achieve *conversational awareness* of the differences between NewCo's and CoreCo's business models. The three elements of the forgetting challenge are not difficult to understand, nor are they difficult to explain to others. So it is tempting to think that an effective training program for NewCo's staff would be sufficient to free NewCo from the past.

It is not. Conversations are fleeting. And organizations have powerful sources of memory.[3]

One such source of memory is *instincts*. Strategic experiments place managers under a great deal of stress, and they present a far more ambiguous environment than most managers in established corporations are accustomed to. Under conditions of stress and ambiguity, people naturally gravitate toward the familiar—that is, they rely on instinct— without being aware of it.

Unfortunately, people's instincts are grounded in what has made CoreCo successful in the past. Thus, leaders naturally look first to customers they already know. They naturally create value propositions that are similar to what they already offer, and they naturally try to use or re-create existing processes.

The instincts of individual managers are not the only source of organizational memory. Another source is the nature of relationships between managers. These are established in ways that facilitate operation of the old business. If you move the same managers to the new business, the relationships are still there. In other words, established patterns of interaction persist.

CoreCo's norms about organizational status are another important source of memory. Often, within organizations, certain areas of expertise are accorded higher status than others. Such social hierarchies are not easily disrupted. Without careful orchestration, the norms of organizational status will persist. NewCo may end up dominated by people who have expertise that is valuable for CoreCo but less so for NewCo.

Planning templates can also reinforce CoreCo's business model by emphasizing measures of performance relevant only for CoreCo. The tendency of CoreCo's measures of performance to reinforce memory are magnified if they are tied directly to compensation incentives or promotion criteria. Further, the way CoreCo reviews business results and evaluates individual performance can reinforce the assumption of reliable predictability that is inappropriate for NewCo.

That is not all. CoreCo's information systems may be highly efficient in delivering the right data to the right people at the right time, but if the same systems are used for NewCo, such data may serve only to reinforce CoreCo's assumptions about why it succeeds. Often-told stories about why the company has been successful can do the same thing.

Memory defines what an organization will and will not do. Erasing memory is the crux of the forgetting challenge.

The Forgetting Challenge for CMT

CMT needed to forget much of what had made Corning successful. All three aspects of the business model needed to change. For one thing, CMT would be selling to an unfamiliar customer. It would approach neither industrial manufacturers, as most Corning divisions did, nor low-level laboratory administrators, as the Life Sciences division did.

CMT's value proposition had to depart from that of other Corning businesses. Corning sold most of its products by emphasizing that it had the highest possible quality based on proprietary science. Although quality was a consideration for CMT, it needed to emphasize cost and convenience most heavily. Also, Corning was not the first mover in this nascent and undefined market, and it did not have the strongest intellectual property in the industry.

Processes needed to change as well. First, CMT needed to reconsider Corning's highly regarded innovation process. The process worked well for new products based on proven science, within an existing business model. But microarray manufacturing was based on emerging science, and the microarray opportunity departed from Corning's business model. It would require a more flexible innovation process. Second, CMT would have to abandon the Corning Life Sciences sales process. Because microarrays had to work with other equipment for genomics experimentation, senior laboratory administrators did the buying. As a result, sales discussions would become more consultative, and the sales cycle would lengthen.

In addition to dealing with a dramatic change in the business model, CMT had to reevaluate the competencies it needed to emphasize. Corning's past success had depended on excellence in glass manufacture. Was this the critical differentiator for CMT? By comparison, how important was expertise in molecular biology? Clearly, it was more important than it was in the existing Life Sciences division. CMT's organizational design needed to reflect this difference, if it was to forget.

The final element of Corning's forgetting challenge proved particularly difficult: Corning had to deal with a much higher level of ambiguity than it was accustomed to in its core business. For example, how much of a barrier did existing competitive patents represent, and how quickly would other competitors enter the market? How quickly could Corning establish reliable manufacturability, and at what cost? How easily could Corning influence the evolution of industry standards, and how would these standards affect customers' perception of value? Resolving these uncertainties would require that Corning hold its managers accountable on the basis of much more subjective criteria. We examine this shift in later chapters.

Table 2-2 summarizes the forgetting challenge for CMT.

TABLE 2-2

Key elements of the forgetting challenge for CMT

Business model	• New customers: senior administrators at laboratories • New value proposition: cost, convenience • New processes: more flexible innovation process; longer, more consultative sales process
Competencies	• New competency set: heavy reliance on new life sciences expertise
Uncertainty	• New degree of uncertainty: predictions of results much less reliable

Building the CMT Organization

Although the key elements of the forgetting challenge for CMT are clear in hindsight and in view of our framework, they were not so clear when Corning's senior executives were establishing CMT's organizational DNA. The late 1990s were an era in which expectation exceeded practical reality in every quarter. A new age appeared to be dawning. New technologies, particularly the Internet, were carrying the economy to unprecedented heights. Investors and executives alike became intoxicated with the promise of quick riches.

Corning was caught up in the frenzy. In the early 1980s, the company had pioneered fiber optic cable, the backbone of modern telecommunications networks and the heart of the Internet. By 1998, the fiber business accounted for more than half of Corning's revenues, and the business was still growing rapidly. Network operators were on a building binge, trying to stay ahead of the anticipated explosive growth in Internet traffic. In fact, the market had become so important that Corning had changed its organizational structure so that the head of fiber was a peer of the head of Corning Technologies, a grouping that included all other Corning business divisions.

At a time when most of their attention was directed toward the fiber market, senior executives at Corning did what was most expedient. They assumed that what had worked for Corning so far would work for CMT. An effort to create a distinct organizational DNA for CMT would have been a serious distraction. Career Corning executives had a great deal invested in the existing rules for staffing and promotion, the prevailing norms for assigning organizational status, and the typical approaches to judging business performance. It would have been natural for them to resist special treatment for a new unit.

Therefore, in making staff, structure, systems, and culture choices for CMT, Corning replicated its organizational DNA (with one exception, as you will see).

Staff

CMT's leaders filled positions by arranging transfers from several existing groups within Corning. Sources included the massive R&D facility in Corning, New York, and Corning's research facility in France, the Fontainebleau Research Center (FRC), which had helped support some of the early research into microarrays.

Another critical resource was Costar, an innovative Boston-area supplier to biotechnology laboratories that Corning had acquired in 1993, an earlier move into the rapid-growth segment of the life sciences market. In fact, it was a Costar scientist who had initially explored the DNA microarray opportunity, with help from the FRC.

Arranging the transfers was not difficult; many employees sought by CMT were intrigued by the exciting opportunity. Soon a staff of several dozen was pushing CMT forward.

Even with these internal resources, CMT leaders recognized that they would have to substantially increase CMT's expertise in molecular biology. And this is the one area in which they made an alteration to the existing DNA: they hired a number of outside experts in the field. One of their first hires was a respected researcher known in academic and industry circles around the world. Although the move added expertise in technical positions in research, development, and sales, it was insiders, and not outsiders, who filled the management-level positions at CMT.

Structure

CMT adopted Corning's overall organizational model. Corning included multiple independent and decentralized business units, such as Corning Life Sciences, that housed functions like sales, marketing, and manufacturing. A centralized research group and a centralized development group were shared by all the business units.

Corning reassigned three executives to lead the CMT venture—one as head of research, another as head of development, and a third as head of the CMT business unit. The three CMT heads reported to Corning's heads of research, development, and the Life Sciences business unit, respectively (see figure 2-1). Although it may seem odd that Corning named no single person to head CMT, this practice reflected Corning's standard approach to innovative product development efforts.

However, within the CMT business unit, as within other Corning business units, there was independence. For example, the CMT sales team was fully dedicated to microarray sales and did not report directly to other sales groups.

Systems

One of the most powerful elements of organizational DNA is the norm for using predictions in plans as a basis for judging business performance. Although CMT involved significant uncertainties, Corning

FIGURE 2-1

Initial CMT organizational structure

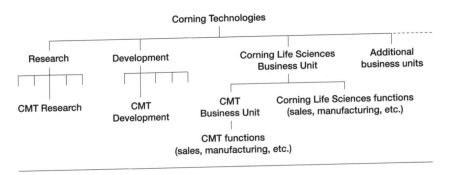

did not shift from its strong culture of accountability to plans. The CMT team members believed the numbers in the plans. They had been produced by a reputable outside consulting team, and Corning senior executives had used the consultant's work to justify the investment in CMT. The plan included a specific set of development deadlines based on Corning's experience with its five-stage innovation process.

To the CMT leadership group, the plans represented what was possible if all employees simply did their jobs. That belief was strengthened through CMT's hiring approach. When interviewing internal and external candidates, CMT leaders looked for people who were bullish about the market for DNA microarrays and about Corning's ability to succeed in it. In fact, no one who expressed skepticism about CMT's business projections was hired.

Culture

Neither Corning's nor CMT's leaders endeavored to create a distinct culture for CMT. Further, given that CMT operated under shared leadership and had connections to many existing groups within Corning (such as the Costar business and the FRC), no unique culture naturally arose. Table 2-3 summarizes CMT's organizational DNA choices.

CMT's First Two Years

CMT's first two years illustrate how bright promise can lead to bitter disappointment when an organization does not effectively cope with the forgetting challenge.

TABLE 2-3

CMT's initial organizational DNA

Element	Description
Staff	• Management positions were filled by internal transfers. Only technical life sciences positions were filled by outsiders. • CMT staff remained within existing R&D subgroups, located in multiple facilities.
Structure	• Leadership was shared by three managers—a research head, a development head, and a business unit head. Each reported to a different senior executive—heads of research, development, and Corning Life Sciences. • The CMT sales team operated independently from Corning Life Sciences.
Systems	• The plan was believed to be accurate and was used as the basis for accountability. • Standard expectations were adopted in the five-stage innovation process.
Culture	• CMT's culture was undifferentiated from Corning's.

At first, the CMT team members proceeded with confidence. They believed that they had unique skills. In fact, in speaking with others in the industry before launching the business, they kept hearing that the life sciences aspects of the process were straightforward. The real challenges related to the physical sciences—the very areas where Corning had an edge. Every aspect of manufacturing the microarrays looked well within reach. CMT leaders motivated their teams to work hard, knowing that potential competitors such as Agilent and Motorola were chasing the same opportunity.

Within months, the program achieved its first success. CMT offered researchers who printed their own microarrays a much-improved *unprinted* glass slide (without DNA adhered to it) with a special coating. Customers were thrilled with the improved consistency that they achieved in printing their own microarrays. Already, Corning had proven that it could leverage its expertise in specialty glass manufacture to create value for genomics researchers. However, the CMT leaders still had their eyes on what they viewed as a much bigger prize: the printed microarray.

Meanwhile, the outlook for Corning's fiber optics business was becoming rosier still. It was the exuberant late 1990s, and every business opportunity seemed golden. Ambitions for CMT escalated. CMT was the innovative new unit that could revitalize the Life Sciences division.

It could even be the next big win for Corning as a whole, comparable to Corning's success in fiber optic cable. This was audacious thinking, given how profitable the communications market had been for Corning. In fact, CMT's five-year revenue projection leaped from $100 million to $250 million. One CMT financial manager recalled the planning atmosphere that year. "It seemed as though everything was growing at 70 percent per year. So if you didn't project $250 million in five years, you heard 'Guys, not enough zeros.'"

The CMT leaders urged their team forward, feeling that if they simply stuck to the plan that they knew was achievable, success would certainly follow. But CMT soon faced unanticipated difficulties.

CMT struggled to achieve reliable manufacture of printed microarrays. The challenges of working with DNA were different from those presented by other fluids Corning had worked with in the past. For one thing, because the biotechnology industry was just emerging, DNA fluid purchased from different vendors had chemical inconsistencies. These variations disrupted manufacture because no single glass coating would consistently adhere to DNA from different suppliers.

Corning's order to one vendor was the largest it had ever received; to deliver, the vendor had to alter its manufacturing processes, and that in turn affected Corning's printing process, leading to further setbacks. Corning's proven methods for identifying and correcting manufacturing problems were also confounded by the peculiarities of DNA. One day the process appeared to be working fine, and the next a mysterious new problem arose.

Soon CMT started missing deadlines established in the business plan. The leadership team knew that missing the plan would not be taken lightly. Falling short was seen as failing.

Naturally, CMT leaders did not want to fail, and this affected their perceptions of what was happening. They viewed their struggles as minor setbacks and consequently urged their team to work harder to get back on schedule. The alternative would have been to reexamine the fundamental decisions they had made so far—and that would create major delays and eliminate even the most remote possibility of hitting their numbers.

Despite many late nights, CMT did not catch up. Soon everyone's expectations had been dashed. In an environment of perceived failure, the cohesiveness of the leadership group frayed. The standard five-stage innovation process that defined how research, development, and business units worked together was not delivering as expected. Disagreements arose and were often settled by reverting to what had worked in the past.

Under the cloud of perceived failure, tensions within CMT and between CMT and Corning disrupted productivity and learning. For example, many employees who were assigned to CMT continued to identify with (and remain physically located within) existing Corning subgroups. As a result, rivalries within Corning—between the research facilities in France and in the United States, and between the acquired Costar group and Corning Life Sciences—were imported to CMT. These rivalries usually generated productive tensions. But under the conditions of ambiguity and disappointment present at CMT (and common within strategic experiments), tensions accelerated and became debilitating.

Unproductive tensions also arose between CMT and Corning Life Sciences. The general manager of Corning Life Sciences was directly responsible for CMT. Thus, he tended to view CMT primarily in terms of its potential to impact the Life Sciences business in the short term, and the fact was that CMT was a huge drag on profitability.

Antagonism also developed between the CMT leadership team and the molecular biology experts that CMT had hired from outside Corning. The scientists thought that the managers were too weak in the life sciences. In particular, they took issue with the way the leadership team assigned resources and evaluated outcomes, two crucial activities of general managers. The biologists believed that when problems arose on the manufacturing line, too many experts were being assigned to relatively unimportant problems and that the wrong types of experts were being assigned to others.

The biologists also disagreed with management's insistence on extremely high quality standards, which led to delays in launching products. Although they tried to convey the idea that "10 percent wrong" in the world of biotechnology was "not a big deal," such low levels of quality were unheard of in Corning's other product lines. In fact, Corning had learned from experience in other markets that it was critical to get a product right the first time. Corning had even been through a lengthy quality initiative to ensure that the value of achieving high quality was deeply embedded in the Corning organization.

In the middle of 1999, following turnover of some senior staff, two senior leaders at Corning took a hard look at CMT. They noted CMT's missed deadlines and the signs that the team members were not working well together. They began discussing what had gone wrong and what they would have to do to fix it.

Understanding What Went Wrong

To summarize, CMT ran into the following difficulties:

- The leaders perceived that CMT was failing, unjustifiably, because it fell short of highly speculative expectations.

- Startled by unexpected results, CMT leaders stuck to the plan rather than reevaluate fundamental assumptions.

- They lost team cohesion and, as a result, defaulted to existing routines, including a structured and linear five-stage innovation process.

- They proved ineffective in solving emergent technical problems.

- They insisted on meeting quality standards higher than customers demanded.

- They were opposed by a powerful manager who was concerned about hitting short-term profitability targets.

All these problems were failures to forget, and all of them were inevitable from the moment CMT adopted Corning's organizational DNA. In the paragraphs that follow, we show how each problem was a result of this choice.

Perceptions of Failure

First, consider what, more than anything else, precipitated CMT's unraveling: perceptions of failure that arose from unrealistic expectations. This was a direct result of the fact that CMT was expected to deliver on plan—just like the other, more mature Corning divisions. Perhaps the most difficult transition that corporations must make in managing strategic experiments is adjusting to higher levels of uncertainty. Specifically, leaders must learn to react differently to disparities between predictions and outcomes. Falling short of plan should not immediately be viewed as failing. Leaders must forget strict norms of accountability to plans.

When outcomes fall short of predictions, it may be the result of poor management, or it may be the result of a lousy prediction. After all, with strategic experiments, there are few facts to base predictions on. Predictions are based on some fact, but they may more strongly reflect management aspirations, or whatever is necessary to attain funding. And aspirations are malleable; recall that the five-year revenue forecast more than doubled before CMT had even produced its first salable microarray.

Note that in several ways, the CMT leadership team made the situation worse by acting to raise expectations and make them even more rigid. They let their ambitions be shaped by a desire for CMT to be as important to Corning as fiber optics. They eliminated any penchant for rethinking the plan by hiring only those who were committed to achieving the plan as initially stated. They used the speculative threat of an imminent competitive entry to motivate, making it that much harder to back off their own demands for getting to market quickly.

They also accorded strong validity to the consulting firm's projections even though nascent markets are inherently unpredictable. They became overconfident, listening to outside life scientists telling them that the real challenge in DNA microarray manufacture was in Corning's area of expertise, even though molecular biologists would naturally see the greatest challenges in unfamiliar disciplines. And they spent all available resources to build a large team quickly.

Each of these actions made it more difficult for CMT's leaders to back off from expectations than it would have been had they taken a more cautious approach and invested in smaller increments.

Sticking to the Plan

Next, consider how CMT's leaders reacted to shortfalls—by sticking to the plan. They could have questioned the original predictions. Unfortunately, explicit discussion of the quality of predictions in plans is not the norm within most corporations. Such discussion would undermine CEOs' ability to hold their managers accountable. If a shortfall is not easily explained by an obvious change in the business environment (for example, the economy entering a recession or a strong new competitor entering the market), managerial underperformance is accepted as the cause.

Three years later, still frustrated by the early results from CMT, one of CMT's leaders told us, "Those projections were not real. They were aspirations." But they were quite real in the sense that they affected decision making. Rather than rethink what was realistically possible, the CMT leadership team simply worked harder to get back to the plan. After the expectations for CMT had been formalized in the annual planning process, they were considered sacrosanct. If CMT's leaders had suggested that the plan's fundamental assumptions needed to be reassessed and that the targets needed to be revised downward, it would have been perceived as an admission of failure.

Lack of Team Cohesion, and Defaulting to Existing Routines

CMT's reporting structure, with three leaders reporting to three different senior executives, led directly to a lack of team cohesion, as well as a tendency to rely on existing routines. Such organizational structures, designed to allow for specialization through division of labor, can work well for relatively predictable processes. Roles and responsibilities can be defined with some precision, and interaction between leaders becomes routine.

But transferring such an arrangement to a dissimilar and unproven business model is inadvisable, and it was ineffective for CMT. There were too many unexpected decision points, each requiring a joint deliberation. There were conflicts, and the natural approach to settling them was to revert to existing norms—to what had worked in the past. Thus, shared leadership makes forgetting unlikely.

Inability to Solve Emergent Technical Problems

CMT's approach to staffing, which relied heavily on internal transfers, affected its ability to respond to technical issues. Although the CMT leaders recognized the need for new expertise in molecular biology, they hired outsiders only at the technical levels and not the management levels. The power within CMT centered on insiders, and their expertise was in specialty glass manufacture. Of course, CMT needed this expertise, but it needed better balance between people who held this traditional expertise and people who brought in knowledge of molecular biology.

The CMT research group was headed by a Corning insider who had expertise in traditional Corning fields. He was selected because he had more experience in the life sciences than any of his peers, but he had been out of that field for seven years. The alternative would have been to look outside Corning for one or more knowledgeable molecular biologists having managerial experience. The search would likely have taken months. Still, it would have been healthy for CMT because it would have given the life sciences perspective greater influence in a critical managerial domain: choosing how to deploy resources to solve technical problems.

Hiring outsiders in managerial positions was not an obvious choice, particularly because assigning high-profile positions to outsiders was counter to Corning's established culture. As a 150-year-old company, it was justified in thinking that its existing management practices had merit. Part of its approach was to encourage long careers; Corning was a close-knit company in which the founding family still played an important role. The company valued long-term, high-trust relationships and face-to-face interaction. Senior executives were expected to closely monitor the career paths of their subordinates. This set of practices had worked for Corning historically, but these are exactly the types of practices that must be reconsidered when strategic experiments are initiated.

Insisting on Quality Standards That Exceeded Customer Needs

CMT's inaccurate perceptions of customer needs were also a direct result of its approach to staffing. Because CMT was staffed at the management level by insiders, they naturally sought to meet the exceptionally high manufacturing standards that were typical of other Corning product lines (but were unrealistic for microarrays). An organizational design that enabled molecular biology experts to wield greater influence would have prevented the problem.

Opposition from a Manager Concerned About Short-Term Profits

The head of the CMT business unit should not have reported to the head of Corning Life Sciences. General managers of mature businesses are preoccupied with demands that are inconsistent with the needs of strategic experiments. They may even view NewCo only in terms of how it can help CoreCo. And they are always cognizant of the fact that NewCo drags down CoreCo's profitability. In the case of CMT, these conflicts of interest aggravated the tensions that disrupted its progress.

We have focused on how Corning's DNA, replicated for CMT, led directly to these failures to forget. However, in the sales function, CMT was able to forget. Throughout Corning, sales groups from the various business units tended to work independently. CMT's sales

TABLE 2-4

Outcomes of CMT's initial organizational DNA

Element	Choice	Result
Staff	• Management positions were filled by internal transfers. Only technical life sciences positions were filled by outsiders.	• Too much power vested in Corning's traditional areas of expertise led to ineffective problem solving and overemphasis on quality.
Structure	• Staff remained within existing R&D subgroups, located in multiple facilities. • Leadership was shared by three managers—a research head, a development head, and a business unit head. Each reported to a different senior executive—heads of research, development, and Corning Life Sciences. • The CMT sales team operated independently from Corning Life Sciences.	• Lack of group cohesion. Natural reversion to existing routines. • Overemphasis on short-term profitability. Reinforced existing roles, responsibilities, and patterns of interaction among research, development, and business unit, when a new, more iterative process was needed. • Sales team succeeded in developing its unique, tailored approach to market.
Systems	• The plan was believed to be accurate and was used as the basis for accountability. • Standard expectations were adopted in the five-stage innovation process.	• Results short of plans were viewed, unrealistically, as failures. When CMT fell short of plan, it simply worked to get back to plan rather than discuss possible flaws in the fundamental assumptions in the plan.
Culture	• CMT had no distinct culture. It was undifferentiated from the core business.	• Also contributed to a lack of cohesiveness and natural reversion to existing routines.

group was not influenced heavily by the existing Corning Life Sciences sales group, and it included several outside experts. As a result, it developed new practices and processes appropriate for CMT. The team researched the market, spoke with potential customers, and developed a sales model that called for a six- to twenty-four-month sales cycle—much longer than the norm for Corning Life Sciences.

Table 2-4 summarizes the problems that resulted from CMT's adoption of Corning's organizational DNA.

Soon, the issues that CMT was struggling with came to the attention of Corning's senior management team. Chapter 3 discusses the changes they made and describes how those changes helped.

Chapter Three

TAMING THE ELEPHANT

THIS CHAPTER continues the story of Corning Microarray Technologies (CMT). We show how Corning reconstructed the CMT organization with a new and distinct DNA and explain why progress accelerated as a result. Then we present a set of general recommendations for overcoming the forgetting challenge.

Major Restructuring and Change in Leadership

During a period of senior staff turnover in 1999, Corning promoted Fred Allen to lead Corning's development group and appointed Martin Ford to the position of president of Corning Technologies (of which Corning Life Sciences was a part).[1] The two senior executives thoroughly analyzed the issues faced by CMT and began making changes.

First, they redefined the role of the CMT business unit leader, making this person the sole leader of the strategic experiment and responsible for research, development, and business unit operations. In addition, they recognized that plans for CMT needed to be flexible. It followed that a different approach was needed for judging CMT's business performance. They anticipated that innovation would not proceed as it normally did at Corning, in a linear and predictable fashion. Instead, the CMT innovation process would be iterative and unpredictable.

Therefore, they also changed to more subjective criteria for evaluating the CMT leader's personal performance. The CMT leader would not be evaluated on the basis of short-term deadlines and costs. Rather, he would be evaluated on the basis of how quickly he learned and made adjustments. They expected this leader to actively consider and reconsider fundamental business questions such as, what is the value proposition? What are our costs likely to be? What is our competition likely to offer? In other words, Ford and Allen anticipated that the CMT leader would face both scientific and business uncertainties and would resolve them over time.

Ford also felt that Corning had not appointed the best possible leader for CMT, so he named Greg Brown, a Corning veteran of nearly two decades, as the new head. Ford had monitored Brown's career for many years and admired his ability to get scientists, engineers, and businesspeople to work together.

Ford also chose to be more closely involved in managing CMT. He expected regular direct reports from Brown, although CMT was still organizationally a part of the Life Sciences division. Later, Ford would formally shift the reporting relationship so that Brown reported directly to him (see figure 3-1). This change effectively broke the conflict of interest between CMT and Corning Life Sciences.

In addition, Ford and his colleagues agreed to move all CMT staff located in Massachusetts to Corning, New York, to build more productive relationships. (One R&D team working on an advanced manufacturing approach remained in France.) This action ensured that the

FIGURE 3-1

Revised CMT organizational structure

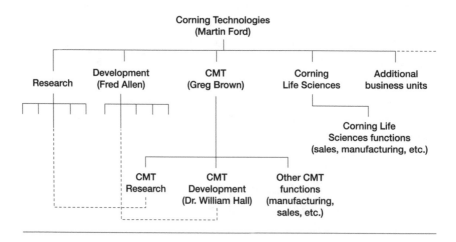

loyalties of the relocated employees were fully behind CMT and not other subgroups within Corning and that they could achieve the rapid learning that was crucial for a strategic experiment. In the process CMT lost several talented scientists, including the Costar scientist who had first pushed for Corning to invest in the microarray business.

Brown made additional changes to the organization, replacing CMT's head of development with William Hall. An outsider who had a PhD in molecular biology, Hall had spent several years managing genomics research for a pharmaceutical company. Brown also hired a molecular biology expert to work full-time with vendors to establish industry standards for DNA supplies. Both moves would help balance the perspectives of the life scientists with those of the entrenched Corning physical scientists.

These changes took several months, but it was time well spent. Table 3-1 compares CMT's organizational DNA before and after the changes that began in late 1999.

TABLE 3-1

Major changes to CMT's organizational DNA

Element	Before	After
Staff	• Management positions were filled by internal transfers. Only technical life sciences positions were filled by outsiders. • Staff remained within existing R&D subgroups, located in multiple facilities.	• Outsiders were hired for influential management positions. • More staff were located in the same facility. • CMT leader was replaced with a manager regarded very highly within Corning.
Structure	• Leadership was shared by three managers—a research head, a development head, and a business unit head. • Each reported to a different senior executive—heads of research, development, and Corning Life Sciences. • The CMT sales team operated independently from Corning Life Sciences.	• All CMT function heads reported to the leader of CMT. • CMT's leader reported directly to the president of Corning Technologies.
Systems	• The plan was believed to be accurate and was used as a basis for accountability. • Standard expectations were adopted in the five-stage innovation process.	• Plans were viewed with greater flexibility, and managerial performance was judged subjectively. • Innovation process was treated as iterative.
Culture	• Culture was undifferentiated from the core business.	• Greater emphasis was placed on experimentation and learning.

CMT's Second Life

Despite the loss of some staff, CMT's rate of progress improved. The change in leadership reset expectations. Revenue expectations remained high, but everything was pushed back roughly one year.

With goals that again seemed achievable, the team rebuilt solid working relationships. Perceptions of failure had been expunged, and Brown brought conflicts to the surface and worked them out. Later, when the team again ran into unexpected hurdles in manufacturing printed microarrays, Brown chose a different path from the one his predecessor had chosen. Rather than urge his team members to work harder to get back to plan, Brown accepted that they were already working hard and focused them on working together to diagnose and fix the problem. With everyone located in the same place, testing and diagnosis proceeded more smoothly. Knowing he would be evaluated on the basis of how quickly he learned and made adjustments, Brown frequently kept Ford up-to-date on setbacks, lessons, and new directions.

In addition, the influence of molecular biology experts improved decision making and technical troubleshooting. It also reduced quality expectations to achievable levels that still satisfied customers. As a result, CMT launched its first microarray product in September 2000, only four months after the arrival of Hall.

The product allowed researchers to experiment with the DNA of yeast. Experiments on organisms with genetic codes simpler than that of humans, such as yeast, had been common two years earlier when CMT first began developing the product. But as the science progressed, interest shifted to more complex organisms. The completion of the mapping of the human genome, something that happened a few months before the CMT product launch, accelerated this shift. As a result, revenues from this first product were disappointing, although customers thought that from a technical standpoint the microarrays were a home run. Such feedback was gratifying for the team, and it lent credence to the notion that CMT's earlier quality standards had been unnecessarily high.

There were still struggles. The research team in France appeared to be hampered by the physical distance between the point of development (the FRC) and the point of manufacture (Corning, New York). Technology transfer was occasionally incomplete and inaccurate, and manufacturing trials were subject to long delays, although a new head of manufacturing reduced many of them. CMT continued to miss development milestones, but in the new scheme this was not viewed as failure. The team members became adept at identifying the things that they did not know and were willing to revisit old decisions. This flexibility was another reflection of the new mind-set, which emphasized learning and not adherence to original plans.

By the middle of 2001, CMT was on the cusp of producing microarrays containing human DNA samples. The market still appeared promising, and there was no significant new competition. Prospects for CMT appeared bright indeed.

CMT's Unexpected Demise

However, strategic experiments, like independent new ventures, are often subject to powerful forces that are beyond their control. Entrepreneurs worry about the fickle IPO window (the interval during which investors are willing to take risks on new stock issues), which closed rapidly as the NASDAQ plummeted in 2000 and 2001. Similarly, leaders of strategic experiments must worry about the performance of CoreCo. They depend, after all, on CoreCo's operating earnings to finance their continued activities. Such funding is limited, because investors loathe any significant dent in earnings.

Worries about available capital were the farthest thing from anyone's mind at Corning in 2000, as fiber sales rocketed Corning's stock price to a peak of $340 in September, up from only $70 a year earlier. But things quickly changed as telecommunications companies recognized that they had massively overbuilt core infrastructure in anticipation of a much greater rise in Internet traffic than materialized. Through the summer of 2001, orders for Corning's fiber optic cable plummeted.

The shock to Corning's finances was unlike anything the company had ever experienced. Over the next twelve months, Corning was forced to cut more than one-fourth of its workforce, close seven major manufacturing plants, slash capital spending, suspend dividend payments, and issue new shares of stock and convertible debt to raise about $1 billion in new capital. (Corning revenues had peaked at $7.1 billion in 2000.)

As Greg Brown prepared for the 2002 budget cycle, best-case forecasts for CMT were still showing a $30 million loss. Martin Ford asked

Brown to explore options for keeping the venture alive on less than half its existing budget. Although few situations strain the cohesiveness of a management team like demands for severe budget cuts, CMT division heads readily devised a plan for a $15 million budget that would allow the venture to continue to make progress, albeit at a slower rate.

Unfortunately, the financial condition had become so strained that Ford was forced to suspend CMT funding altogether.

Brown was evaluated positively for his performance at CMT and was soon assigned to another business unit. This was an important step. Corporations need talented managers to run strategic experiments. If the cost of failure is too high, they will shy away from such assignments.

By the end of 2003, Corning's Life Sciences division was still selling unprinted glass slides for researchers who printed their own microarrays. The company's finances were improving, but it was not clear whether Corning would be able to resurrect its efforts to manufacture microarrays.

Final Analysis

Under the new organizational structure, CMT was able to overcome the forgetting challenge. By having Brown as its single leader and having him report directly to the senior staff, CMT avoided adopting the pressures and norms of the core business. When Brown hired an outside molecular biology expert to a leadership position, it gave CMT an internal voice able to challenge the unnecessarily high quality standards that Corning naturally insisted on.

Because CMT was no longer tightly integrated with centralized R&D groups, it was able to jettison the rigid structure of the innovation process and make progress by following a more iterative path. Moreover, the management team treated projections as though they were guesses, and not as though they were a nonnegotiable basis for judging performance. In essence, what had worked for CMT's sales team, in microcosm, worked for CMT as a whole: independence, flexibility, and a balance of inside and outside perspective.

Greg Brown led with the recognition that there were likely to be many mistakes and unexpected hurdles. He was not hell-bent on achieving expectations that had little basis in fact or directly relevant experience. Leadership in the context of strategic experiments calls for humility. It calls for leaders who can admit that they do not have all the answers, who can acknowledge that they do not even know what is possible and what is not, who are willing to warn that the strategic experiment might very well fail—and can inspire hard teamwork anyway.

Although we cannot judge with any certainty what might have happened to CMT if not for the collapse of the fiber market, it is our judgment that the forgetting challenge was the most significant of the three challenges for Corning, and that CMT was well on its way to succeeding.

Recommendations for Overcoming the Forgetting Challenge

Based on the experience of CMT and the other strategic experiments profiled in this book, it is clear that if any strategic experiment is to overcome the forgetting challenge, it must have a unique organizational DNA.[2] The differences between NewCo's and CoreCo's DNA are dramatic. It is much easier to underestimate the level of change needed than it is to overestimate.

Selections of staff, structure, systems, and culture must be considered carefully. Our recommendations relating to each of these elements are shown in table 3-2 and described in detail next.[3]

Hire Outsiders

Hire outsiders, at both the operational and the management level, so that there is a mix of insiders and outsiders. Give strong consideration to hiring an outsider to lead NewCo.[4]

It is unrealistic to expect that long-term employees of CoreCo will easily abandon CoreCo's business definition unless they are regularly challenged by an outside perspective. Only outside hires can give this external perspective. And an outsider at the top of NewCo— well versed in competencies that NewCo needs but CoreCo does not have—can effectively challenge the existing assumptions, values, and decision biases. With the authority and influence that come with the leadership position, this leader can identify and eliminate those assumptions that are sensible for CoreCo but are irrelevant for NewCo.

It is true that some strategic experiments led by insiders have succeeded, and certainly CMT performed better under its second leader, who was an insider just as the first had been. Still, the choice to hire an

TABLE 3-2

Recommendations for overcoming the forgetting challenge

Element	Description
Staff	• Hire outsiders at both the operational and the management level so that there is a mix of insiders and outsiders. Very strong consideration should be given to hiring an outsider to lead NewCo.
Structure	• The head of NewCo should report to an executive more senior than the head of CoreCo. • Over time, NewCo must create its own version of roles and responsibilities that define how the major business functions (such as marketing and product development) interact. At least until an effective and stable structure is established, NewCo should operate under a single leader and not report to any centralized functional groups.
Systems	• The basis of accountability for NewCo executives should be shifted from performance against plan to a more subjective set of criteria, including how quickly NewCo demonstrates that it can learn from experience and make adjustments. • Performance metrics appropriate to CoreCo should not be applied to NewCo without careful consideration. Particular care should be taken with the profitability metric.
Culture	• NewCo must develop a unique culture, starting with a nearly blank slate. It should borrow only the most abstract and universal elements of CoreCo's culture (for example, the value of integrity or teamwork). And it must start with a culture of experimentation and learning, which may directly oppose CoreCo's culture of accountability to plans.

insider is usually not made through careful consideration but by default. An internal transfer is quick and easy and causes minimal internal dissent.

Some executives have argued that an outsider cannot succeed at the top of NewCo because she does not have a track record with the senior executive team. As a result, this person will have difficulty getting support from existing groups within CoreCo. Where there are conflicts with CoreCo—say, competition for limited capital—an outside leader may have little chance to prevail.

This concern is valid, but the leader of NewCo should not be fighting these battles alone. She should report directly to an executive on the senior staff who is well respected, well connected, and responsible for ensuring that NewCo is appropriately supported. We have much more to say about this person's role in chapter 5.

Have the NewCo Head Report to a High Point

The head of NewCo should report to an unconventionally high point within the corporation. She should report to an executive more senior than the head of CoreCo.[5]

In many organizations, status is commensurate with resources under command, the number of people managed, or the number of years of tenure. It is thus unorthodox to have the head of NewCo—someone with few resources and probably an outside hire—report to someone on the senior staff. Nonetheless, the head of NewCo must be made a peer of the head of CoreCo on the organization chart, even though NewCo may initially represent only one one-hundredth of CoreCo's budget.

The alternative—having the head of NewCo report to the head of CoreCo or someone even lower on the organizational chart—exposes NewCo to several dangers. The general manager of CoreCo is a powerful executive immersed in the existing business and is likely to reinforce CoreCo's orthodoxies. Further, the head of CoreCo is likely to have conflicts with NewCo over resources, priorities, and philosophies. In fact, he may view NewCo strictly in terms of how it can advance CoreCo's needs. Any leader who is evaluated and compensated on the basis of short-term profitability against targets will view NewCo's budget in this light and will feel a need first and foremost to minimize any negative impact by NewCo on CoreCo's operating earnings. The only way around this is for funding decisions to come from higher in the organization.

Establish New Norms for Functional Interactions

Over time, NewCo must create its own version of roles and responsibilities that define how the major business functions (such as marketing and product development) interact.[6] At least until an effective and stable structure is established, NewCo should operate under a single leader and should not report to any centralized functional groups such as sales or product development.

The processes required for NewCo to deliver value may be dramatically different from those in CoreCo. It may be expedient to adopt CoreCo's norms for interactions within and among functions, but NewCo must have the flexibility to learn through experimentation which structure and which routines will work best. Until such routines are established and roles and responsibilities solidified, NewCo will operate most effectively under a single point of leadership. For example, CMT needed to abandon the rigidly defined five-stage innovation process along with its definitive expectations for the centralized research, development, and manufacturing functions. To accomplish this, CMT needed a single leader.

Change the Basis of Accountability

Do not judge the leader of NewCo on the basis of performance against plans. Instead, judge him based on a more subjective set of criteria, such as effort, quality of decision making, and ability to adjust to changing conditions and lessons learned. We will have much more to say about how the senior management team can ensure an environment of discipline and accountability, even without judging NewCo by the numbers, in chapters 6–9.[7]

Disciplined accountability for performance against plans simply cannot work in NewCo's uncertain environment. Traditional planning systems were designed to implement a proven strategy by ensuring accountability under the presumption of reliable predictability. Planning systems for strategic experiments, by contrast, should be designed to hasten discovery of a winning strategy by supporting learning, given the unpleasant reality of reliable unpredictability. But no such system is in wide use.

As the CMT story shows, when a company adheres to the presumption of reliable predictability, the results for NewCo can be disastrous. Forecasts for NewCo are treated as though they are much better than they really are. In fact, when a promising forecast is accepted as part of NewCo's business plan, the perception that NewCo is succeeding can strengthen dramatically—on the basis of the forecast alone. In companies that have strong accountability to numbers in plans, the expectation is that what is written in a plan can be achieved if managers simply do their jobs.

When outcomes fall short of predictions, NewCo should evaluate, learn, and reset expectations, but this is easier said than done. Failing to measure up to a forecast can dramatically affect how senior executives perceive NewCo's performance, with disastrous consequences. The ensuing perception of failure can lead to unnecessary and disruptive changes in NewCo's strategy, leadership, organizational structure, or all of these.

Leaders of strategic experiments must avoid setting rigid expectations. They need to focus on what is achievable in the near term and minimize talk about long-term revenue projections. They must recognize that their plans are based on untested assumptions and proceed accordingly.

Match NewCo's Performance Measures to NewCo's Business Model

Do not apply CoreCo's performance metrics to NewCo without careful consideration. Take particular care with the profitability metric.

Strategic experiments can easily go astray when NewCo is measured based on CoreCo standards. In the CMT story, the quality measure is illustrative. Critical success factors vary from one market to another, as do cost structures. For this reason, measures and their associated standards within CoreCo are often not relevant for NewCo. They should be supplanted by measures that help managers continuously refine judgments about NewCo's probability of success.

For any strategic experiment, the one measure most likely to be judged on the basis of CoreCo standards is the bottom line—profitability. This was not problematic for CMT but could have become an issue after CMT launched human DNA microarrays and generated its first major revenue stream.

There are two reasons that using the profitability measure for strategic experiments can be problematic. First, there is never an unambiguous method for calculating it. Internal transfer costs for resources that NewCo borrows from CoreCo can be allocated in several ways. Because of such ambiguity, NewCo's decision making should not be driven by profitability measures but by incremental cash flows, at least until NewCo is a proven and stable business.

A bigger problem with the profitability metric is the difficulty of knowing when to insist that NewCo achieve profitability. Because there is no obvious choice, strategic experiments are often faced with demands for profitability at arbitrary times—a poor practice. Sometimes NewCo is assigned a grace period, after which it is on the hook. Demands for profitability can also be driven by the rhythm of the annual planning cycle or by changing business conditions within CoreCo, even though CoreCo's business cycle likely has nothing to do with NewCo's long-term prospects.

Encourage NewCo to Develop a Distinct Culture

Culture is a pattern of shared values, beliefs, and decision biases within an organization that establishes norms for behavior. In successful organizations, the culture strengthens over time as certain values and beliefs become strongly correlated with positive results. But NewCo is experimental and has no record of success. Thus, NewCo must start building its culture from a nearly blank slate. The values, beliefs, and decision biases that are supportive of CoreCo's business model may or may not be relevant to NewCo. Therefore, until NewCo's business is proven, NewCo's culture must remain fluid. Only those elements of culture that are nearly universal (such as the importance of teamwork, for example) should be transferred from CoreCo to NewCo.

NewCo also needs a culture of experimentation and learning, even though this may directly oppose CoreCo's culture of accountability to plans or emphasis on continuous process improvement.[8] Supportive cultural norms include valuing creativity and flexibility, favoring quick decisions (as opposed to multilevel hierarchical approvals), seeking rapid performance feedback and using it to openly examine past decisions, sharing information frequently and openly across functions, and being willing to take risks. CMT made some modifications in this direction after its leadership change.

A Framework for Assessing the Intensity of the Forgetting Challenge

Some innovation initiatives, such as continuous improvement efforts or new-product launches, do not involve a significant forgetting challenge because the business model remains the same. But every strategic experiment faces a difficult forgetting challenge. NewCo needs DNA that is dramatically different from CoreCo's.

Still, among strategic experiments, there is variation in the intensity of the challenge. The degree of difficulty depends on two things: the fundamental drivers of the forgetting challenge and the organizational intensifiers of the forgetting challenge. Table 3-3 and figure 3-2 guide you in assessing the magnitude of the forgetting challenge.

This assessment is worthwhile because some of our recommendations are variable. When the intensity of the forgetting challenge is high, the recommendations should be followed more aggressively. For

TABLE 3-3

Assessing the intensity of the forgetting challenge

This table is used in conjunction with figure 3-2 to assess the intensity of the forgetting challenge.

	Do you agree with these statements? (1 = strongly disagree, 7 = strongly agree, or NA)	Rating (1–7)
Fundamental drivers of the forgetting challenge	1. NewCo serves an unfamiliar customer.	
	2. NewCo offers a value proposition that emphasizes different fundamental elements such as cost, quality, convenience, and service.	
	3. NewCo requires processes that are fundamentally different from CoreCo's processes in various functions (sales, marketing, manufacturing, etc.), or the relationships *between* functions are substantially altered.	
	4. NewCo requires competencies that CoreCo does not possess.	
	5. NewCo faces significant uncertainties. Customer desires, technology, and competitor behavior are evolving quickly and are difficult to predict.	
	Calculate the average rating (excluding NAs) to determine the magnitude of the fundamental drivers of the forgetting challenge. On the horizontal axis of figure 3-2, a score of 4 defines the midpoint between "low" and "high."	
Intensifiers of the forgetting challenge	1. The corporation has a strong culture of accountability to plans.	
	2. The corporation has only one business model.	
	3. All business units within the corporation are at similar points in the business life cycle (i.e., start-up, rapid growth, expansion, maturity, decline).	
	4. CoreCo has well-established standards of business performance that do not apply to NewCo, often because NewCo has a different cost structure.	
	5. The corporation has a well-defined culture specific to its business and has effective socialization mechanisms built into its hiring and acquisition processes.	
	6. The corporation has a history of promoting primarily from within.	
	Calculate the average rating (excluding NAs) to determine the magnitude of the intensifiers of the forgetting challenge. On the vertical axis of figure 3-2, a score of 4 defines the midpoint between "low" and "high."	

FIGURE 3-2

Intensity of the forgetting challenge

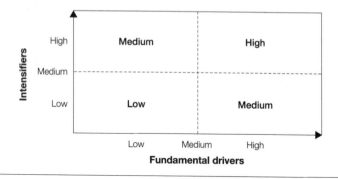

example, you might increase the proportion of NewCo's staff hired from outside the corporation, or you might abandon even more of Core-Co's standard performance measures in favor of ones customized to NewCo's business model.

Our recommendations are not intended as a cookbook recipe. Every strategic experiment is unique, and organizational DNA choices must be pondered in the context of a specific opportunity and a specific organization. We suggest, however, that in considering NewCo's organizational design, the recommendations here—and not CoreCo's existing design—should constitute the starting point. Alterations should be made only on the basis of strong context-specific arguments.

Because of the need for dramatic organizational change, it may take months to build NewCo. Taking the time that is needed is usually a better choice than rushing to market, even when there is evidence that competitors may beat you to market. The first-mover advantage argument is often overstated.

Each of the strategic experiments that we studied faced forgetting challenges of varying magnitudes. As we probe other stories of strategic innovation in this book, we will not leave the forgetting challenge behind. Although subsequent chapters focus on borrowing and learning, we periodically review the impact of the forgetting challenge and the power of organizational DNA to overcome it.

Chapter Four

WHY TENSIONS RISE WHEN
NEWCO BORROWS FROM CORECO

O VERCOMING the forgetting challenge is necessary but not sufficient. To have the best possible chance at success, NewCo must also borrow CoreCo resources.[1] This requires a delicate balance. New-Co must be distinct from CoreCo, because a distinct organizational design enables NewCo to forget. At the same time, NewCo must not be isolated from CoreCo. The two business units must be linked, even though interactions between NewCo and CoreCo will inevitably create frictions. Only when NewCo is both distinct from and linked to Core-Co can NewCo both forget and borrow.

The story of New York Times Digital (NYTD), the Internet division of The New York Times Company (hereafter, "the company") is illuminating. (The company owned many much smaller media properties in addition to the *New York Times*, and NYTD operated several Web sites. However, for simplicity, we focus here strictly on the *Times* newspaper and NYTimes.com.)

The NYTD story has many parallels to the CMT story. Initially, the company replicated its organizational DNA for NYTD. Later, recognizing that the new business was too wedded to the constraints of the established one, the company reorganized NYTD, almost completely overhauling its DNA. The division began operating much more independently and as a result was able to explore new territory.

Still, no investor would bet on NYTD if it were to walk away from the *New York Times* brand, write its own news, or ignore relationships with the advertising community that the newspaper had developed over decades. NYTD could be fully effective only if it learned how to leverage these resources, even as a separate entity.

For some time, it struggled to do so. In this chapter, we examine the root causes of difficulties that arise when NewCo is linked to CoreCo.

Entering the Internet World and Struggling to Forget

In 1995, an employee in the information systems group at the *New York Times* who was responsible for keeping an eye on emerging technologies warned, "This Internet thing is going to be huge. It is a tremendous opportunity. We have to get on the bandwagon!" CEO Russ Lewis agreed. He launched a strategic experiment, at the time dubbed the New York Times Electronic Media Company, to explore what the world of the Internet would be all about.

Recognizing that his company did not have all the skills it needed for the endeavor, Lewis immediately initiated an external search for an executive who could lead it. He hired Martin Nisenholtz, an expert with a long career in interactive media. In doing so, Lewis took an important step in overcoming the forgetting challenge. However, in every other way, the new business was formed with DNA nearly identical to that of the core business.

For example, Nisenholtz reported directly to both the general manager and the editor of the newspaper rather than to a senior executive at the corporate level. A respected journalist with a long career at the *Times* was named director of editorial operations. The rest of the staff came through internal transfers, including the team of four that created the basic software to publish the first edition of NYTimes.com. The planning cycle was fully integrated with that of the core business. Although Nisenholtz brought an outsider's viewpoint, the new operation was closely supervised by powerful executives from the newspaper and thus inherited the newspaper's conservative culture and values.

The approach of keeping the new business closely integrated with the existing one was not without benefit. Even though no one knew what the future of Internet journalism was, the newspaper employees generally viewed the NYTimes.com operation as credible, precisely because it was closely supervised by newspaper staff. This would not necessarily have been the case if the new unit, like the long-established broadcast division, had reported directly to corporate. As a result, efforts to coordinate NewCo and CoreCo operations proceeded relatively smoothly.

But being part of an established organization also created limitations. At first, Nisenholtz and some of his colleagues had ambitions to create an entirely new and separate newsroom. In his view, an entirely new medium demanded that the processes of news gathering, production, and presentation be fundamentally reexamined. The notion had merit, but Nisenholtz had to settle for a much narrower focus for NYTimes.com. The newspaper would be responsible for all the journalism, and NYTimes.com would be, in essence, a software operation.

The NYTimes.com team repurposed newspaper content for the Internet by altering headlines, adding hyperlinks, resizing photos, and changing captions. They updated the Web site throughout the night until the final edition of the paper went to press. They also found new ways to make the Web site more valuable. They experimented with various ways to package content, tested the nascent multimedia capabilities of the Internet, and explored the possibilities of interactivity. Occasionally, they integrated information or databases from outside sources with their own content.

Each year, the company increased the resources allocated to NYTimes.com. But Nisenholtz acutely felt the constraints of working for an established corporation. In particular, the newspaper management team was concerned about diverting resources to an experimental business that had only a distant and uncertain hope of returning a profit. Nisenholtz, by contrast, felt that he needed to spend much more money to fully capitalize on the possibilities of the Internet. He felt as though he were running nothing more than a "newspaper.com" operation, when something much more radical was possible. He did not have the technology infrastructure to support the type of Web site he visualized, nor did he have the type of staff he needed.

Soon, he would have a powerful ally on his side—Wall Street. In the first three years in the life of NYTimes.com, the NASDAQ had doubled. Valuations of technology stocks were surging. The buzz in the financial press was all Internet. Soon Nisenholtz was not alone in wondering whether the company was devoting sufficient resources to NYTimes.com, or whether there was sufficient active and creative dialogue about the direction in which the Internet operation could go. Competitors appeared to be investing heavily.

Lewis soon received a proposal to take the company's Internet operations public with a special equity security known as a *tracking stock*. This financial strategy would allow the company's Internet activities to be valued more like technology stocks than newspaper stocks. The investment bank making the proposal estimated that the stock would have an appealing valuation. In fact, to Lewis, it was shockingly high. To make it work, he would have to consolidate the company's major Internet operations as a separate division.[2]

The Creation of New York Times Digital

The company formed NYTD as a distinct business unit that had its own income statement and was a peer with other major business units, including the *Times*. Nisenholtz was named the head of NYTD, reporting directly to Lewis. But that was not the only change. Responding to concerns that the Web sites needed more freedom to explore the vast potential of the Internet, Lewis mandated broad reorganization and increased investment.

Nisenholtz subsequently made a number of changes. He established his own policy team for NYTD, including an executive vice president, a CFO, legal counsel, and vice presidents for business development and human resources. He also created a new organizational structure within NYTimes.com. The initial organizational structure for NYTimes.com had borrowed a great deal from traditional newspaper norms, including traditional newspaper titles. In the new structure, new titles were adopted, and a new *product manager* role was created to accelerate product development and cross-functional teamwork. (At NYTimes.com, a *product* was any new and unique way to package content and advertising on the Web site or in e-mail to users.) Product managers also analyzed how the products were being used and continuously improved them. The nature of Internet technology gave NYTimes.com a luxury that the newspaper never had. NYTimes.com was able to gather lightning-fast feedback after launching new products by monitoring the use of each page of its Web site.

To enable the development of more sophisticated products, Nisen-holtz upgraded NYTimes.com's technology infrastructure. Before the organizational change, NYTimes.com had to compete with the news-paper department to get its technology projects prioritized. Soon after the reorganization, NYTimes.com had constructed its own platform.

NYTD also changed its hiring approach, looking outside the corpo-ration to fill new positions. Hiring was challenging in the late 1990s. The lure of stock options on the planned NYTD tracking stock was critical in attracting people who had the profile NYTD sought: young, bright, ambitious, and with dot-com or technology experience. The staff grew to nearly four hundred people, and at that point nearly three-fourths of them were outsiders.

NYTD made a distinct effort to shape culture as the new hires arrived. It wanted to make clear that NYTD was a different company, with a different set of objectives and values from those of the *Times*. Specifically, NYTD wanted to create an experimental culture that min-imized bureaucratic controls, procedures, and paperwork. Rigid pro-cesses were not allowed to develop. A spirit of openness was empha-sized. Further, NYTD did not try to eliminate any redundancies in its Web site operations through centralization of certain operations. NYTimes.com moved into a new building in Manhattan about ten blocks from the newspaper headquarters. The office design included glass walls around executive offices and large open spaces to encourage conversation, cooperation, and teamwork.

NYTD developed a bottom-up approach to budgeting. Ideas for new products came from throughout the organization. There was a lot of guesswork in the financials that supported the plans. The senior pol-icy team evaluated and selected or rejected the plans based on loose net-present-value analysis and professional judgment. The corporation developed revenue and profitability targets for NYTD, but they were frequently revised as the environment changed.

To summarize, Nisenholtz and his colleagues made organizational choices that closely mirrored the six recommendations of chapter 3. Specifically, NYTD did the following:

- Hired extensively from outside the corporation.

- Reported to a high point in the corporation. (NewCo and CoreCo were peers.)

- Developed its own internal organizational logic.

- Allowed financial expectations to be revised as the environment changed and more was learned.

- Focused on performance information most relevant in its own environment.

- Developed a different culture, starting with a focus on experimentation.

As a result, NYTD overcame the forgetting challenge. Note that NYTD also moved to separate office space. Several companies we studied believed that separate physical space helped NewCo develop into a distinct organizational entity.

There was an explosion of creativity following the reorganization. NYTimes.com expanded dramatically in scope and functionality. The new organization was so successful in coming up with fresh ideas that the ability to hire and train people was the chief constraint on the rate of investment in new products.

One major enhancement was building a *continuous news* function. This group of journalists was responsible for adding *New York Times* style and perspective to breaking news reports from around the world and publishing on the Web site as quickly as possible. The *Times* was no longer tied to a daily publishing cycle. At times, it chose to break exclusive stories on NYTimes.com. This arrangement helped minimize the chance of being scooped by the broadcast media, which could go on the air at any time.

NYTimes.com developed a distinct business model. It began to understand that its customers were different from those of the newspaper. Whereas the bulk of *Times* readers still came from within the New York metropolitan area, NYTimes.com users were dispersed worldwide. Traditional newspaper advertisers were slow to adapt to the Internet, so NYTD sold advertisements to technology companies and through newly rising Internet-only advertising agencies. In addition, users of the Web site acted differently from readers of the newspaper. Newspaper readers tended to browse entire sections, whereas Web site users often conducted more targeted searches for specific bits of information.

NYTD also developed processes that departed from *Times* norms—in particular, the fast-paced continuous news function, as well as a product development process that involved a high level of collaboration be-tween business and editorial staff. NYTD also built a different balance of competencies from those at the *Times*, with a heavier reliance on technology expertise than journalistic know-how. And NYTD adapted to the rapidly changing world of the Internet, accepting the uncertainty inherent in the environment by allowing frequent updates of plans.

Tensions Between NYTD and the Newspaper

Although NYTD reaped tremendous benefits from operating much more independently, it could not survive, or even operate, without the core business. NYTimes.com relied on the *Times* brand and borrowed most of its content from the *Times* newspaper. In addition, there were clear synergies to be gained in advertising if NYTimes.com could col-laborate with the newspaper in selling large ad packages and in shaping a new combined offering for classifieds. But after the reorganization, tensions developed between NYTD and the core organization, and these tensions disrupted borrowing.

There were several sources of friction. Because NYTD had made it clear that it was trying to build a different kind of organization, interac-tions between the two took on an "us versus them" undertone. (NYTD communicated that it aimed to be fast-moving, antibureaucratic, and willing to take risks and experiment—as though that were new and dif-ferent. But of course the *Times* aspired to be the same and winced at the implication that it was not.) Further, it was easy to resent the attention that the business media lavished on the technology industry. Additional coverage of NYTD's proposed stock offering further heightened antagonisms, because some people felt that a few newcomers stood to get rich on the back of a brand that had been built over decades. (In fairness, NYTD employees' jobs were much less secure, and many had given up a chance to participate in the company's pension plan to have a chance to receive options on the tracking stock. As it turned out, it took longer than expected to get the tracking stock ready for public offering. By the time it was ready, the NASDAQ had declined dramat-ically and the offering was withdrawn.)

There were additional sources of unease within certain functions. The newspaper department that was least enamored of NYTD was circulation. Its fear was hardly irrational. Making newspaper content available on the Internet at no charge gave readers a powerful reason not to subscribe to the print version of the newspaper.

The group that sold display advertisements (as opposed to classifieds) also was nervous about the NYTD sales group, which was eager to take advantage of the existing sales relationships to sell advertising space on the Web. Many of the salespeople had developed relationships over years or even decades and naturally wished to protect them. In addition, they didn't understand the new media as well, and neither did their clients, so it was a difficult sell. The commission structure encouraged dedication to the much larger newspaper packages. Finally, some believed that the only way their clients would make room for Internet advertising was to reduce their budgets for print advertising.

The editorial staffers of the newspaper were also concerned. Their anxieties focused on the high level of collaboration allowed between business staff and editorial staff at NYTimes.com. In the newspaper industry, respect for a "Chinese Wall" between business and editorial had become a sacred principle, one that ensured that the integrity of journalists was not corrupted by commercial pressures. At the *Times*, journalists were barred from speaking to managers on the business side of the organization and were even prohibited from visiting certain floors of the corporate headquarters. (NYTD managers understood the principle, but they thought that much less drastic controls were sufficient, given NYTD's limited journalistic role.)

Tensions heightened as the economy started to slump in late 2000. Newspaper operations were particularly sensitive to the state of the economy because advertising tended to be one of the first things that corporations cut. The company's operating profits dropped sharply. As a result, NYTD's losses as a fraction of the company's operating profits doubled to nearly 20 percent in less than six months. In early 2001, it was easy for some newspaper managers to resent the fact that NYTD was losing millions while they were pinching pennies.

The March to Profitability

With the tracking stock abandoned and the corporation's cash flows deteriorating, NYTD was suddenly under intense pressure to achieve profitability. Martin Nisenholtz had anticipated the pressures, and he quickly initiated conversations that led to two layoffs, cutting the staff nearly in half and reducing the breadth of features offered on the Web site.

The layoffs were sobering after the ebullience of the dot-com run-up. In retrospect, Nisenholtz acknowledged that in 1999 and 2000 he had expanded operations beyond what was sustainable. But he had no regrets about the organizational change. It had enabled him to hire a talented staff and build a sophisticated technology infrastructure—the foundations of the business.

From a financial perspective, the layoffs were successful. NYTD achieved profitability late in 2001. It was fortunate to do so, because the economic environment after September 11, 2001, was a strain for the corporation. NYTD barely escaped a proposal to reintegrate the organization with the newspaper. In fact, few newspapers retained separate Internet divisions through this period.

In subsequent years, NYTD enjoyed a period of stability and calm, and it continued to grow and increase its profitability. The senior management team, the *Times*, and NYTD all worked together to improve the effectiveness of the links between NewCo and CoreCo.

Tensions are inevitable between NewCo and CoreCo. Up to a point, tensions are healthy. They show that people are engaged and really care, and they are more likely to place real issues on the table. But even though tensions can be productive, they can also escalate and disrupt borrowing.

The tensions between NYTD and the newspaper were not unique. Such tensions are part of the challenges of managing strategic innovation. Smartly managing the tensions that arise between NewCo and CoreCo is the crux of the borrowing challenge. Unlike other companies in our research, which struggled to create effective cooperation, The New York Times Company succeeded. Healthy and productive levels of tension were achieved and maintained.

In summary, NYTD evolved from integrated to isolated to distinct but linked, as shown in figure 4-1. At first it could borrow but not forget. After the reorganization it could forget but struggled to borrow. In time, it learned to do both. NYTD became the model of the distinct but linked strategic experiment that is able to simultaneously forget and borrow. This reflects great credit on the company's management team. By 2004, NYTD was earning more than $30 million annually on revenues of approximately $100 million.

FIGURE 4-1

NYTD's organizational evolution

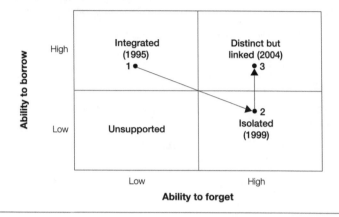

Understanding the Root Causes of Tensions

Tensions cannot be managed effectively if they are not anticipated. Based on our research at The New York Times Company and other organizations, we offer the following observations about the root causes of tensions:

- Tensions rise when CoreCo perceives that NewCo will cannibalize CoreCo revenues.

- Tensions rise when CoreCo perceives that NewCo could render a CoreCo competence obsolete.

- Nervousness is inevitable when CoreCo perceives that NewCo might damage crucial CoreCo assets, such as brands or customer relationships.

- Early on, revenue growth for NewCo often increases losses. This can elevate tensions as CoreCo managers loudly question the wisdom of allocating capital to a business incurring a loss. Bonuses tied to corporate profits exacerbate the situation.

- Resource scarcity heightens tensions, so tensions rise when there is a downturn in the core business. CoreCo is likely to disagree on priorities for allocating capital, manufacturing capacity, employee time, and other resources.

- CoreCo managers can become angry if they are inexperienced with or unaware of the differing needs of units at different stages of the business life cycle. Examples include the need to evaluate business performance differently, the need to place more emphasis on flexibility than efficiency, and the need to hire, promote, and compensate based on different criteria. In fact, if NewCo managers receive large bonuses when NewCo succeeds, CoreCo may specifically resent the fact that NewCo's success was dependent on CoreCo resources.

- NewCo, if designed properly, feels foreign to CoreCo. This can make it difficult to establish trust.

- CoreCo managers may become jealous of NewCo, especially if NewCo starts to receive strong public endorsements from analysts, the press, outside consultants, or the CEO. CoreCo managers have worked for years or decades to advance, and now CoreCo may appear inferior to a younger and sexier division.

- Comments or attitudes based on stereotypes about the capabilities of new and old companies, such as "Big companies cannot be agile or entrepreneurial," can be hurtful and destructive. Or CoreCo employees may naturally grant respect and credibility only on the basis of size and resources under command, and this can be hurtful to NewCo employees, who do not want to feel marginalized, small, unprofitable, or unimportant.

- Tensions may rise if NewCo needs to alter some CoreCo processes. CoreCo may be so disciplined about process efficiency that it is unwilling to do so.

How great are the tensions likely to be between your core organization and its strategic experiment? Any or all of these sources of tension may play a role.

Critically, sources of tension are dynamic. They will evolve as NewCo passes from infancy, to winning a first customer, to rapid growth, to profitability, and to maturity. Because anticipating tensions is the key to overcoming the borrowing challenge, it is crucial to understand the

FIGURE 4-2

Dynamics of tensions between NewCo and CoreCo

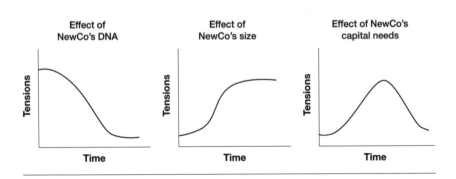

forces that elevate or ameliorate tensions. As shown in figure 4-2, there are three primary dynamic forces.

First, through the long maturation process, NewCo's DNA will naturally evolve to something closer to CoreCo's DNA. Eventually, New-Co will act like a mature business, focused on optimizing profitability rather than exploring new territory. This gradual convergence reduces tensions.

Second, increases in NewCo's size aggravate tensions. When New-Co is very small, tensions will be minimal, simply because NewCo is an inconsequential activity for most CoreCo managers. But as NewCo grows and demands more through its interactions with CoreCo, tensions naturally rise.

A third major force is the balance of NewCo resource needs and the corporation's resource availability. NewCo is in greatest need of resources during its growth phase, especially that part of the growth phase that precedes profitability. Tensions are likely to be greatest during this interval—and even worse if deterioration in CoreCo's business environment weakens profitability and thus resource availability. As NewCo nears profitability, its capital needs decline, as do tensions.

In chapter 5, we shift from diagnosing the root causes of borrowing problems to developing strategies for overcoming them.

Chapter Five

TURNING TENSION INTO A PRODUCTIVE FORCE

T HIS CHAPTER outlines a three-step approach for overcoming the borrowing challenge. First, select the right links between New-Co and CoreCo. Second, establish a cooperative environment for borrowing. Third, monitor interactions and intervene as necessary to keep tensions healthy and productive. We conclude by identifying six borrowing strategies along with the unique challenges associated with each.

Select the Right Links

CoreCo likely has a vast range of assets that look valuable to NewCo. For example, NewCo may desire to leverage CoreCo's brands, expertise, manufacturing facilities, information systems, and networks of customers, suppliers, or distributors. To do so, it will want to create links that can take on a variety of operational forms. NewCo may want to coordinate shared use of an existing asset, to create joint teams to share knowledge, to merge NewCo processes with existing CoreCo processes, or even to create new processes.

The resources of the corporation are so vast and so attractive that some corporations approach the borrowing challenge with the notion that NewCo will have the best chance to succeed if it borrows as much as possible from CoreCo. This approach is a common mistake. Links should be selected carefully. Each is a significant endeavor, one that will likely challenge the senior management team. Each link increases the risk that NewCo will be overexposed to CoreCo's DNA and will have trouble maintaining its distinctiveness. Borrowing can easily go too far.

Choose Only the Most Powerful Links

NewCo should be linked to CoreCo only where NewCo can gain a crucial competitive advantage.

Usually, no more than two links meet this criteria. Incremental cost reductions are never sufficient justification for creating a link. When you seek such benefits, a partnership with a third-party provider of services for start-up organizations can be a better approach.

NYTD was highly unusual in that it had four important links to the *Times*. NYTD leveraged the newspaper's journalistic content (and thus its brand), it coordinated sales calls with key newspaper customers, it developed new products jointly with the newspaper, and it created a joint offering of print and digital classifieds. All these lent crucial competitive advantages to NYTD.

Links should be created early in NewCo's life. To ensure that it can forget, you may be tempted to isolate NewCo at first and plan to create links later. But an independent NewCo will only become more entrenched in its independence as it grows and succeeds, and integration will only become more difficult.[1]

Avoid Sharp Conflicts of Interest

Links should be avoided where conflicts between NewCo and CoreCo are acute.

For example, although there might have been benefits to cooperation between NYTD and the newspaper's circulation department, such a link would have been especially difficult to manage because of the perceived direct threat NYTD posed to circulation revenues.

Avoid Links to Support Departments

Links to support departments (such as human resources, information technology, finance, legal, or purchasing) may seem convenient, but the money saved will not make or break NewCo. In fact, policies established within functions such as human resources and finance have powerful impacts on an organization's DNA. It is worthwhile to duplicate these functions within NewCo.

It appears particularly important that NYTD created its own human resources, finance, and information technology functions. Establishing new practices in these areas helped NYTD create the kind of organization it needed so that it could forget. NYTD retained its own separate senior policy team even as it worked hard to create links to the *Times* in other areas.

Consider, on the other hand, the early years of a strategic experiment at General Motors (GM). When GM designed OnStar to commercialize in-vehicle information, navigation, and telecommunications services, it emphasized the importance of exploiting the vast resources of the firm. Many links were established between OnStar and GM. Some worked well, but in other cases incompatibilities were too great. Three links were particularly problematic: in IT, purchasing, and HR.

The computer system in OnStar's call center was the heart of OnStar's business. Even though IT played a much less critical role for GM as a whole, the IT link was strong. In fact, OnStar's IT head reported to both OnStar and GM's IT department. Following GM practice, OnStar created the smallest possible IT group—only enough personnel to manage agreements with outside programmers and system integrators.

But the practice of outsourcing as much as possible made it hard for OnStar's staff to build thorough knowledge of its own system, OnStar's most crucial asset. Every enhancement had ramifications throughout the system, which many people had worked on but few had a full understanding of. The group had a difficult time keeping up with demands for new functionality, and soon a major reconstruction of the system was necessary.

Although GM's purchasing group had succeeded in saving billions for the corporation through a rigorously controlled bidding process designed to ensure competition among suppliers, the complexity of OnStar's needs and its inability to specify exactly what was required made the purchasing system ineffective. The purchasing system also worked on rhythms appropriate for the multiyear product development cycles that characterized GM's core business, but OnStar needed to move more quickly.

Moreover, GM's human resources group defined specific compensation norms for all positions. As a result, OnStar had a hard time attracting talented IT experts to Detroit in the middle of the dot-com craze.

Because standard processes and decision biases in IT, HR, and purchasing were contrary to OnStar's needs, OnStar would have been better served to isolate itself from these functions and develop its own processes. Nonetheless, without intense competition for several years, OnStar was able to overcome many frustrations and continued to expand its subscriber base.[2]

Link, Don't Outsource

Be wary of proposals for outsourcing entire functions to CoreCo rather than creating a jointly managed link.

Such an approach can make it hard for NewCo to forget. For example, had NYTD not built its own sales group but instead relied strictly on the *Times* display ad sales group, it likely would have called only on traditional customers and conveyed the digital value proposition in the same terms as the print value proposition. Because NYTD had its own independent sales team, it had the flexibility to define a different approach and leverage *Times* sales relationships with certain customers.

Establish a Cooperative Environment

After you have identified links, the senior management team should not simply leave the details to the general managers of NewCo and CoreCo to work out on their own initiative. This is another common mistake.

Senior management involvement is crucial. There are too many natural conflicts of interest between the two GMs. The heart of CoreCo's general manager is likely to—and should—remain closely aligned with the interests of CoreCo. Because the general manager of CoreCo manages a much larger business than NewCo and probably has much longer tenure within the organization, he will tend to have a stronger negotiating position and will resolve points of dispute in favor of the shorter-term interests of CoreCo. Furthermore, coordinating NewCo and CoreCo is demanding and requires an ability to think in two extremely different contexts. Even with the best interests of NewCo in mind, the general manager of CoreCo does not have sufficient time for it.

In the approach we recommend, little interaction between general managers is necessary because effective borrowing can usually take place at the operational level (see figure 5-1). Working through the hierarchy is neither necessary nor desirable.

FIGURE 5-1

Selected links between NewCo and CoreCo at the operational level

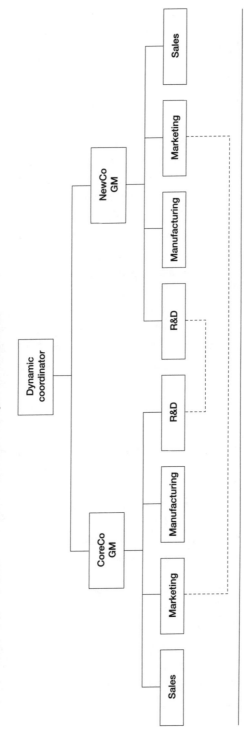

Coordination at operational levels is most likely to be successful if the senior management team takes the following five steps, starting when NewCo is created.

Reinforce Common Ground

Redouble efforts to strengthen common values that inspire both NewCo and CoreCo.

Inevitably, the NewCo and CoreCo cultures will have conflicting elements. For example, the *Times* newspaper viewed its premium subscription price as a proper reward for high-quality content, whereas NYTD did not charge readers at all. Such conflicts are inevitable, and should be balanced with a "metaculture" consisting of values shared by both NewCo and CoreCo. Common values will be nearly universal, but this does not diminish their ability to unify. Examples include teamwork, collaboration, communication, mutual respect, loyalty to a shared brand, respect for diversity, and the necessity of always judging the performance of the corporation from both a short-term and a long-term perspective. At The New York Times Company, Russ Lewis constantly reinforced the company's "Rules of the Road" (see figure 5-2), which capture many of these values.

FIGURE 5-2

The New York Times Company's "Rules of the Road"

Rules of the Road

Success at The New York Times Company means more than achieving our financial and journalistic goals. All of us should conduct ourselves in a manner consistent with the following tenets of behavior:

- Treat each other with honesty, respect and civility.
- Strive for excellence—don't settle for less.
- Embrace diversity.
- Contribute your individual excellence to team efforts.
- Take risks and innovate, recognizing that failure occasionally occurs.
- Information is power; share it.
- Accept responsibility; delegate authority.
- Give and accept constructive feedback.
- Maintain perspective and a sense of humor.

Source: The New York Times Company

Keep NewCo Close to Home

Although it is helpful to make NewCo's office space distinct and separate from CoreCo's, the two should not be so far apart that coordination of borrowing is highly inconvenient.

One manager at The New York Times Company commented that about one mile of separation was ideal—far enough to have your own culture, close enough to get support when you need it.

Change Narrow Incentives

Reconsider compensation and promotion incentives that reward CoreCo performance so strongly that it is likely CoreCo managers will resist supporting NewCo.

The senior management team should consider at least partly replacing such incentives with ones that reward CoreCo managers based on the combined performance of NewCo and CoreCo. Doing so does not guarantee unqualified support. CoreCo employees may be predisposed to conclude that what is best for the corporation is to feed CoreCo with resources and starve NewCo. Still, achieving cooperation is easier if incentives reward results at the aggregate, corporate level. Another helpful step is to include an assessment of each manager's skill in collaborating with other business units in her individual performance reviews.

Replenish CoreCo Resources

Agree to maintain CoreCo's resource base at a level high enough at least to maintain current performance.

If CoreCo is being run as efficiently as possible, there are no slack resources. CoreCo's general manager will naturally worry that any diversion of resources to NewCo will cause CoreCo's performance to suffer. The senior management team must reassure CoreCo's leader that they intend to make it as easy as possible to be supportive of NewCo. It should be a minimal distraction, so that CoreCo's manager can focus on managing CoreCo as well as possible. CoreCo is a large, established business, and a full-time responsibility.

Assure the leader of CoreCo that his business will get access to additional resources to enable CoreCo to give NewCo the support it needs. In return, simply ask him to help persuade CoreCo employees to take a positive attitude toward NewCo, which NewCo could play a crucial role in CoreCo's future.

Some observers believe that cooperation from the general manager of CoreCo is so important to NewCo that it may be advisable to replace her if she does not fully support NewCo.[3] We view this approach as far too risky. NewCo is an experiment, and CoreCo is the foundation. The experienced general manager of CoreCo is too valuable an asset for the corporation to lose. Instead, neutralize her concerns about how CoreCo will be affected.

Examine Transfer Pricing Policies Closely

Ensure that CoreCo's income statement is properly compensated through fair transfer pricing policies.

The task of examining policies for allocating costs between NewCo and CoreCo proves strikingly important, even though decisions within NewCo should not be affected by any calculation that relies on an internal cost allocation. Instead, decision making within NewCo should focus on risk-return assessments informed by incremental cash flow analyses.

But cost allocations between NewCo and CoreCo affect motivations and emotions. Tensions can be reduced if CoreCo managers feel that they are being fairly compensated for their efforts to support NewCo and if joint revenues are shared appropriately. Clearly, the need for a perception of fairness is much more pronounced if bonus formulas remain in place that are tied to business unit profitability.

Some corporations that we observed set low transfer prices to give NewCo the best possible chance at success. But this approach can accelerate tensions by giving CoreCo an incentive to prioritize the needs of full-paying external customers ahead of NewCo's.

Setting too high a transfer price can also be detrimental. NewCo needs credibility within the corporation. Within most corporations, there is nothing that lends more credibility then being able to demonstrate that you are profitable—or on a path that is rapidly taking you to profitability. When NYTD attained profitability, it was a momentous event. There was great joy. NYTD suddenly had much greater credibility when it interacted with the newspaper, even though the measurement of NYTD's profitability was sufficiently ambiguous that it could be debated for hours.

NYTD paid a fixed fee plus a royalty to the newspaper for use of its content, but there was little in the way of definitive benchmarks to tie the actual terms to. Nor was there an attempt to account for NYTD's use of the *Times* brand. (It would be hard even to know the direction of an appropriate payment. Did NYTD benefit from use of the brand, or did it actually enhance the brand to the benefit of the newspaper?) In addition, there was no effort to compensate NYTD for new subscriptions generated through the Web site. On the other hand, NYTD inherited the company's existing business of selling digital copies of newspaper archives, an operation sufficiently profitable to have a dramatic impact on NYTD's profitability.

Ambiguous or not, NewCo's profitability is a powerful symbol. The senior management team must find a cost allocation policy that fairly compensates CoreCo for the resources it lends NewCo and gives NewCo the best possible shot at achieving profitability.

Monitor Ongoing Interactions

Careful selection of links and a solid effort to create a cooperative environment do not guarantee that borrowing will proceed smoothly. The task of monitoring ongoing interactions between NewCo and CoreCo, and intervening as necessary to keep tensions at healthy and productive levels, is best delegated to a single senior executive to whom the general managers of both NewCo and CoreCo report. We will call this executive the *dynamic coordinator* (DC).

The role of the DC is demanding. It takes a level of commitment, time, and energy far out of proportion to the size of NewCo. The DC must be influential and respected within the corporation. In larger corporations, he must define the combined priorities of NewCo and CoreCo, must compete with other business units for capital to support NewCo, and must garner the support of other senior executives to endure the years of losses that may be necessary.

In smaller corporations, the DC may be the CEO or a member of the CEO's staff. The DC should be skilled enough to understand the different needs of start-up and established organizations and preferably should have experience in both environments. The DC must always be mindful of the following six priorities.

Maintain NewCo's Distinct Character

The DC should ensure that NewCo's organizational DNA is stable and is not diluted over time through interaction with CoreCo.

Because CoreCo is larger and more powerful, it can easily infect NewCo with its own DNA. To help prevent this, the DC must constantly explain the rationale for differences between the two organizations. For example, the business performance of a new and experimental business must be evaluated differently from that of a mature one. For CoreCo, accountability to plans must be emphasized, whereas for NewCo the emphasis should be on experimentation, learning, and adaptability. Further, NewCo and CoreCo managers may be compensated differently, with different trade-offs between risk and return. The DC must reinforce the notion that these differences are fair and appropriate.

Coach in Two Contexts

The DC must coach and support two general managers facing fundamentally different challenges.

Because it is often best to hire an outsider to lead NewCo, the DC must not let CoreCo's general manager socialize the leader of NewCo into "the way things are done around here."[4] Tensions between these two leaders can be sharp, particularly if there is potential for cannibalization of revenues or disagreements about resource priorities in an environment of tight financial constraints. These disagreements can become untenable in joint business planning meetings. Therefore, it is wise to hold planning and business performance reviews separately for CoreCo and NewCo.

Counter Destructive Tensions

The DC must monitor the health of the operational interaction between NewCo and CoreCo and must counter tensions before they turn destructive.

Some of the root causes of tensions deal with substantive concerns of business strategy. An effective option for the DC is to gather and present hard data, such as direct customer feedback, that ameliorates those concerns. For example, analysis that demonstrated that NYTD was not appreciably damaging circulation revenues—and was perhaps even helping, because many new subscriptions were coming through the Web site—was helpful in reducing tensions between NYTD and the newspaper.

Many of the root causes of tension are less substantive. The DC must be prepared to bridge communication gaps and misunderstandings between very different organizations. For example, if tensions flare over differences in compensation between NewCo and CoreCo, the DC must remind CoreCo employees of the unique risks faced by NewCo. If

CoreCo managers react poorly to the excessive attention that NewCo receives from the press, analysts, or even the CEO, the DC can remind CoreCo managers that their business is the bedrock on which the corporation rests. NewCo is interesting and exciting, but far from proven. If people are offended by stereotypical comments about the differences between new and mature companies, the DC can work to establish common values and promote an atmosphere of mutual respect.

To help arrest tensions before they arise, the DC can get involved in staffing. People at interaction points between NewCo and CoreCo must be mature. In almost every organization, there will be some who are not. They will be too wedded to their own needs or points of view, unable to view a situation from the other side's perspective, or more interested in personal power or control than they are in what is best for the corporation.

Empower NewCo

The DC must manage the balance of power between CoreCo and NewCo.

In many organizations, power naturally gravitates to CoreCo because it is larger, it is profitable, and it is established (see figure 5-3). The DC must oppose this tendency, because for links to be effective, NewCo usually needs to have greater authority (though not always, as you will see in the next section). An effective DC uses influence carefully to help NewCo maintain the authority it needs, without formally subordinating one side to the other.[5]

FIGURE 5-3

Balance of power between CoreCo and NewCo

Power balance

Natural progression over time

CoreCo

NewCo

The DC must often supply an opposing force

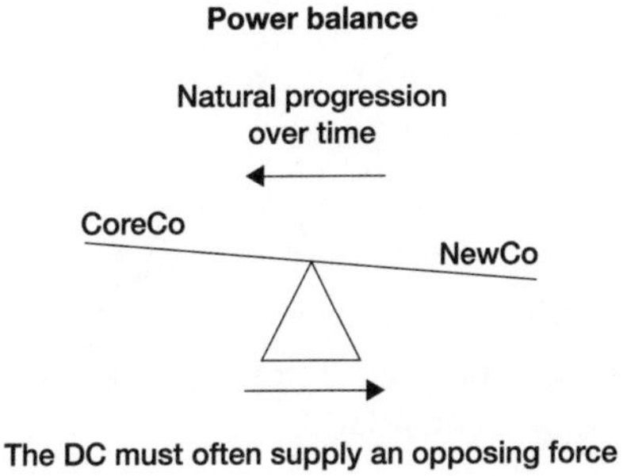

Manage Expectations

The DC should set NewCo's performance targets conservatively and shape performance perceptions carefully.

The willingness of CoreCo to assist NewCo depends heavily on how CoreCo perceives NewCo's performance. Objectively, NewCo's performance is highly ambiguous; it depends heavily on long-range projections. As a result, performance perceptions can swing quickly, based less on data than on ongoing politicking and social interaction within a company.

It is common for leaders of strategic experiments to make bold promises. When those promises are not fulfilled, as is often the case, the consequences can be disastrous, including a complete loss of confidence in NewCo or a premature decision to discontinue NewCo's funding. The DC should strive to maintain a perception that balances the possibility of a tremendous win for the corporation with reasonable levels of uncertainty regarding the total resources required and the time to profitability.

Be Ready to Adjudicate

The DC should intervene as a coach and mediator when NewCo and CoreCo cannot resolve differences on their own.

To the extent possible, the DC should avoid exercising overbearing authority. When adjudicating disagreements, it's best to ensure that advocates of both NewCo and CoreCo feel that they have been heard and own the solution to the greatest extent possible.

Figure 5-4 summarizes our general recommendations for borrowing. We now turn to recommendations for specific borrowing situations.

Six Borrowing Strategies

CoreCo can help NewCo in many ways. For example, there are three generic ways that NewCo might leverage CoreCo's business processes: it might borrow the output of an existing process, coordinate its processes with CoreCo's, or work jointly with CoreCo to create a new business process. In addition, NewCo might borrow three kinds of assets from CoreCo: brands, expertise, or physical assets. Each type of borrowing presents unique challenges.

FIGURE 5-4

Recommendations for overcoming the borrowing challenge

1. **Choose only powerful links**

    Choose links that lend NewCo a crucial competitive advantage.
    Avoid links with heavy conflicts of interest.
    Avoid links that easily import CoreCo's DNA to NewCo.
    Link, do not outsource entire functions to CoreCo.

2. **Establish context for borrowing**

    Reinforce values that NewCo and CoreCo share.
    Keep NewCo geographically close to CoreCo, if possible.
    Change incentives that strongly reward localized performance.
    Replenish CoreCo resources.
    Examine policies for internal accounting transfers carefully.

3. **Moderate ongoing interactions (DC)**

    Maintain NewCo's distinctiveness.
    Coach two GMs facing distinct challenges.
    Counter tensions before they become destructive.
    Empower NewCo in most interactions.
    Manage expectations of NewCo's performance.
    Adjudicate irreconcilable differences.

Borrow the Output of an Existing Process

The most straightforward link is when NewCo borrows (actually, purchases) the output of an existing CoreCo process. For example, NYTD purchased newspaper articles from the *Times*. When the outputs transferred from CoreCo to NewCo are intermediate products—not available on the open market—this type of link represents a strong competitive advantage for NewCo over independent start-ups. The *Times* sold archives to other information services, but NYTD was unique in the level of flexibility it had in deciding how the newspaper articles were used.

The challenge for the DC in establishing such a link is to set a fair transfer price. In some situations, it may be possible to seek competitive outside bids for a similar product to establish a fair transfer price. If deals are structured so that CoreCo receives more money as NewCo grows, CoreCo is given a direct stake in NewCo's success, and this practice can reduce tensions. The structure of the agreement between NYTD and the *Times* had this effect, because it included both a fixed charge and a royalty.

Coordinate a NewCo Process with a CoreCo Process

Merging CoreCo and NewCo processes can also confer competitive advantage for NewCo over independent start-ups, which find it much more difficult to strike the partnerships needed to enable similar activities. The DC must be directly involved to reconcile competing goals and priorities and perhaps to influence CoreCo to follow NewCo's lead.

NYTD benefited from two such links. The first was in selling display advertisements. NYTD joined the newspaper sales staff on sales calls to major corporate accounts. At first, the newspaper sales team saw risks in doing this. They wanted to protect relationships with clients that they had nurtured for years. In addition, the NYTimes.com sales team was much younger, and its sales revenues were growing quickly, much more quickly than newspaper revenues. It is understandable that the newspaper sales team was uncomfortable.

Balancing egos can be a delicate task for the DC. A completely unproven NewCo can readily be marginalized by the core company. On the other hand, a NewCo that is apparently headed for a big success is likely to be resented by CoreCo. Corning experienced the latter difficulty when trying to leverage sales relationships at life sciences laboratories to get introductions to senior administrators who purchased genomics experimentation systems. The CMT sales team members had been told they were chosen because they were the best; they represented the future of Corning Life Sciences. They were a bit too willing to share this belief with their sales colleagues in the core business. As a result, they were quickly resented, and coordination suffered.

The senior management team at The New York Times Company took several steps to achieve healthy coordination of sales processes. First, the managers made it clear that their intent was to establish a clear market value for Internet advertisements. Under no circumstances were digital packages to be heavily discounted or given away to secure larger print packages. In addition, the senior management team redoubled its efforts to establish a common set of values (see "Rules of the Road," figure 5-2). They also altered individual performance reviews for certain key managers, giving heavier emphasis to effectiveness of collaboration across business unit boundaries.

NYTD also had some success merging its product development process with that of the newspaper. In fact, it encouraged the journalists on the *Times* staff to actively consider how they could use the Web site operations to reach a wider audience and do so in new ways. This practice gave the paper journalists a new outlet for their creativity, with lower risk than was inherent in launching a new section of the newspaper. One of the first results of this effort was a product known as *Deal Book*, an e-mail newsletter sent to a subscriber list that distributes late-breaking news related to mergers and acquisitions.

It took time, but eventually the staff of journalists at the *Times* saw many ways in which they gained personally from working with NYTD. This illustrates a common phenomenon: the benefits of interaction between NewCo and CoreCo often accrue mostly to NewCo early in NewCo's life, but then reverse later in life. DCs can increase the willingness of CoreCo employees to work with NewCo at its earliest, most experimental stages if they can convey this point convincingly.

Create New Processes That Benefit NewCo and CoreCo

Occasionally, NewCo and CoreCo can collaborate to create a new process or product. Doing so has the potential of combining competencies and resources in ways that no competitor can match. The DC should actively look for such areas of opportunity; they may not happen organically. After the development of a new process or product begins, the DC must remain involved, reinforcing values shared by both organizations and emphasizing collaboration and communication. The DC can anticipate that settling on the roles and responsibilities of the individuals on the two sides will be particularly contentious.

NYTD and the *Times* had exactly such an opportunity in the area of classified ads. The Internet was having a profound impact on the need for classifieds. eBay became an alternative to selling personal items through the classifieds, and the rise of Web sites like Monster.com and hotjobs.com provided alternatives to placing recruitment ads in the newspaper. Classifieds were a crucial source of ad revenue for the newspaper industry. In fact, one reason the company had created NYTimes.com and its other Internet operations in the first place was to find ways to protect this source of revenue. In its first related initiative, the company entered into a multiparty industry partnership formed to create an online classifieds offering. Unfortunately, the network had trouble moving quickly, and the company withdrew.

The experience was costly in that it allowed competitors to establish themselves. By late 1999, the company needed to quickly come up with an effective response. The senior management team formed a joint committee to frame a combined offering from The New York Times Company and NYTimes.com. Directors of business development from both sides led the effort to create a new offering over a few months, considering everything from doing nothing to acquiring Monster.com.

There were opposing viewpoints—some thought print classifieds were dying, others thought they would always play an important role—but the team arrived at a solution. It created a joint offering in which the newspaper staff sold classified recruitment packages that included both print and digital, and NYTD managed the technology, production, and presentation of the online recruitment section. Disagreements became most difficult when the time came to assign specific responsibilities, and this was the point at which senior management engagement was most needed.

Share a Brand

Brands are valuable, but building new brands is expensive and risky. To be able to borrow a brand, such as the *New York Times* brand, is an immense advantage for a strategic experiment over an independent start-up.

Although it's usually a good idea for the DC to exercise her influence to empower NewCo over CoreCo to ensure that links work effectively, caution is advisable when dealing with brands, which are particularly vulnerable to mistakes. As a result, when NewCo borrows a CoreCo brand, the DC must ensure that there is sufficient oversight to protect it. Hasbro, the focus of chapter 7, did not do so. As a result, NewCo created products that contradicted some attributes of the brand and used the brand in ways that were contrary to established licensing agreements.

At the same time, giving CoreCo too much power can be dangerous. Will the link become a conduit for things best forgotten? Can NewCo's DNA be maintained if CoreCo is given authority over a certain aspect of its operations? The DC must ensure that the CoreCo manager who is given oversight of NewCo's use of the brand has a clear and limited role (he should have no unchecked veto power on NewCo initiatives) and understands the need for NewCo to develop its own business practices. The DC must build a close relationship with this manager and be alert to actions that may be unhealthy for NewCo.

Protecting the *New York Times* brand, one of the most valuable and recognizable in the world, was of paramount concern for the senior executive team. It became a much greater concern when NYTD was established as a separate and independent organization and began to encourage cross-functional collaboration among journalists and businesspeople.

The company protected the brand by assigning an experienced *Times* journalist to manage editorial operations at NYTimes.com, even after NYTD became its own business unit. That journalist was committed first and foremost to maintaining the high quality and accuracy of content on NYTimes.com. He had day-to-day control over how content was altered and presented on the Web site, and he remained loyal to the standards and norms of the newspaper. At the same time, he was accountable to the head of NYTD, an effective check on his authority.

Borrow Knowledge

Independent start-ups must build expertise from scratch, either through trial and error or by hiring individuals who may or may not coalesce as a team. Either approach is expensive and far from foolproof. Therefore, strategic experiments that effectively borrow existing corporate competencies gain an important advantage.

But giving NewCo access to CoreCo's expertise requires more than just encouraging people to talk with one another. DCs can maximize the transfer of knowledge if they follow these principles:[6]

- Two specific attitudes must not be allowed to fester: "knowledge is power" (so why share it?) and "not invented here" (so why listen?). Knowledge givers in CoreCo must be treated as heroes, and knowledge receivers in NewCo must have their ears open. If NewCo managers are allowed to feel that CoreCo is only a graying dinosaur—and not the cutting-edge organization that NewCo is—no knowledge transfer will take place. And because strategic experiments are often in a race with the competition to get to market, this is not the time for reinventing the wheel.

- It is unwise to rely on information technology alone to transmit information. Although it's advisable to try to document knowledge wherever possible, some knowledge always remains only in the heads of experienced employees. Thus, interpersonal interaction is necessary. Interaction between executives perceived to have roughly equal power and influence is most successful.

- It is more effective, when possible, to transmit information in the context of actual work and with a specific objective than it is to establish interaction only for the purpose of transferring knowledge. Regardless of the context, it is important to be aware that the technical staff of CoreCo may use a unique language that is foreign within NewCo, and vice versa. Often, it is necessary to identify specific employees who understand both languages to act as intermediaries.

- Liberal use of internal personnel transfers from CoreCo to New-Co can ensure effective knowledge transfer. (As noted earlier, however, these transfers must be balanced with the appointment of outsiders, particularly at the management level, so that NewCo can overcome existing strategic orthodoxies.) Some knowledge is transferred with the people who move, and their established relationships with CoreCo provide a foundation for additional sharing of expertise.

- To build cooperation between NewCo and CoreCo, DCs should point out that knowledge often flows both ways. It is not just a one-way street in which NewCo exploits the core. However, benefits usually flow primarily toward NewCo early in its life, and in the other direction only after NewCo starts to succeed. CoreCo may not see immediate benefit, but it often will in the long run.

When it comes to the challenge of borrowing knowledge, revisiting the case of Corning Microarray Technologies is instructive. As you will recall from chapter 2, CMT needed Corning's expertise in specialty glass manufacturing—specifically, in adhering tiny quantities of fluid to glass. Consequently, Corning needed to combine expertise from several units in several locations. The company needed robust knowledge flows among its new team of microbiologists, its established research facility in Corning, New York, its existing advanced life sciences division in the Boston area, and its research facility in France.

The complex arrangement did not serve Corning well. With geographic distance limiting interpersonal interaction, personnel relied heavily on information technology to communicate. Loyalties were split between the needs of CMT and the needs of the respective divisions, and competing loyalties fermented "knowledge is power" and "not invented here" attitudes. Information sometimes flowed slowly, held up by competing priorities.

After Corning executives reorganized CMT in 1999, most of the people involved were assigned to Corning, New York, a tactic that increased interpersonal contact and minimized delays in information flow. The company's hiring of an outside molecular biologist at a senior management level helped to equalize the power associated with expertise in the physical and the biological sciences. He was also an effective communicator who was able to interact with all groups involved.

Borrow Manufacturing Capacity

In many industries, high capital costs for building manufacturing facilities are insurmountable barriers to entry for start-up ventures. Strategic experiments have an advantage if they can integrate their operations with CoreCo so that they benefit from existing capacity. This was not an opportunity for NYTD, but it was for other companies in our research.

The DC has two significant roles when NewCo borrows manufacturing capacity. The first is simply to keep an eye on capacity constraints. At Analog Devices, a company we will examine in chapter 10, CoreCo experienced an unexpected growth spurt. Because bringing additional capacity online was a lengthy process, the company operated close to its manufacturing limit for several quarters. The manufacturing managers were ready to discontinue production for NewCo because it was not yet profitable. Only active intervention by the senior management team kept NewCo alive.

The second issue is to ensure that a good learning environment for NewCo is created within the existing manufacturing facility. Given the discipline required to meet CoreCo production demands, it may be difficult for CoreCo employees to give any focused energy to improving NewCo's experimental processes. The learning rate can be accelerated if it is possible to isolate NewCo's processes and keep the same team working on NewCo's production from one day to the next.

Assessing the Intensity of the Borrowing Challenge

Every strategic experiment faces a difficult borrowing challenge. Even if there is only one link between NewCo and CoreCo, the DC's role is important and demanding. In our judgment, helping NewCo overcome the borrowing challenge is the highest-leverage intervention point for the senior management team. Still, some strategic experiments will be more demanding than others.

The two factors that determine the intensity of the borrowing challenge are the total number of links between NewCo and CoreCo and the presence of fundamental drivers of tension between NewCo and Core-Co. The senior management team, and the DC in particular, should take the time to assess the intensity of the borrowing challenge using figure 5-5 and table 5-1. In this way, they can gauge their expectations of the amount of time they need to dedicate to NewCo.

In the next four chapters we turn to the learning challenge. However, we will not leave behind the forgetting and borrowing challenges. Case studies in chapters 7 and 8 offer brief opportunities for review.

FIGURE 5-5

Intensity of the borrowing challenge

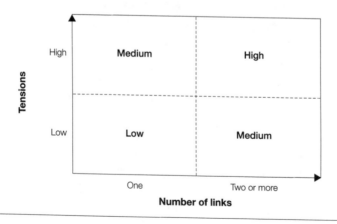

TABLE 5-1

Assessing the intensity of the borrowing challenge

This table is used in conjunction with figure 5-5 to assess the intensity of the borrowing challenge.

Do you agree with these statements? (1 = strongly disagree, 7 = strongly agree, or NA)	Rating (1–7)
1. CoreCo perceives that NewCo could cannibalize CoreCo revenues.	
2. CoreCo perceives that NewCo could make a CoreCo competence obsolete.	
3. CoreCo perceives that NewCo has the potential to damage CoreCo assets such as brands, customer relationships, or distribution networks.	
4. NewCo will put a significant dent in the corporation's earnings. Typically, NewCo's losses rise even as it is succeeding in growing revenues. CoreCo managers are likely to question the wisdom of allocating capital to a business incurring a loss. Bonuses tied to corporate profits exacerbate the situation.	
5. Capital is scarce, or could become scarce if CoreCo faces a downturn. CoreCo is likely to be resistant to allocating capital, manufacturing capacity, employee time, or other resources to NewCo.	
6. CoreCo managers are inexperienced with or unaware of the differing needs of units at different stages of the business lifecycle such as: (a) the need to evaluate business performance differently, (b) the need to place more emphasis on flexibility than efficiency, (c) the need to hire, promote, and compensate based on different criteria. If NewCo managers receive large bonuses when NewCo succeeds, CoreCo will likely resent the fact that NewCo's success was dependent on CoreCo resources.	
7. The corporation has only one business model.	
8. Establishing trust between NewCo and CoreCo is likely to be difficult, because the differences between NewCo and CoreCo are so great that the two organizations are unlikely to coalesce around a set of common values.	
9. NewCo and CoreCo managers, in showing pride for their business units, are likely to propagate stereotypes about differences between established and start-up businesses. For example, NewCo may assume that big companies cannot be agile or entrepreneurial, while CoreCo insists that status should be based solely on resources under command. Such attitudes rarely constitute healthy rivalry. They can easily disrupt cooperation.	
10. CoreCo is so disciplined about process efficiency that it is unlikely to be willing to alter processes or experiment on NewCo's behalf.	
Calculate the average rating (excluding NAs) to determine the likely magnitude of tensions between NewCo and CoreCo. On the vertical axis of figure 5-5, a score of 4 defines the midpoint between "low" and "high."	

Chapter Six

WHY LEARNING FROM EXPERIENCE
IS AN UNNATURAL ACT

WHEN EXECUTIVES wrestle with the decision to invest in high-potential new businesses, many of them naturally wish for more information. It would be comforting to believe that the decision to invest is made on the basis of data and rational calculation. But estimates of how emerging industries will develop are unreliable at best. For example, when AT&T consulted McKinsey & Company in the mid-1980s for advice on the cellular telephone market, McKinsey concluded that the worldwide potential was 900,000 units. Today, 900,000 new subscribers become mobile-phone users every three days.[1]

The essence of strategic experiments is that much more is unknown than known. No amount of research and planning can resolve the unknowns in advance. The future of an emerging industry is simply unknowable.

Despite this unsettling reality, companies must occasionally take risks on strategic experiments if they wish to stay ahead of the competition. The winner is not necessarily the company that starts with the best plan. Rather, it is often the one that learns and adapts the quickest. Even if a strategic experiment is designed to overcome the forgetting and borrowing challenges, it can stumble if it cannot learn.

Unfortunately, strategic experiments present extremely challenging contexts for learning. Although established companies have a wide range of advantages over independent start-ups, our research has shown that strategic experiments are handicapped by numerous *learning disabilities*. In this chapter, we describe the nature of the learning challenge, and we identify four types of learning disabilities.

What Must Be Learned?

Organizational learning has attracted a great deal of energy and investment in recent years. A sign of the times: many corporations now have chief learning officers or chief knowledge officers. Knowledge may not show up on the balance sheet, but it is one of the most valuable assets that many corporations possess. Rapid advances in information technology have made it possible to gather and process huge amounts of data. Entire industries have emerged to give companies the capability to mine the data effectively and turn a mountain of data into usable business intelligence.[2]

However, in the context of managing strategic experiments, the meaning of *learning* is very specific. Leaders of strategic experiments have a focused learning task: they must improve their ability to predict New-Co's performance. This is the crux of the learning challenge. In fact, whenever we speak of learning in this book, we are referring to this specific learning task.

Just how important is this task? The rate at which predictions improve is directly related to the rate at which NewCo is able to zero in on a winning business model—or abandon a failed project. Faster learning also leads to lower risk exposure, reduced capital needs, and minimal time to profitability.

Initial predictions are always wrong. Sometimes they are dramatically wrong. Estimates for market size of new industries are frequently off by as much as a factor of 10. This means that total resources allocated can be off by just as great a multiple. Over time, however, such wild guesses become informed estimates. Later, informed estimates become reliable forecasts (see figure 1-2 in chapter 1).

To improve predictions, NewCo's leadership team must systematically resolve a handful of *critical unknowns* that can either make or break a business. For example, the critical unknowns for Corning Microarray Technologies (chapter 2) were:

- Would a standard compatible with CMT's microarray offering be widely adopted?

- Could Corning's expertise in adhering tiny quantities of fluid to glass be readily transferred to microarrays?

- Could CMT lower costs to a point that would compel laboratories to invest in entirely new systems for genomics experimentation?

Critical unknowns for New York Times Digital (chapter 4) included these:

- What content or services would readers pay for online?

- How valuable would online advertising prove to be, compared to traditional alternatives?

- How quickly would traditional advertisers adapt to the new medium?

- How rapidly would the competition add new features and services to their Web sites, and how much would it cost to keep up?

Experimental businesses face several critical unknowns, often one or two in each of four categories: market, competition, technology, and profitability. Here are some generic examples:

Market: How quickly will the market grow, and when? Will customers be willing to take a risk on new products? Which customers will find the greatest value in our offering?

Competition: Who else will enter this market? How quickly? How aggressively?

Technology: Can we create a great product? Master its manufacture? Will the market accept the standards we are proposing?

Profitability: What price level will the market sustain? How quickly can we reduce per-unit costs as we grow?

Experimentation Is Easy, but Learning Is Hard

Managers of strategic experiments resolve critical unknowns—that is, they learn—only through trial and error. This process of discovery is the only alternative to research and rational analysis, which are of limited value when unknowns are so great. To be ready to learn, you must understand the specifics of how trial-and-error learning works.

Trial-and-error learning is really a process of developing and refining a theory.[3] You may instinctively have a negative reaction to the word *theory*. Perhaps in your mind *theoretical* and *practical* are opposites—but nothing could be further from the truth. Every time a manager makes a decision, the underlying rationale for the decision includes a theory—one that predicts what will happen as a result of the decision. A theory is nothing more than a cause-and-effect story about how planned actions lead to expected outcomes.

We learn by analyzing disparities between theoretical predictions and actual outcomes. In fact, resolving why what you thought would happen did not actually happen is the central activity in trial-and-error learning.

Everyone has some familiarity with trial-and-error learning, even though you may have never thought about it in terms of theories, predictions, and outcomes. Think about when you learned how to ride a bicycle. You got on, you tried pedaling, you wobbled, and you fell over. On an unconscious level, you processed a rich set of data about your actions and their outcomes. You tried again and again, and soon you got it right.

Through trial and error, you learned quickly. You were able to do so because the environment for trial-and-error learning was ideal on three counts.

- *Speed*: Each trial lasted only a few seconds, from start to finish.

- *Clarity*: The outcome of each trial was unambiguous (ouch!).

- *Repetition*: You were afforded the luxury of as many trials as you desired.

When you can try something repeatedly and you get clear feedback within seconds each time, your prospects for learning are excellent. Under such conditions, humans are proficient at working through the process of developing theories, making predictions, and analyzing the difference between predictions and outcomes, without even being aware of it. Indeed, the process of learning from experience can be left to intuition.

Unfortunately, early life experiences, such as learning how to ride a bicycle, shoot a basketball, or play a video game, mislead us about the nature of trial-and-error learning. Most learning environments are not nearly so ideal, and, as a result, learning requires more work:

- *Speed*: What happens when the duration of an experiment is not seconds but hours, weeks, or even years? Our memories fail us. It quickly becomes too hard to recall theory or prediction. Thus, there must be a discipline of clear documentation and rigorous analysis.

- *Clarity*: What happens when results are complex and multidimensional and cannot be reduced to a simple, black-and-white answer? Theories must be deconstructed into many constituent parts and must be validated or invalidated one piece at a time.

- *Repetition*: What happens when each trial is so lengthy, risky, or expensive that only one or a few trials are possible? Learning must be as efficient as possible. In fact, lessons must sometimes be drawn while the experiment is in progress.

Intuition is always important. But learning should not be left to intuition alone in any except the most ideal conditions.

The learning environment for strategic experiments is far from ideal. Months, quarters, even years can pass between the launch of an experimental business and a definitive outcome. Evidence accumulates unevenly along multiple dimensions, and it rarely points unambiguously to success or failure. And repetition is far too expensive to be practical. Typically, you get one chance. Therefore, learning is difficult. And it is hardly intuitive.[4]

In several companies, we have heard managers involved with strategic experiments talk about the need to take an "experiment-and-learn" approach. But this mostly amounts to just talk. What the managers really mean is that they expect to be forgiven if the business does not turn out as they had anticipated. *And they should be*. But forgiveness alone leads only to experimenting, and not experimenting and learning.

Lessons are not magically revealed to those who have opened their minds with an experiment-and-learn attitude. Learning must be a conscious, explicit effort. It requires discipline. It requires accountability. And it requires a structured process.

The Science of Learning

The scientific community has given us such a process, namely the *scientific method*: design an experiment, make predictions on the basis of a theory, conduct the experiment, measure outcomes, and draw conclusions based on an analysis of comparisons between predictions and outcomes. When the scientific method is rigorously applied, theories and predictions are explicit and documented. Analysis of results is thoughtful and thorough. Through disciplined application of the scientific method, scientists have generated volumes of knowledge in fields from astrophysics to zoology.[5]

Scientists seek ideal conditions for experimentation. They look for experiments that can be conducted rapidly; for example, early geneticists studied species that reproduced quickly. Scientists attempt to isolate experiments from outside forces so that results are unambiguous. Physicists measuring the force of gravity, for example, needed to create a vacuum to eliminate the effect of air resistance on falling bodies. Scientists also keep experiments as inexpensive as possible so that they can be repeated; small-scale models of new airplanes are tested in wind tunnels, for example, before full-scale airplanes are constructed.

Nonetheless, in many fields, such ideal conditions are just not possible. To study the impact of a new treatment for cancer, scientists may have to wait many years to get reliable data on outcomes. Did the patients live longer than they otherwise would have? What other factors affected life span? Or consider the study of global warming. Only one "trial" is possible—an ongoing trial that will take many years—and the phenomenon is extraordinarily complex and has many confounding factors.

Just because scientists studying cancer and global warming cannot create idealized laboratory conditions, however, does not mean that they abandon the scientific method. There is no other alternative. Furthermore, the scientific method becomes increasingly important as conditions deviate further from the ideal. Each trial must be gleaned for as many lessons as possible. Sometimes a single trial must be evaluated for lessons even as it is in progress.

Can managers of strategic experiments apply the scientific method? They can and they must. Granted, their learning environment is far from ideal. It is more like the study of global warming than the study of aerodynamics. But there is no alternative.

Science and Business

Science is important in business, and companies that practice good science are often highly innovative. The scientific method has a natural home in research and development departments, just as it does in the test marketing of new products.[6] Further, some of the companies that have excelled in continuous improvement have done so by training factory-floor employees in the scientific method so that they can identify problems, generate experimental solutions, measure results, and so on with little oversight.[7]

In conducting our research, however, we did not observe healthy practice of the scientific method. Nonetheless, we believe that achieving proficiency at learning is a skill well within reach for management teams, even in the far-from-ideal learning environment that characterizes strategic experiments.

In fact, general managers already have a familiar process in place that mimics the central elements of the scientific method: the planning process. For this reason, the design of the planning process is the single most powerful element of NewCo's organizational DNA.

Consider the four major steps of the planning cycle, as shown in figure 6-1:

1. You develop a plan, predicting specific outcomes from the actions specified in the plan.

2. You execute the plan.

3. Later, you measure outcomes and compare them to the predictions in the plan.

4. You diagnose any disparities between predictions and outcomes. This last step is the central learning step.

FIGURE 6-1

Learning is closely tied to planning

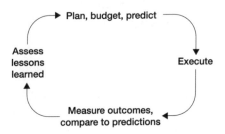

When the learning process is healthy, you analyze predictions and outcomes with detachment, honesty, and rigor. Through the analysis, the cause-and-effect story about planned actions and expected outcomes is explicitly debated. When a specific lesson is identified and documented, the theory is revised, and the predictions are updated.[8] As the cause-and-effect story improves, management teams become increasingly accurate at predicting the future of the strategic experiment.

Our research revealed, however, that few strategic experiments follow this path of gradual improvement. Instead, predictions are altered infrequently, and when they are, they are altered suddenly and sharply. Resource allocations tend to follow the same path: they suddenly lurch up or crash down. These are signs that the learning process is not nearly as efficient and effective as it could be. Why?

The Sacred Prediction

Again, the learning objective for the general manager of a strategic experiment is to refine a theory of business so that predictions of business performance improve over time. The central learning step is to analyze disparities between predictions and outcomes.

Therefore, predictions are at the heart of the learning process. They should be treated with care. When outcome data becomes available, the process of analyzing comparisons between predictions and outcomes should be thoughtful and diligent. But our research showed that predictions are fragile and vulnerable. Predictions fall victim to four specific *learning disabilities*:

- Predictions are ignored (and the learning process is left to intuition).

- Predictions or performance perceptions are manipulated (and lessons learned are distorted as a result).

- Predictions become rigid (and the initial theory of business "locks in" and is not refined as new evidence is gathered).

- Predictions and outcomes are analyzed poorly (and managers draw lessons that are inaccurate or incomplete).

For the learning process to work, predictions must be retained. Moreover, they must be revisable—when there is a specific and documented lesson to justify it.

A first step in overcoming learning disabilities is to be aware that predictions are at the heart of the learning process and that they are often mistreated. However, the mistreatment of predictions is symptomatic of deeper problems. Attacking the problem requires greater understanding of the specific mechanisms through which learning disabilities arise.

Earlier we noted that general managers are already intimately familiar with a process that mimics the scientific method: the planning process. In some ways, this is good news. There is no need to invent an entirely new process from scratch.

But it is also bad news. The basic source of all learning disabilities is the fact that although it is similar, the planning process was not designed to support the scientific method. It was designed for several other purposes, among them allocating resources between competing proposals, motivating leaders with stretch goals, and evaluating individuals' performance. But as you will see, these purposes are not compatible with science. When science and planning collide, learning disabilities arise.[9]

To improve planning for strategic experiments, we must identify the root causes of learning disabilities. There are four:

- Insufficient engagement in the planning process

- A strong culture of accountability for performance

- Self-interest and influence

- Inappropriate planning processes and frameworks

As shown in table 6-1, each of these four root causes can lead to more than one of the four learning disabilities: predictions are ignored, predictions or performance perceptions are manipulated, predictions become rigid, or predictions and outcomes are poorly analyzed. In the remainder of this chapter, we explain each of these root causes in greater detail and make recommendations for countering each one. In chapters 7 and 8, we describe how learning disabilities derailed two strategic experiments.

Insufficient Engagement in Planning

The most basic root cause of learning disabilities is an unwillingness to make a serious investment in planning. When managers prepare plans

TABLE 6-1

Root causes of learning disabilities

	Learning disabilities			
Root causes	**Predictions ignored**	**Predictions or performance perceptions manipulated**	**Predictions become rigid**	**Predictions and outcomes poorly analyzed**
Insufficient engagement in planning	X			X
Culture of accountability	X		X	
Self-interest and influence	X	X	X	
Inappropriate planning processes or frameworks	X	X		X

hastily, they do not see value in them later. This leads directly to two learning disabilities: managers ignore predictions altogether, or at best they conduct a weak and superficial analysis of differences between predictions and outcomes.

Unfortunately, it is common for leaders of risky and uncertain businesses to disdain planning and invest little time in it. They tend to emphasize three reasons, and each has surface validity. Nonetheless, minimal investment in planning leads to minimal learning.

First, they argue that the business is so uncertain that predicting is impossible. So why bother? Predicting business performance under conditions of great uncertainty is unfamiliar and uncomfortable territory for many managers. In a proven business, predictions are based on a simple theory: that the current period will look much like the preceding one. In fact, the notion of a business as an *ongoing concern* is one of the most important assumptions underlying our system of financial accounting. The theory is subconscious, and rarely is it explicitly discussed. Managers forget that there is a theory underlying the predictions at all.

Strategic experiments are not ongoing concerns. There are no simplifying assumptions, so predicting requires that you create a theory. This is more difficult, even daunting. It requires that you get comfort-

FIGURE 6-2

The truth about predictions for strategic experiments

Q: What do these two have in common?

WIZARD   EXECUTIVE DIRECTOR

A: They are both in the business of predicting the future.

able with the great likelihood that the predictions will prove wrong. Predictions may be no more reliable, perhaps, than the premonitions of a carnival wizard gazing into a crystal ball (figure 6-2). And yet predicting is the core of the learning process.

The second reason that managers give for slighting the planning process is that predictions are likely to be wrong. Therefore, they argue, they should ground their decisions not in predictions, but in hard evidence. True, it is good practice to gather as much data as possible before making decisions. In fact, some consulting firms have made fortunes identifying the relevant data and making it more understandable. There is comfort in being able to say that you made a difficult decision based strictly on factual data.

But it is an illusion. Even when there is plenty of data available, there is still at least an implicit prediction of what will result from the decision. There is always a prediction, and there is always a theory—one that explains how the planned action will lead to a desirable outcome. But managers are much more comfortable discussing the data than the prediction (see figure 6-3).

FIGURE 6-3

Confronting the necessity of making predictions can be discomfiting

The third argument that managers tend to make for minimizing attention to planning is that any time spent planning is time not spent doing.[10] Getting to market quickly is a pressing concern for many new and experimental businesses. Managers often work long hours, getting as much done as possible as soon as possible, to beat the competition to the prize. Planning can easily be viewed as nothing more than a distraction.

The problem is that a focus on *doing* locks a strategic experiment into its initial path—a path based on a great deal of guesswork. Only through a disciplined planning and learning process can a strategic experiment gradually iterate toward a successful business model.

Recommendations

To learn, leaders of strategic experiments must recognize that all three reasons are only weak excuses. They must confront the necessity of making predictions if they are to learn. Yes, predictions are inevitably wrong. But it is through the process of making predictions and subsequently analyzing why predictions differ from actual results that learning happens. No one gets better at predicting by avoiding it.

Therefore, planning demands a great investment of time and energy. To help ensure that this investment gets made, senior managers must spend a disproportionate amount of time with new and uncertain businesses. Even though NewCo may have only a small fraction of the revenues of CoreCo, it demands much greater than a small fraction of senior executives' attention.

Further, when engaging in the planning process, leaders of strategic experiments and senior executives alike must adopt a scientific mind-set.[11] They must view a critical aspect of their mission as uncovering the mystery of how to achieve profitability in an emerging industry.

Unfortunately, the notion of an "experimental business" is discomfiting to many. Instead, people use terms such as *new venture* or *high-growth opportunity*. Such language is more reflective of how entrepreneurs view themselves—as bold visionaries leading an adventure to a new and spectacular land. This type of leadership is needed. But it must be combined with an experimental mind-set and a focus on resolving specific uncertainties.

A Strong Culture of Accountability

The central step in the learning process is interpreting disparities between predictions and outcomes. This interpretation is extraordinarily powerful. It not only drives the learning process, but it also controls the direction of the business. When outcomes exceed predictions, we all happily continue doing what we were doing. When outcomes fall short of predictions, changes of some kind soon follow.

But what kind of changes? That depends on how the disparity between prediction and outcome is diagnosed. The diagnosis begins with a fundamental choice that boils down to this: either the outcome or the prediction must be blamed.[12] Outcomes are the direct result of managerial action. Predictions come from theories about how the business is thought to work (figure 6-4).

The problem with a strong culture of accountability is that interpretations of disparities between predictions and outcomes are heavily biased toward managerial underperformance; that is, the prediction is presumed to be correct. It is treated as a manager's pledge, and to fall short is to fail.

FIGURE 6-4

Evaluating performance

Evaluations of performance involve comparing predictions and outcomes. Disparities can be the result of either poor execution or poor predicting.

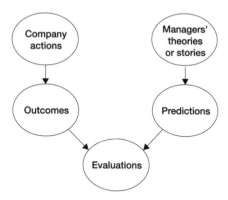

This is a reasonable and powerful approach to managing *proven* businesses, which are reliably predictable. It leads to organizational learning, as underperforming managers are retrained, given increased supervision, or replaced. Business units subsequently learn to bring performance in line with predictions—predictions that have been established based on the experience of those who preceded the current team.[13]

In strategic experiments, however, the bias in interpretation toward managerial underperformance is highly likely to be off the mark. In fact, this bias is directly opposed to what is needed for strategic experiments. The starting assumption must be that the predictions are wrong. For strategic experiments, the learning objective is not to improve performance until it reaches proven standards but rather to discover what standards are possible. In other words, the learning objective is to bring predictions in line with performance, and not the other way around.

When this bias is not adopted, it is likely that one of two learning disabilities will arise. The first possibility is that predictions immediately become rigid, because they are assumed to be correct. Alternatively, senior managers may make some allowance for uncertainty and temporarily relax standards of accountability. In the interim, typically, predictions are simply ignored.

Recommendations

With considerable justification, senior executives often believe that a strong culture of accountability explains a great deal of their companies' success. They know that holding managers accountable for results is powerful. But the alternative is not chaos. It is a different kind of accountability. In chapter 9, we introduce theory-focused planning (TFP), a specific set of tools and techniques for creating accountability for learning. In this section, we explain why the change is necessary.

There is wisdom in the adage, "What gets measured, gets done." Quantitative expectations of performance motivate employees and provide a crystal-clear business focus. In fact, most employees prefer accountability to specific, numerical goals. Objective measures feel intrinsically fair, whereas qualitative assessments are subject to bias. The managers performing the reviews also prefer objective measures because evaluating people is stressful. Without simple, quantitative measures of performance, it is hard to make negative evaluations stick.

There are contexts in which accountability to numbers works well. Salespeople are often measured against quotas. Evaluations of taxi drivers can be weighted heavily to their safety records. And field goal kickers are assessed on their percentage of successful kicks. But there can also be perverse consequences. Software programmers measured on the number of lines of code they write may produce inelegant and buggy modules. Research scientists whose bosses count patents may generate obscure inventions with little practical utility. And executives measured by stock price may find ways to inflate the stock this year while hurting the company in the future.

In fact, the jobs that are most effectively reduced to single quantities are the ones that are the most one-dimensional. The broader a person's responsibilities, the more complex and subjective the evaluation. Measurement becomes more ambiguous. There are more stakeholders with a wider range of needs. Evaluations come at specific points in time, but there are always short-term versus long-term trade-offs. It is nice to be able to tie evaluations to objective measures, but it is a luxury. It is not the norm. There is always a heavy dose of subjectivity in evaluating general managers and senior executives. At best, you can heavily weight the evaluation based on performance against prenegotiated predictions of what is possible. For mature businesses with plenty of consistent history on which to base predictions, this is reasonable. For strategic experiments, it is not.

Senior executives are naturally reluctant to take any action that they perceive will damage accountability.[14] We believe, however, that the *worst* thing a senior executive can do is to hold NewCo's leader accountable to plan.

Skeptical? Consider first that initial predictions are inevitably wrong. They are wrong even with the best intentions, when NewCo's leader makes an earnest effort to make the best prediction possible. But such an earnest effort is not even likely. NewCo's leader has great incentive to make projections as low as possible (without going so low that NewCo is no longer able to obtain funding). That way, he will have the best chance of meeting expectations. Of course, this type of maneuvering goes on in every negotiation of performance targets. But with strategic experiments, the range of justifiable numbers is much wider. The risk is that all energies are expended in gaming the negotiation process, rather than codifying a clear, testable theory of performance.

Accountability to plan also creates undesirable behaviors after plans are in place. When it becomes clear to NewCo's leader that he will fall short, he will perceive failure.[15] As a result, he will withhold information and withdraw from open conversations about business performance. Worse, he will quietly redouble his efforts to get back on plan— even if changes in the environment have rendered it obsolete—to prove that he is not failing. He will not question fundamental flaws in plans, he will not experiment with needed changes in direction, and he will ignore changes in the environment. He will avoid the one thing that you need him to do most: reevaluate the plan. And that means that he will not learn.

Rather than backing away from holding NewCo's leader accountable, senior executives must shift the *basis* for accountability. Instead of being accountable for performance against plans, managers of strategic experiments should be accountable for learning. When NewCo learns quickly, it converges on a working business model quickly. It minimizes time to profitability, minimizes risk, minimizes capital needs, and maximizes the probability of a big win.[16] TFP, explained in chapter 9, ensures that theories of performance are clearly articulated and that predictions are reviewed frequently (at least quarterly; potentially monthly), with a particular eye toward predictions that can quickly resolve the handful of critical unknowns that can make or break the business. When the process is well managed, predictions are revised *only* when all parties (at a minimum, NewCo's general manager and her supervisor) agree that there is sufficient evidence that addresses a critical unknown. Predictions cannot be changed on a whim. TFP is a disciplined process.

Consider the different behaviors that the senior executive who is supervising NewCo can engender when he commits to a process like TFP. First, he will change his own behavior. He will want to make a fair evaluation of NewCo's leader. Therefore, he will take business performance review meetings very seriously, knowing that he is unable to observe the leader of NewCo every day and knowing that the numbers will not speak for themselves. He will fully engage in the learning process by discussing theories, assumptions, predictions, outcomes, and critical unknowns. Through this discussion, he will be able to contribute his years of experience to the learning process. Predictions will not be revised ad hoc, they will only be revised with his buy-in. Through intense interaction, he will be able to evaluate NewCo's leader's performance in a much more meaningful way, albeit one that is more qualitative.

By committing to TFP, the senior executive supervising NewCo can also change the behavior of the leader of NewCo by demonstrating that he understands the unpredictable nature of strategic innovation. Therefore, he will evaluate her based strictly on the speed, rigor, and discipline that she brings to the learning process of analyzing disparities between predictions and outcomes—and not on whether she actually hits her numbers. Therefore, she is more willing to step back, reassess, and redirect. An entirely different dynamic can develop. Open, free, and candid discussion about the future—rooted in predictions and outcomes—becomes much more likely. In fact, she will involve her entire management team in the discussion, and learn as much as she can from their insights. Further, she will willingly share bad news, because she knows that she will not be penalized, and that doing so is the only way to demonstrate that she is committed to learning. She will be eager to demonstrate the quality of her thought processes, because that is how she will be evaluated. She will proactively provide candid analyses of changes in the environment, reexamine fundamental assumptions in plans, and take risks as needed to find new paths to success.[17] See table 6-2 for a comparison of the behaviors motivated by each approach to accountability.

TABLE 6-2

Comparison of behaviors encouraged by two approaches to accountability

Accountable to plan	Accountable to learning—through disciplined and rigorous execution of theory-focused planning
Focus on favorable negotiation of targets	Focus on clear articulation of a theory of business performance
Assume plan is correct	Quickly test assumptions in plan
Hide bad news	Eagerly share bad news
Avoid conversation	Engage in conversation
If falling short, redouble effort to hit plan	If falling short, reexamine assumptions, observe changes in the environment, and revise plan if and only if there are clear lessons learned
Avoid risks	Resolve critical unknowns through controlled experiments and carefully examined risks

Self-Interest and Influence

Learning follows from honest and detached interpretations of disparities between predictions and outcomes. Unfortunately, it can be difficult to be honest and detached, because these interpretations create favorable or unfavorable perceptions of both personal and business unit performance. These perceptions, in turn, are central in the ongoing competition for prestige, power, and resources.

The associated motivations can easily overpower the drive to learn from experience. In an effort to build influence or diminish the influence of a colleague, executives may try to spin the perceived level of performance of a strategic experiment. This can take the form of questioning the validity of past predictions so that they are likely to be ignored, manipulating predictions or performance perceptions, or insisting that existing predictions never be changed. Because the actual performance of a strategic experiment is ambiguous, the perceived performance can be dramatically altered through the influence of powerful executives.[18] The potential for self-interest to distort the learning process is high.

Three key actors are active and influential in shaping NewCo's perceived performance: the general manager of NewCo, the general manager of CoreCo, and the executive to whom the general manager of CoreCo reports. Each of these key actors faces a different political reality composed of different pressures, different fears, and different ambitions (see table 6-3). In our research, we observed that the path of strategic experiments is altered at least as often by these factors as it is by rational assessment of lessons based on a careful comparison of predictions and outcomes.

Recommendations

To achieve learning, these three players must work together to fight any intrusions of self-interest into the learning process. Awareness of the issue is crucial. With awareness, managers will at least explicitly consider conflicts between self-interest and organizational needs. On the other hand, when managers are unaware of how the pursuit of self-interest can have a negative impact on the organization as a whole, there is nothing to stop them from this pursuit.

Business performance reviews are crucial moments. To ensure that predictions are not ignored, all key executives must remain committed to understanding the basis for past predictions and analyzing what has changed since then. They must be alert to efforts to manipulate performance perceptions and must ensure that stories about how NewCo is performing are grounded in relevant evidence. They must also encourage revision of predictions when the evidence dictates it.

TABLE 6-3

The three key executives are driven by distinct fears and ambitions

Executive	Primary fear	Primary ambition
General manager of NewCo	Losing resources or support before fulfilling vision	To be a bold, visionary leader, a hero
General manager of CoreCo	Losing organizational influence to upstart business unit—NewCo	To achieve maximum possible growth for CoreCo (even if at the expense of NewCo)
CEO	Allowing culture of accountability to crumble	To achieve breakthrough performance for corporation as a whole while delivering consistent earnings to investors

In addition, planning meetings for mature businesses should be held separately from those for strategic experiments. The two evaluations are made on the basis of completely different criteria. Even for the dynamic coordinator, who is involved in both NewCo and CoreCo, it may be too difficult to quickly switch from one conversation to the other. For the GM of CoreCo, who is fully immersed in managing a mature business, it may be impossible.

Inappropriate Planning Processes and Frameworks

We cannot overstate the importance of having the right framework and set of tools for analyzing disparities between predictions and outcomes. The templates used in the planning process become the perceptual filters that determine which data is gathered and how it is presented.[19] This in turn has an enormous impact on subsequent analysis and conclusions.

When you use a poor set of planning templates, any number of analytical errors become far more likely. Research shows that humans and organizations are naturally subject to many analysis pitfalls when trying to explain organizational performance:

- A bias for simple, linear explanations of cause and effect.

- An overemphasis on recent events to explain current causes (when more distant history may actually be more important).

- An assumption that cause-and-effect relationships in familiar contexts (CoreCo) also hold in unfamiliar ones (NewCo).

- An assumption that big effects have big causes. (Suppose you made two investments to improve performance, and the second cost ten times as much as the first. It would be natural to attribute any performance improvement to the second investment.)

- A bias for ignoring failures.

- A bias for paying too much attention to major events (entry of a new competitor, an unexpected manufacturing crisis), especially those with strong metaphorical power, such as changes in leadership.

- A bias for attributing success to our own actions.

- A bias for attributing failure to the actions of others or to bad luck.

Research also shows that it is particularly difficult to avoid these pitfalls when we are analyzing single case histories, such as strategic experiments. Furthermore, in low-probability, high-consequence events (such as strategic experiments), emotions run high, and drawing logical inferences is that much harder.[20] One part of overcoming these pitfalls is simply to be aware of them.[21] In addition, a proper analytical frame is essential.

The conventional planning process was designed to implement a proven business model in a relatively static and stable environment. Managers of strategic experiments have a much different goal: they must test an experimental business model in a dynamic and uncertain environment. As a result, the tools, templates, and frameworks built into the conventional planning process are not up to the task. They call attention to the wrong measures, present information in the wrong formats, and ask the wrong questions at the wrong times. The inevitable result is poor analysis and unsubstantiated conclusions.

Furthermore, each corporation customizes its planning templates to emphasize measures and standards that are appropriate to CoreCo. These measures and standards likely have little relevance for NewCo, however, and they make it much easier to misinterpret results or manipulate perceptions of performance.

Finally, planning processes and templates have built-in time frames. The norm is to review fundamental business questions annually. However, in strategic experiments, fundamental questions must be addressed much more frequently. It is dangerous to allow a full year to pass while ignoring predictions and their underlying theories.

Recommendations

A new approach to planning is needed, one that is customized to the dynamic and uncertain environments in which high-growth-potential businesses compete. The approach must include tools and frameworks that assist management teams in discussing predictions and the theories used to generate them. Fluency in discussing theories and predictions is generally very low. Beyond debating forecasts for market growth, predictions are not a normal part of the everyday general management dialogue. As mentioned earlier, we have developed such a planning process, called theory-focused planning (TFP), which is the focus of chapter 9.

Figure 6-5 summarizes our recommendations for overcoming each of the four major learning disabilities.

FIGURE 6-5

Overcoming the four learning disabilities

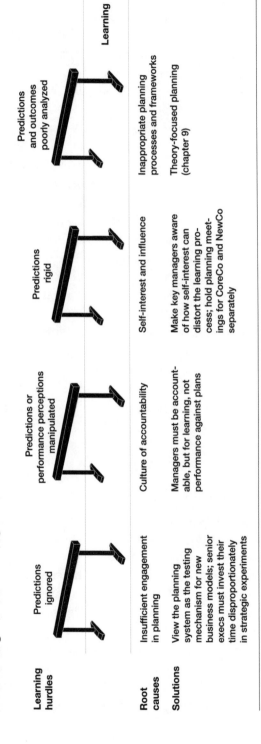

Learning hurdles	Predictions ignored	Predictions or performance perceptions manipulated	Predictions rigid	Predictions and outcomes poorly analyzed
Root causes	Insufficient engagement in planning	Culture of accountability	Self-interest and influence	Inappropriate planning processes and frameworks
Solutions	View the planning system as the testing mechanism for new business models; senior execs must invest their time disproportionately in strategic experiments	Managers must be accountable, but for learning, not performance against plans	Make key managers aware of how self-interest can distort the learning process; hold planning meetings for CoreCo and NewCo separately	Theory-focused planning (chapter 9)

In chapters 7 and 8, we further explore the real and sometimes disastrous impact of learning disabilities by showing how they hindered the evolution of two strategic experiments: Hasbro Interactive and Capston-White's Document Management and Production Services. Both companies were reasonably successful in overcoming the forgetting and borrowing challenges. Their struggles were defined by the learning challenge.

Chapter Seven

How Being Bold,
Competitive, or Demanding
Can Inhibit Learning

In 1951, after nearly thirty years as a manufacturer of a variety of small products in Pawtucket, Rhode Island, Hasbro unexpectedly struck gold. A toy inventor sold Hasbro a quirky idea for $500 and a 5 percent royalty. Mr. Potato Head was nothing more than a set of plastic noses, ears, eyes, moustaches, glasses, hats, and so on that children could use to decorate potatoes or other foods. (Later, after parents complained of finding rotten vegetables behind their sofas, a plastic spud was included in the package.) No one could put their finger on the appeal of this product, but it was a runaway hit. Hasbro's future was in toys.[1]

By the mid-1990s, Hasbro was headed by Alan Hassenfeld, grandson of the company's founder. Hasbro had continued to introduce new toys, including another famous blockbuster, G.I. JOE. In addition, the company had expanded into games by acquiring Massachusetts companies Milton Bradley and Parker Brothers. Hasbro product lines leveraged well-known brands (some Hasbro built and owned, some it licensed) including Monopoly, Batman, Nerf, Play-Doh, Raggedy Ann, Candy Land, Scrabble, and Barney. The toy industry had evolved into a two-horse race: Hasbro versus Mattel. G.I. JOE versus Barbie. Both companies were of similar size. In 1996, Hasbro's revenues were $3 billion, and Mattel's were $3.8 billion.

Hasbro Interactive

In the mid-1990s Hasbro formed Hasbro Interactive, an experimental business focused on video games for PCs. But the roots of Hasbro's experimentation with video games came much earlier. Toward the end of the 1970s, game industry executives were nervous—very nervous—because of the rapidly rising popularity of video games. Were traditional board games doomed? By the early 1980s, Atari's video game system was familiar to every child in the United States. After purchasing the game console, which used standard televisions for display, users could purchase new video game cartridges at consumer-friendly prices of less than $40. Numerous third-party developers offered games for Atari's console.

In response, Hasbro developed a practice of working with outside software developers to create video games for Atari and other platforms. The game development group conceived of ways to convert Hasbro's popular board games into a video format, did some high-level design and visual work, and turned the rest over to outside contractors. The company's most technology-savvy employees monitored the outside work. Hasbro always proved a successful toy or game first and then considered translating it into a video game.

This remained the company's approach until the rising capabilities of the personal computer appeared to make it a viable competitor with other game platforms. By the mid-1990s, high-capacity CD-ROM drives and advanced multimedia capabilities came with most new PCs, and PCs could be found in most homes. The PC appeared to be the new video game platform of choice.

By 1995, Hasbro's toy and game divisions had developed a few CD-ROM products in a decentralized, ad hoc manner. Tom Dusenberry, a longtime employee of Parker Brothers, began speaking with Hassenfeld about taking a much more aggressive approach. A talented visionary, Dusenberry was able to build enthusiasm for futuristic ideas. Hassenfeld charged Dusenberry with building a new division, Hasbro Interactive, and accelerating Hasbro's production of video games for PCs.

Dusenberry had started on the loading docks at Parker Brothers and had been promoted through positions in manufacturing, marketing, and sales. He had stayed connected with developments in video gaming throughout his career. He viewed Hasbro Interactive as his big opportunity. Tremendously ambitious, he believed that if the market was indeed as explosive as he anticipated, he would eventually succeed Hassenfeld as Hasbro's CEO.

Forgetting and Borrowing at Hasbro Interactive

Hasbro created Hasbro Interactive as a separate and independent division that reported to the vice chairman. The CFO also provided oversight. Hasbro Interactive operated on Hasbro's regular planning cycle, although planning meetings were separate from those in other divisions. Dusenberry lured a few of his peers away from Hasbro's games division, but he knew that Hasbro did not have all the skills that he would need. He hired the best software developer he could find—one well known in the industry—to lead the product development effort, and he recruited numerous video game experts to work with him. Dusenberry operated independently, with the freedom to develop a strategy, build a new organization, and execute. He set up shop about a two-hour drive from corporate headquarters, where a new and distinct culture developed.

Given these organizational decisions, Hasbro Interactive was well constructed to leave behind those portions of Hasbro's success formula that did not apply to the interactive gaming market. Hasbro Interactive offered a new value proposition, developed new approaches to sales, marketing, and product development, and built new competencies.

Dusenberry also succeeded in borrowing where needed. In fact, borrowing was crucial because the entire venture was based on the premise that existing products and their associated brands could readily be translated from traditional toys or board games to computer games. To ensure that branding remained consistent, Dusenberry hired insiders familiar with Hasbro's brands and established ongoing interaction with marketing teams at Hasbro. The senior team at Hasbro set a tone for those interactions: brands needed to be protected, but they were not *owned* by the core business.

As mentioned in chapter 5, a link created for purposes of lending a brand to NewCo is an exception to the rule that NewCo should be empowered over CoreCo in each link. In one instance, the Monopoly brand suffered from insufficient coordination between NewCo and CoreCo, and this situation might have been prevented had Hasbro brand teams been given a more formal oversight role. Otherwise, the link was effective, despite tensions that arose when both sides endured periods of disappointing performance.

There was also potential for a link in sales, though limited. Hasbro Interactive's most important customers were major retailers such as Wal-Mart, which also accounted for a large fraction of Hasbro sales. But major retailers assigned the purchasing of video games and board games to different departments, and standard terms of sale were entirely different.

The Early Years

At first, Hasbro Interactive kept things simple. Its focus was strictly on Hasbro's strongest product lines. Early CD-ROM titles included Tonka trucks, Candy Land, Play-Doh, Mr. Potato Head, Battleship, Yahtzee, and others. Monopoly and Scrabble won industry honors.

As a result, Hasbro Interactive was a quick success. It broke even or came close to doing so through 1997. Revenues more than doubled that year from $35 million to $86 million, and two Hasbro Interactive titles were on the industry's top ten list. In addition, Hasbro Interactive's products endured longer than those of its competitors. Blockbuster games from other companies may have sold more copies at their peak, but they never lasted as long.

In 1997, Hasbro Interactive handily exceeded its financial targets, and employees received generous bonuses. Several new cars appeared in the company lot in early 1998. The business model worked. Dusenberry found himself frequently in front of Wall Street analysts, touting the potential of Hasbro Interactive. The market for technology stocks was accelerating, and ambitions for Hasbro Interactive grew in parallel. The division planned to double revenues again in 1998.

But to get there, Hasbro Interactive would have to be much more aggressive. It would have to walk away from the relative predictability of its established business model and pursue much more experimental possibilities. It was at this point that the learning challenge became directly relevant. Unfortunately, Hasbro Interactive was not prepared to learn.

Hasbro Interactive's Bold Expansion

In 1998 and 1999, Dusenberry bet on several new opportunities that would take the business far beyond translating existing Hasbro properties to an interactive format. Hasbro Interactive did the following:

- Purchased licenses to produce games based on the television shows *Wheel of Fortune* and *Jeopardy*

- Purchased rights to all Atari video game properties, hoping to resurrect interest in classics from the 1980s, such as Missile Command and Asteroids

- Purchased rights to additional well-known video games such as Pac Man and Dig Dug

- Created a sports division and signed a five-year licensing deal with Formula 1

- Acquired Microprose for $70 million, adding $20 million per year to the product development budget (a 50 percent increase)

- Acquired Avalon Hill for $6 million, gaining a number of additional game properties that could be translated to an interactive format

- Acquired Europress, moving Hasbro Interactive for the first time into educational products

- Announced for the first time an intent to develop its own games from scratch

- Planned to expand the number of platforms for which games would be developed, including a highly anticipated new platform from Sega known as Dreamcast

That was not all. The Internet, with its quickly advancing capabilities, could hardly be ignored. Hasbro's properties seemed ideal for early adoption on the Internet because they did not require sophisticated graphics.

At the time, many established corporations were trying to cash in on the extremely high Internet valuations by creating their own Internet ventures. Outside market research agencies were estimating the future size of the Internet gaming market to be north of $1 billion. Such projections were based on the notion that people wanted to play multiplayer games on far more occasions than they could find partners. Therefore, the ability to connect with people around the world for a game of Risk or Monopoly would attract millions.

Hasbro established a Games.com business unit in 1999. Initially, Games.com was separate from Hasbro Interactive, but the two were consolidated in 2000. Hasbro struck a partnership with a soon-to-be-launched Internet portal backed by high-profile investors, including Paul Allen of Microsoft, and built a $100 million game development studio in California.

Overall, the expanded ambition was consistent with the anything-is-possible atmosphere of the late 1990s. But the way that Hasbro Interactive pursued growth brought a great many additional unknowns into the business. No longer was Hasbro Interactive's business model reliably predictable. Instead, it was reliably unpredictable.

Consider some of the new unknowns: Could video game users be attracted to old video game titles? To what extent and how quickly would video game players migrate to the Internet? How much would they be willing to pay? How soon could advertisers be attracted to video game Web sites? How quickly and aggressively would Hasbro competitors invest in video games? Would the PC really become the dominant gaming platform, or would new alternatives arise?

In addition, how easily could Hasbro Interactive identify winning concepts when the starting point was something other than a proven traditional Hasbro game? For example, Avalon Hill games tended to be complex. Would they translate to video effectively? And how would the cost characteristics of complex games differ from Hasbro's games—that is, how much more expensive would they be to maintain and update?

Even more questions arose. As Internet and computer graphics capabilities advanced, how much would product development times increase? How much more costly would it be to develop a single video game? Finally, in the frothy dot-com environment, would Hasbro Interactive be able to attract and hire a sufficient number of software developers to fulfill its ambitions?

Full Speed Ahead! (Crash)

These unknowns needed to be resolved for Hasbro Interactive to zero in on a workable business model. Instead of iterating through various experiments, however, Dusenberry ventured forth as aggressively as possible for as long as possible, with an unquestioned belief in Hasbro Interactive's potential. Partway through the dramatic expansion, he was further emboldened by a strong finish in 1998. Revenues were just short of $200 million, more than double the revenues of a year earlier. And the division was still profitable.

Soon, there was talk of Hasbro Interactive reaching $1 billion in revenues within as little as three years. This was an audacious target; it would vault Hasbro Interactive into position as one of Hasbro's major divisions. Initially the goal was only conversational, but it affected decision making. It fueled ambition. Dusenberry's excitement about the prospect of running such a large business was transparent to his colleagues. Although some senior executives at Hasbro were nervous about the risks inherent in trying to grow so quickly, no one acted to put a stop to this bold goal.

No one could know it at the time, but as the $1 billion ambition coalesced, Hasbro Interactive entered a new period in its history—the beginning of the end. Briefly, here is what happened.

Dusenberry viewed the positive results for 1998 as validation of the aggressive expansion of Hasbro Interactive. But 1998 was more likely a reflection of the original business model than it was a result of the new activities, many of which were still in the development stage.

Subsequently, results in the first quarter of 1999 were disappointing because of unexpectedly high returns of unsold product from retailers. Senior executives at Hasbro became much more alert. They had many questions. Concerns heightened when Hasbro Interactive reported a significant loss at the end of 1999—in the tens of millions of dollars. The pressure was on for Hasbro Interactive to show quick returns from its expanded investments.

But losses inevitably precede profits in any strategic experiment. Patience is required. Unfortunately, Hasbro's core businesses suffered a bit of a decline, and this increased pressures on Hasbro Interactive to restore profitability. The division could not easily do so. A great deal had been invested in experimental opportunities, and Dusenberry did not want to abandon them before they had a realistic chance to succeed.

The end came late in 2000, when turnover in Hasbro's senior management team led to a change in sentiment toward Hasbro Interactive. For the first time, Dusenberry's constant efforts to internally promote the long-term potential of Hasbro Interactive failed to sustain funding for the business. Hasbro Interactive was sold to an outside buyer for only $100 million.[2]

Had Hasbro Interactive been engaged in a learning process throughout, a more favorable outcome would have been likely. Specifically, Hasbro Interactive would have been able to pare only the failing parts of its business.

But Hasbro Interactive's learning disabilities prevented this option. The details of what happened at Hasbro Interactive in its later years are instructive. They show how learning disabilities alter the course of strategic experiments. They also show how behaviors that in many contexts are viewed positively—being bold, competitive, or demanding—can lead to predictions that are ignored, are manipulated, or become rigid and thereby cause strategic experiments to falter.

Ignored Predictions

Any of the four root causes of learning disabilities can lead to predictions being ignored. Three played a role in the Hasbro Interactive story.

Inappropriate Planning Processes or Frameworks

Recall that the learning process is embedded in the planning cycle. Therefore, the frequency of the planning cycle places an upper limit on the rate of learning. But frequent engagement in planning is not the norm in most corporations. In fact, the frequency of the customary planning cycle is perhaps the most obvious disabler of learning. Conventional practice is to cycle through the planning process only once per year, and this was the norm at Hasbro.

Although it is true that many corporations, including Hasbro, constantly check outcomes against plans, even as often as weekly, these generally are quick "status checks" to see whether anything has gone wrong. If a problem is noticed, it is isolated and fixed quickly. But these reviews are less useful in strategic experiments because no accepted standards exist for what constitutes a "problem." Disparities between predictions and outcomes must be viewed with an eye toward reexamining critical unknowns and fundamentally reassessing strategy. This review must happen at least quarterly, or even monthly. But common practice is to ask fundamental questions of strategy only once per year.

Insufficient Engagement in the Planning Process

Dusenberry did not emphasize planning. He was required to submit a plan once per year, but these plans were quickly out of date. Decisions to expand Hasbro Interactive's operations did not conveniently coincide with the annual planning cycle. It would have taken an unusual effort to keep revising plans, and Hasbro Interactive did not make the effort. In fact, Dusenberry charged Hasbro Interactive's finance group with heavy analysis of potential acquisitions, and this left even less time than usual for planning.

It showed. An interim corporate review of Hasbro Interactive's plans in 1999 showed that the functional plans within Hasbro Interactive were not well coordinated. (For example, the marketing plan for a new product would forecast revenues beginning before the product development group's planned release date.)

Not only were plans out of date and out of sync, but also minimal performance information was gathered to compare with predictions. Hasbro's information systems frustrated Dusenberry. They were optimized for the toy and game business, but terms of trade in software were very different. For example, software retailers demanded much more flexible terms for returns of unsold product. In addition, Hasbro was in the midst of a major information systems overhaul during Hasbro Interactive's growth period, and that made gathering information much more difficult.

In the face of such limitations, Hasbro Interactive needed to increase its commitment for thoughtfully tracking and analyzing its business. But Dusenberry did not make this a priority, for several of the reasons discussed in chapter 6. Most of all, Dusenberry viewed planning as a distraction. Hasbro Interactive was in an all-out race to capture a share in an emerging market, and it needed to focus on the future.

Self-Interest and Influence

Some Hasbro employees felt that Hasbro Interactive was purposely dodging planning tasks because the division wanted to prevent potentially negative information from becoming transparent. In fact, leaders of strategic experiments often try to limit performance information, and for legitimate reasons.

Performance perceptions are powerful game pieces in the ongoing struggle for influence and control within any organization. The head of NewCo must constantly be concerned about building and sustaining the political will for continued support of an experiment. To help achieve this goal, the leader naturally desires to maintain the perception that NewCo is excelling.

Performance assessments of a strategic experiment are highly ambiguous, and quick judgments based on limited information can be damaging. Understandably, leaders of strategic experiments perceive the political environment surrounding them as full of risks. They run relatively small businesses that lose money—sometimes a lot of money. Losing political influence could quickly lead to losing funding and losing one's job as well.

Therefore, some leaders of strategic experiments deliberately create as much ambiguity as possible. They might limit the flow of performance information. They might openly question the value of original predictions by pointing out the paucity of supporting data and experience. They might even focus a planning discussion on the ambiguity of internal accounting allocations. Shared costs are always present between Core-Co and NewCo, and they can never be divided in an unambiguous way.

All this helps create as much wiggle room as possible. With greater ambiguity, leaders of strategic experiments can create favorable stories about how well the business is doing.[3] As a result, they can take the business in whatever direction they feel it needs to go.

Dusenberry tried to minimize energy expended on planning and reviewing performance. One tactic he used was to shift attention from the short term to the long term. He talked often of Hasbro Interactive's potential to grow to a $1 billion business in only a few years. By doing so, he was deflecting attention from any evidence that could demonstrate that his business was underperforming. It was always easier to make projected long-term performance appear attractive than it was to rationalize short-term disappointments.

But analyzing the long term does not lead to learning. There are too many uncertainties, and too little evidence, to say anything conclusive. For managers to learn, the analysis must focus on comparisons between short-term predictions and short-term outcomes. Based on conclusions drawn from this analysis, managers can adjust short-term resource allocations, and gradually zero in on a winning approach.

Learning requires transparency. Information, especially about surprises and negative outcomes, must be collected and shared with openness and candor. Information must be considered a friend and not an enemy. The dynamic coordinator must ensure that performance information is viewed rationally and not abused for political jockeying.

Manipulated Predictions or Performance Perceptions

When predictions are manipulated, the process of rationally analyzing disparities between predictions and outcomes is disrupted. At Hasbro Interactive, two root causes led to the manipulation of predictions.

Inappropriate Planning Processes and Frameworks

Heads of strategic experiments may perceive that keeping the performance of their businesses ambiguous can work in their favor, but this strategy can backfire. The question "How is the business performing?" is so instinctive, and so pervasive, that it is bound to be answered in one way or another. The lack of an answer creates a vacuum, and that vacuum will inevitably be filled, often in a way that disrupts learning.

On the initiative of a new senior executive, starting in early 1999, Hasbro held monthly meetings to review the performance of *all* of Hasbro's business units. Heads of all units attended, including Dusenberry. (Hasbro Interactive had previously been reviewed separately, by the CFO and vice chairman.) The meetings naturally engendered an atmosphere of competitiveness. All units reported a standard set of "value drivers" used by the corporation, such as growth rates, margins, inventory turns, and the like.

Not seeing any alternative, everyone in the room naturally evaluated Hasbro Interactive exactly as they would evaluate any other Hasbro division.[4] When Hasbro Interactive's returns from the retail trade were excessive by toy and game standards, it looked bad—even though terms of trade were much different in software. When Dusenberry argued that product development expenses at Hasbro Interactive could be capitalized rather than expensed, a practice common in the software industry, others became uncomfortable because the practice was unfamiliar in toys and games. Moreover, the group emphasized profitability in the short term. The argument seemed to be, "If the business is not profitable today, it is not a good business." Although it was important for Hasbro Interactive to show evidence that it was on a long-term path to profitability, immediate profitability is not a realistic benchmark for experimental businesses.

Thus the measures that shaped the perceived performance of Hasbro Interactive were not those that could help resolve critical unknowns. Instead, they were convenient measures that the executives accustomed to managing mature toy and game operations understood—and readily latched on to, because they made their own business units look superior to Hasbro Interactive. This situation is not uncommon. Over time, measures of performance become powerful within an organization. They have proven relevant for many years, and they seem inherently fair.[5]

In effect, working from Hasbro's universal planning framework, the other business heads shifted the basis for assessing the performance of Hasbro Interactive. They manipulated the existing predictions (an action Dusenberry facilitated by discounting them himself), substituting accepted measures and expectations from the core business.

Precisely because of these types of dynamics, we think it advisable to hold business performance reviews for experimental businesses separately from those for mature businesses. It is too difficult to try to train executives who are fully devoted to managing a large, mature business to temporarily shift to a different evaluation approach when an experimental business is being discussed. Misinterpretations are likely.

Self-Interest and Influence

Hasbro Interactive had revenue projections in place in early 1999 when talk of $1 billion in revenues arose. The revision upward to $1 billion was not based on a reassessment of evidence nor on an analysis of what it would take to get to $1 billion. Instead, it followed from a desire to "sell" the business.

Both the senior executives and Dusenberry played roles. The former were using the potential of Hasbro Interactive to impress investors and elevate the stock price; the latter was simply trying to acquire greater resources and build influence within the organization.

Emotional factors also played a role. Predictions can easily lock in to round-number benchmarks, such as $1 billion in revenues. Competition, too, can fuel the escalation in expectations. When Mattel acquired The Learning Company, it immediately increased its interactive revenues to nearly $1 billion, and Hasbro executives felt the need to keep up. (In a well-publicized business disaster story, Mattel would later sell The Learning Company for nothing more than a share of future earnings.)

This process of inflating predictions disrupts learning. Predictions should be modified only following an analysis of the disparities between predictions and outcomes.

Rigid Predictions

When the learning process is healthy, predictions are gradually modified as evidence is gathered. But two of the root causes of learning disabilities can prevent the adjustment of predictions, even as evidence accumulates.

A Culture of Accountability

Hasbro had historically practiced a relatively forgiving approach to accountability to plans because of the inherent unpredictability of the toy business. At the prodding of a senior executive hired from the outside, however, Hasbro had started holding managers more accountable to plans, and this made it unlikely that predictions for Hasbro Interactive could be revised.

Leaders of strategic experiments often play a role in the solidification of expectations. In part because they want to be seen as bold and visionary, in part because they need to keep others excited about the business's long-term prospects, and in part because of pressure from demanding bosses that hold them accountable for results, they frequently reaffirm commitments to the long-term numbers.[6]

But initial long-term projections—and early decisions—are based on big assumptions. Subsequently, these big assumptions become perceived realities as hard work, big dreams, and fear of competition magnify emotional attachments to existing objectives. Even in the face of disappointing results, leaders often escalate commitments rather than stop to reevaluate. Perceptions of success therefore remain concretely adhered to initial expectations.

Dusenberry was wedded to his expansive view of Hasbro Interactive's potential. When it became clear that 1999 revenues would fall short of plan, Dusenberry reaffirmed his belief in the $1 billion goal.[7] He insisted on staying on course.

In selecting leaders of strategic experiments, senior executives face a tough paradox. It is natural to select leaders who have strong track records. At the same time, executives with strong track records are the ones who have the least exposure to failure. They are also most likely to become defensive in the face of evidence suggesting that an experimental business is off course.

Self-Interest and Influence

Internal dissent at the top of CoreCo can solidify expectations, as senior executives compete for power and influence. Here is how it might work: suppose one senior executive has given vocal support to a strategic experiment, claiming it could be hugely important for the company's future and urging investment. A second senior executive might see this as an opportunity to get ahead of the first executive if the risky experiment founders. At the first sign that NewCo is in trouble, the second executive will associate the first executive with failure as often as possible. In doing so, he will remind others of the executive's past support for NewCo and will reinforce the original high predictions of NewCo's performance. Such maneuvering can reasonably be inferred at Hasbro.

With the organization's best interests at heart, CEOs can also solidify predictions. In an effort to support an experimental business, a CEO may speak loudly of its potential—as Hasbro's top executives did—both to insiders and to outsiders. The intent may be to get investors excited, or it may be to increase CoreCo's support for NewCo and thus improve links between them. But doing so can lock in an aggressive prediction. The voice of the CEO is powerful, and expectations stick.[8]

Going Guardrail-to-Guardrail

Any prediction that is rigid is damaging. The most dangerous rigid predictions are long term. The decision to invest in a strategic experiment is often made on the basis of long-term projections of market size, revenues, and potential profitability. As a result, whether or not the new business is actually growing at a rate that validates these initial projections can be one of the most watched indicators.

Such long-term projections, however, do not support learning as the strategic experiment proceeds. It takes too long for evidence that can concretely confirm or reject these projections to accumulate. Plans should lay out what is expected to happen month-by-month or quarter-by-quarter. Short-term, revisable predictions serve as the basis for ongoing learning.

That said, there is nothing wrong with having a bold, long-term revenue target. In fact, such targets can be motivational, even inspiring.[9] They can help in obtaining internal support or financing. In the long term, organizations rarely exceed their aspirations. So *not* having a bold long-term goal is tantamount to making a commitment *not* to achieve anything grand. But bold long-term goals that are used to motivate need to be coupled with rational short-term predictions that are used to support learning.

The heavy focus on a long-term, rigid projection—the $1 billion revenue goal—was very damaging for Hasbro Interactive. Visualize a race car driver repeatedly losing control, brushing the guardrail on one side of the road, and then overcorrecting and slamming into the guard-rail on the other side. In the context of a strategic experiment, the equiv-alent of going guardrail to guardrail is optimistic overinvestment fol-lowed by abandonment—exactly the story of Hasbro Interactive. Such a pattern is the opposite of the gradual-zeroing-in pattern that marks a healthy learning process. Predictions that are both rigid and long term lead to guardrail-to-guardrail decision making.

Here's why. It's difficult to evaluate the probability of actually hitting a long-term goal. It is a judgment call. As a company invests more in an experimental business (and places a heavier drag on the income statement), pressures build for proof that the goal can be reached. As-sessments of "maybe" or "possibly" become less tolerable. Senior man-agement teams eventually split into an "Aggressive" faction that favors continued investment, and a "Prudent" faction that favors severe re-duction in investment or even abandonment.

Initially, the group favoring continued investment will be stronger. But tensions rise when, inevitably, experimental businesses do not pro-ceed according to plan. The Prudents will use any negative surprise to build their case. Unable to admit defeat or even weakness, the Aggres-sives redouble their commitment. Tensions rise further.

The decision-making atmosphere can polarize in this way even while the actual odds of success change very little. It takes time for evidence to accumulate, and much remains unknown for several quarters. But rational assessment of evidence is an early casualty as these tensions escalate. Misinterpretations become likely, and it is often on the basis of such misinterpretations that Prudents gain enough strength to take over.

In waiting for victory, the Prudents become frustrated. The sudden release of accumulated frustration exaggerates their decision making, and the support for the experimental business goes from one guardrail to the other.

That is what happened at Hasbro Interactive. Through a period of senior-management turnover in mid-2000, one of the strongest mem-bers of the Prudent faction rose to the post of president and chief oper-ating officer. This development gave the Prudents their victory. Long a conservative voice concerned about overinvestment in Hasbro Interac-tive, the new COO quickly chose to exit the business entirely.

This may or may not have been the best decision for Hasbro. Many factors were involved. But at least part of Hasbro Interactive's opera-tions were proven profitable in the division's early years, and that part was now gone. Further, Hasbro had not learned from its investments beyond this profitable model. As a result, it was not able to separate the profitable aspects of its experiment from the unprofitable ones. The division was viewed as an all-or-nothing proposition. For this reason, it was viewed as a failure.

A more objective path would have focused on short-term predictions and outcomes. Hasbro Interactive had few clear short-term predictions other than product development deadlines. When these deadlines were missed, a general unease arose that the business perhaps was not doing well, but these missed deadlines did not lead to a reassessment of what was planned or what was possible. Some Hasbro executives conjectured that the rising complexity of game platforms might be responsible for the long product development times, but this insight did not lead to a reevaluation of key planning variables such as pricing, total investment required, or time to profitability. This type of analysis could have helped Hasbro Interactive pare down its business to a few profitable activities, enabling Hasbro interactive to remain a part of Hasbro.

We continue the discussion of learning disabilities in chapter 8, where we analyze another strategic experiment, this one in the computer industry.

Chapter Eight

How Being Reasonable, Inspiring, or Diligent Can Inhibit Learning

I N 1996, Capston-White (CW), a leader in computer printers and related technologies, reassessed its strategy. CW focused on the corporate market, and key accounts were now at risk. Copier companies, which had served a distinct market for decades, were launching new products that performed multiple document functions, including printing, faxing, copying, and scanning, thus competing directly with CW. The new machines also were designed to be integrated directly into corporate IT networks.

To respond to the threat, CW began developing its own multifunction devices. It also decided to borrow the copier industry's services strategy. Corporations typically outsourced the management of their copiers to the copier suppliers. Rather than purchase the copiers, they paid by the page, and the copier company took care of everything: installation, maintenance, repairs, and so on. By contrast, the computer printer industry sold products, and purchasers were then on their own. Only basic customer service was included with the printer purchase.

But printing devices were becoming much more complex as they performed more functions. It seemed logical that corporations would soon want services for their fleets of printers. CW consulted outside market researchers, who supported this notion.

So CW launched a strategic experiment: its own services business, dubbed Capston-White Document Management and Production Services (DMPS). It offered its corporate clients contracts that included leased machines, on-site maintenance and repair, and ongoing monitoring of printer use. DMPS intended to gradually add services as it proved the business.

Reducing corporations' costs and improving the convenience of routine printing were admittedly not the sexiest ideas on earth. But neither was Tom Stemberg's plan to open a new chain of superstores that sold pens, paper clips, envelopes, and other office supplies at discounted prices—and Staples became an icon of entrepreneurship.

DMPS faced a difficult learning challenge, one well worth study. CW made a high-risk investment of millions of dollars just to get started, with no promise of any return. Many unknowns existed:

- How quickly would the market for printing services develop? (A related unknown: How popular would complex, networked, multifunction devices become?)

- What range of services would be needed to attract customers?

- What was the best process for developing new services?

- What sales approach would work—through printer distributors, through an internal technical sales force, or through a consultative sales force?

- What was the best way to deliver services—through distribution partners or via an internal staff?

- What was the best way to define the service offerings? What would they cost to deliver? What price would customers bear?

- To what extent would product sales and service sales be correlated? Could CW offer to serve only CW printing and imaging devices, or would it need to service devices from any vendor?

Two years into the life of the business (a period we will refer to as stage 1), results were disappointing. The management team concluded that it had made a mistake in choosing to rely on CW's distributors to sell and deliver the new services. In addition, the team decided that to

FIGURE 8-1

Range of services for DMPS

Low complexity

- Call center resolutions
- Warranty repairs and replacement

Medium complexity

- On-site management of fleets: installations, upgrades, maintenance, repair
- Complete leasing and outsourcing on per-page basis
- Integration with internal IT help desks
- Usage monitoring by workstation or application
- Automatic installations and removals to optimize overall printing assets
- Rapid-response-time services for mission-critical printers

High complexity

- E-commerce systems
- Integration of enterprise resources planning systems

make the value proposition compelling, the service offerings needed to be radically expanded to include consulting services. (See figure 8-1 for a list of services.)

Both conclusions led to an increase in the level of investment in the venture in stage 2. CW had to hire and train new personnel for selling, delivery, and consulting, and it made a significant acquisition to help expand its range of services. The company also built a cutting-edge IT infrastructure that would allow many of its services to be delivered remotely, over the Internet.

Unfortunately, two years later, results were still disappointing. CW sought additional advice from outside consultants and market research firms, and both sources continued to believe that a market existed for the services CW offered.

However, the stage 2 losses were staggering. Shell-shocked, the company chose a more conservative approach (stage 3). It laid off one-third of the DMPS workforce and again focused on selling and delivering basic services as efficiently and effectively as possible with in-house sales and delivery teams. (It did not return to selling and delivering services through distributors.)

Although the business gathered momentum with this approach, two years later a major merger between CoreCo and another industry leader led to another reevaluation—and a significant organizational

FIGURE 8-2

The four stages in the history of DMPS

Stage	Strategy
1	Limited services, sold and delivered through distribution partners
2	Expanded services, sold and delivered by internal staff
3	Limited services, sold and delivered by internal staff
4	Expanded services, sold and delivered through a reorganized internal staff with a new management team

restructuring (stage 4). New leadership within the company again became convinced that to be compelling, DMPS had to offer more complex consulting services. CW also chose to modify its processes for developing services; to offer services for both CW and non-CW printers; and to build a new, more consultative sales force.

The outcome of this latest change in approach has not yet become clear. However, when we review the four-stage history of DMPS (summarized in figure 8-2), two interesting questions arise: was DMPS learning? Was it learning as quickly as possible?

Lessons Learned—Too Slowly

DMPS was learning, but not as quickly as possible. It took too long to zero in on a workable model, and the changes from one stage to the next were much more dramatic (guardrail to guardrail) than necessary. And, each change was more painful than it should have been. Changes in strategy came only at a high cost: each time, the leader of DMPS was reassigned and a new leader was appointed.

Another way to look at the health of the learning process is to consider how quickly DMPS was able to resolve the critical unknowns we have discussed. By the end of stage 1, it had discovered only that selling and delivering services through its existing distribution partners did not work. DMPS experimented with different ranges of services in stages 2 and 3, but it was only in stage 4 that DMPS adopted an approach that would enable it to test many of the remaining critical unknowns.

Further, one of the most important critical unknowns—when the market would develop—was not explicitly tested. This omission became an expensive mistake in stage 2, when DMPS invested heavily in anticipation of explosive market growth.

Because leaders of strategic experiments often use thorough market research to validate initial investment, they may not always view whether and when a market will develop as a critical unknown. They should. Market research into nascent industries can be misleading. Forecasting *that* a new market will develop is difficult enough; putting a date on *when* it will develop is nearly impossible, because many outside forces are at play that cannot be easily assessed.

In retrospect, the forces delaying the development of the market were clear. DMPS's target customers—chief information officers—had their hands full in the late 1990s. Sure, CIOs were intrigued by the possibility of outsourcing the management of their printers, and market research repeatedly confirmed that interest. But when they would actually get around to purchasing those services was another question. They had their normal jobs of automating internal processes. Plus, they had to deal with two demanding one-time projects: overcoming the Y2K problem and preparing for the conversion to the euro. What's more, they were under new pressures to generate breakthrough business strategies based on the Internet.

Furthermore, the DMPS value proposition was predicated on the growth of complex, networked multifunction devices that could print, copy, scan, fax, and more, in the high-volume environment common in corporate copy centers. But the market for such devices, while indeed expanding, was growing more slowly than expected. In fact CW's first launch of a product into this market was a serious disappointment.

By 2001, the Y2K and euro conversion issues had passed, the dot-com bubble had deflated, and the general economy was slumping. Now CIOs were much more interested in finding ways to cut costs. Therefore, DMPS services became more attractive. But even then, most companies had no idea how much they were spending overall on printers, paper, and toner because these purchases were decentralized. DMPS had to educate its potential customers about the value it could provide, and this took time. There was no clear evidence that a market was developing until late in stage 3.

Why didn't DMPS learn more quickly? Part of the problem was that DMPS struggled in its effort to forget. It instinctively adhered to the successful business model of the core business. In addition, DMPS suffered from learning disabilities. Although the precise mechanisms were distinct from those at Hasbro, the effect was the same: predictions were ignored, they became rigid, and they were manipulated.

The Forgetting Challenge at DMPS

Recall that one of the most difficult tasks associated with the forgetting challenge is to abandon the existing business model. Recall also that overcoming the learning challenge involves gradually zeroing in on a working business model. Thus, forgetting is a prerequisite for learning.

Like CW, many companies choose to expand from products to services in order to sustain growth as their product businesses mature.[1] The transition requires a dramatic shift in value proposition, because interactions with customers become richer and more frequent. Customer satisfaction and convenience become the primary value drivers (as opposed to product quality or price), and they are dependent on those continuing interactions. Excelling in such an environment requires new skills and new processes. In sum, it requires a new business model.

But as constituted in stage 1, the DMPS organizational DNA was nearly identical to CW's. Although some of the leaders brought to bear exposure to the copier industry, the management team as a whole naturally adhered to the CW success formula. Therefore, the starting point for the strategic experiment was much further from an eventual workable model than it otherwise would have been.

The initial business model for DMPS mimicked CW's approach to the products business in three ways: in selling and distributing, in launching new services, and in defining a business focus.

Selling and Distributing

CW believed that an important reason for its ability to generate high profitability in its core business was that the company always sought high human resources leverage. CW kept only the highest-value-added processes in-house—those requiring the greatest intellectual capital, particularly research and product development. Everything else was outsourced.

As an indication of how well it was doing in this respect, CW tracked revenues per employee. The implicit assumption—that high revenues per employee predicted success—shaped DMPS in its early years. In fact, it led to the initial misstep of relying heavily on distribution partners.

Building a large army of service personnel—or a large internal workforce of any kind—was anathema to the way things were done at CW.

CW's distribution partners, which sold and delivered CW products to corporations, had a sales capability in place, with a combined workforce that was as spread out geographically as CW's customer base. DMPS planned to define the services, create the marketing materials to support the sales team, develop the necessary software tools, and train the service delivery teams. This plan was exactly in line with how CW managed its products business.

But DMPS discovered that the distribution partners had little motivation to deal with the services business. They knew products, and they were making good money selling them. Furthermore, customers did not have confidence in the capabilities of the distributors. They wanted a well-known organization such as CW to actually be on-site delivering the services.

It took all of stage 1 for CW to conclude that the distribution approach was ineffective. But if it had been able to forget, it likely would not have started with a model that relied so heavily on distributors, an arrangement that was unusual for a services offering. Two years lost.

Launching New Services

Another example of the misapplication of the product mind-set was CW's approach to launching new services. In the early stages, DMPS sequenced its approach to the market as though it were launching a new product: design the product. Perfect it. Launch it. Market and sell it. This linear approach places a premium on getting product quality as high as possible the first time.

Services, on the other hand, can be launched more loosely, even with vague definitions of the nature of the service. Then the services can improve over time through interaction with customers. DMPS began experimenting with this new approach only in stage 4—six years into the life of the strategic experiment.

Defining a Business Focus: Single-Vendor or Multivendor Services?

In an additional nod to CoreCo's established business model, DMPS initially developed services only for CW printers. That is, if a corporation owned printers from CW and from another vendor, DMPS would manage only the CW printers. Although an ability to support multiple vendors' printers would certainly have been valued by customers, DMPS's business was viewed through the lens of how it could help or hurt the core business. Again, only in stage 4 did DMPS begin experimenting with service offerings that included products from multiple vendors.

DMPS was slow to forget. They were also slow to learn, because predictions were ignored, they became rigid, and they were manipulated. Each of these learning disabilities was caused by one of the four root causes described in chapter 6.

Ignored Predictions

The root cause that led to predictions being ignored was CW's exceptionally strong culture of accountability.

At CW, you made your plans. Period. In an counterintuitive way, this aggressive practice led directly to predictions being ignored. To allow for uncertainties inherent in strategic innovation, the senior management team had developed a specific practice of allowing a grace period during which underperformance was forgiven.

In one way, the rationale was on target. Strategic experiments are unpredictable, and holding leaders accountable to the numbers in the plan is counterproductive. But the method of removing accountability was not on target. What needed to go was the discipline of actually being responsible for delivering the numbers in the plan, but CW threw out the plans, too. Thus, the predictions in the plans did not become the basis for ongoing learning. Planning was nothing more than an exercise for winning funding and approval for an initial strategy.

It is no accident that each stage was roughly two years long. DMPS's grace period was consistently one year. Strategic adjustments were made as a part of the annual planning cycle. For the leaders of DMPS, the first year was a free pass; the second year, you had to deliver. And CW was ruthless in holding its managers accountable. None of the first three DMPS leaders survived for a third year.

Had the succession of DMPS leaders been actively engaged in learning during their respective tenures, they would have more frequently adjusted strategy as part of a process of careful and controlled experimentation.[2] Instead, only the senior leadership team made such adjustments, and it did so only in conjunction with disruptive leadership changes. CW's grace period actually *reduced* the potential rate of learning by one-half because plans were revisited only every other year.

Research shows that infrequent reassessment of strategy is the norm and not the exception. Strategic reassessments are most likely to occur after critical events, such as a major organizational change, a merger that leads to an influx of new people, a change in leadership, a change in resource constraints, a major competitive change, or a sudden decline in performance.[3] At least DMPS insisted on strategic reassessments every two years, but such evaluations should have been much more frequent. The essence of good leadership of strategic experiments is that the strategy is always being reevaluated.

Rigid Predictions

The same root cause—a strong culture of accountability—led naturally to predictions becoming rigid at CW. If predictions are not revisable, learning suffers.

Decision making is also affected. Note that the evolution from stage 1 to stage 2 to stage 3 demonstrates guardrail-to-guardrail decision making, much like Hasbro Interactive. The decision-making pattern resulted from the same underlying cause: performance perceptions that were driven by rigid, long-term predictions rather than by short-term, revisable predictions.

When the grace period elapsed in the second year of each stage, DMPS was evaluated as either succeeding or failing primarily on the basis of progress toward long-term revenue targets—a standard against which DMPS struggled until late in stage 3. These predictions were not treated as revisable. They were solidified by market estimates from outside experts—estimates that should have been presumed wrong—and by CW's practice of holding managers accountable for results. In stage 2, they also were solidified because the DMPS leader at the time was not willing to admit defeat.

The stage 2 leader had committed a great deal of resources to DMPS, with tremendous bravado. She wanted to be seen as bold and visionary, and she needed to get others excited about the venture's long-term prospects. As a result, she continued to redouble efforts to meet the long-term prediction, even when a reevaluation of strategy would have been wiser—because there was little evidence that a market was developing as the research had projected. Driven by rigid long-term predictions, DMPS went from one guardrail in stage 2 (aggressive investment) to the opposite rail in stage 3 (excessive pessimism).

In going guardrail to guardrail, DMPS simultaneously made multiple changes to its strategy, greatly complicating the analysis of lessons learned. Consider the transition from stage 1 to stage 2. Two major changes in strategy were made: DMPS would sell and deliver services itself, and the service offering would be dramatically expanded. It turned out that the first change was on the mark, but the second was several years premature. Thus, the second change was abandoned—but not until stage 3. A practice of testing strategy more methodically (one change, and therefore one controlled experiment, at a time) and more frequently would have enabled DMPS to get from stage 1 to stage 3 much sooner.

Manipulated Predictions or Performance Perceptions

In the Hasbro story, you saw how one of the root causes—the self-interest and influence behaviors of competing business unit heads—can lead to manipulated predictions. Here you will see how a much different influence behavior can also disrupt learning.

Leaders must motivate. One motivation technique is to create drama by telling stories about performance. Stories fall into two categories: success is imminent, or survival is at stake.

Research shows, however, that when people perceive that performance is either near the aspired level or near failure, they are least likely to maintain an experimental mind-set.[4] Instead, they keep their heads down, work hard, and do their jobs to the best of their abilities. They become highly risk averse and are less open to questioning the overall plan. Thus, leaders of strategic experiments can inadvertently dampen any enthusiasm for thoughtful analysis of predictions and outcomes by sending strong motivational messages about how the business is performing.

Throughout stage 2, DMPS's leader reinforced the notion that the business was on track to success. In doing so, she prevented thoughtful dialogue about how the business was doing and whether the strategy needed to be reconsidered. Instead, the answer came from the top: we are on track. Success will follow if we stay focused and execute.

During stage 3, DMPS suffered from the same learning disability, but it took the opposite form. The pain of the significant losses during stage 2 led to cautious, protective supervision in stage 3. DMPS's leader in stage 3 felt that she was under constant probation. The perception from the end of stage 2 was that the business was performing extremely poorly, and that perception endured through stage 3. The layoffs only made people feel less inclined to see the positives in how the business was doing. As a result, the DMPS management team had little motivation to constantly reassess performance and reevaluate strategy. Again, the answer came from senior management: the business was performing poorly. In fact, the team felt doubt from one month to the next about whether funding would continue.

Leaders have a great deal of latitude to alter perceptions of NewCo's performance because its assessment is ambiguous. Competitive data is limited, customer feedback is vague, and costs are difficult to anticipate. The voice of the leader can have a tremendous impact on performance perceptions, and it can be tempting for a leader to motivate people by creating a perception of near-success or near-failure. But doing so blunts any inclination by workers to maintain a questioning mind-set.

A better approach is to reinforce the perception, "We have a long way to go, and it is not at all clear how we are going to get there." Such a statement is honest, and it is appropriately humble given the uncertainties. It also can be very motivating, in a way that engages employees both in hard work and in learning.

A Review of Learning Disabilities

To learn from business experiments, you must thoughtfully analyze the comparisons between predictions and outcomes, and then update predictions based on lessons from the analysis. But as you have seen, many mechanisms can disrupt this process. Predictions are ignored, they become set in stone, or they are manipulated, as are performance perceptions. In all cases, learning suffers.

You have also seen that learning disabilities derive from four root causes. The causal paths from root causes to learning disabilities are sometimes directly tied to key executives such as the general managers of NewCo or CoreCo or a corporate-level executive, and sometimes tied more closely to a company's management systems and culture, as summarized in figures 8-3, 8-4, and 8-5.

Note that management behaviors generally thought to be positive have a role in many of these mechanisms. Chapter 7 explained how being

FIGURE 8-3

When predictions are ignored, learning is disabled

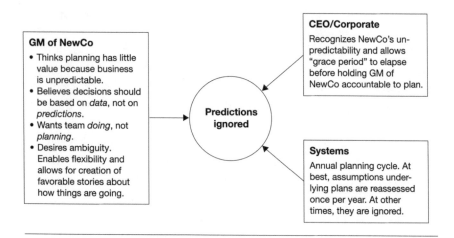

bold, competitive, or demanding can lead to learning disabilities. In this chapter, you have seen that being reasonable by allowing a grace period, and offering inspiring leadership, can also backfire. Next, you will see that misdirected diligence in planning also can be counterproductive.

Poor Analysis of Predictions and Outcomes

We now turn to the fourth learning disability: poor analysis of predictions and outcomes. Corporations have experimented with three planning approaches for strategic experiments: conventional planning, discovery driven planning, and the venture capital planning model. Your choice of approach has dramatic implications for the way you analyze predictions and outcomes.

It turns out that none of these three approaches is appropriate for strategic experiments. DMPS actually tried all three, and its history illustrates the shortcomings associated with each of them.

Conventional Planning

For most of its history, DMPS operated on the same planning system as the rest of CW. This conventional approach was similar to that of every corporation we studied. Three aspects of this planning hindered

FIGURE 8-4

When predictions or performance perceptions are manipulated, learning is disabled

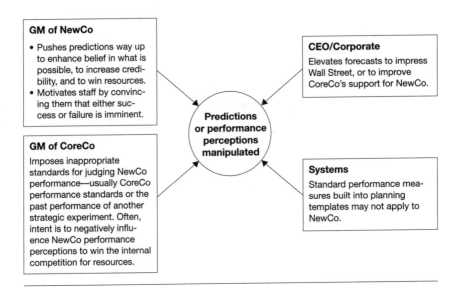

GM of NewCo

- Pushes predictions way up to enhance belief in what is possible, to increase credibility, and to win resources.
- Motivates staff by convincing them that either success or failure is imminent.

GM of CoreCo

Imposes inappropriate standards for judging NewCo performance—usually CoreCo performance standards or the past performance of another strategic experiment. Often, intent is to negatively influence NewCo performance perceptions to win the internal competition for resources.

Predictions or performance perceptions manipulated

CEO/Corporate

Elevates forecasts to impress Wall Street, or to improve CoreCo's support for NewCo.

Systems

Standard performance measures built into planning templates may not apply to NewCo.

learning for DMPS in that they contributed to poor analysis of predictions and outcomes: the plans were too detailed, too little emphasis was placed on analyzing trends, and assumptions were not explicit.

Too Much Detail. Diligent executives managing mature businesses often develop detailed plans because detail is valuable in isolating the cause of disparities between predictions and outcomes. It allows managers to determine, for example, that the profitability shortfall was a result of poor cost control in the subwidget production facility in the west region.

In strategic experiments, such detail does not pay. Predictions are unreliable even at the most aggregate levels. Detail is only a distraction; it creates only an illusion of precision and careful management. It is rather like the practice of measuring first downs in U.S. football. With great fanfare and drama, the officials measure first downs to the nearest fraction of an inch, when the accuracy in spotting the ball at the end of any play is at best plus or minus one foot.

FIGURE 8-5

When predictions become rigid, learning is disabled

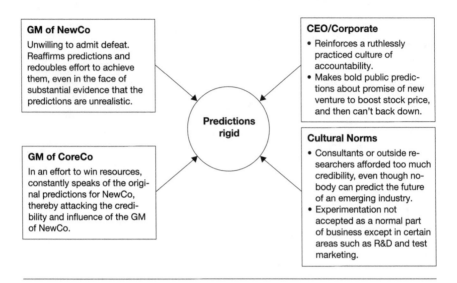

GM of NewCo

Unwilling to admit defeat. Reaffirms predictions and redoubles effort to achieve them, even in the face of substantial evidence that the predictions are unrealistic.

GM of CoreCo

In an effort to win resources, constantly speaks of the original predictions for NewCo, thereby attacking the credibility and influence of the GM of NewCo.

Predictions rigid

CEO/Corporate

• Reinforces a ruthlessly practiced culture of accountability.
• Makes bold public predictions about promise of new venture to boost stock price, and then can't back down.

Cultural Norms

• Consultants or outside researchers afforded too much credibility, even though nobody can predict the future of an emerging industry.
• Experimentation not accepted as a normal part of business except in certain areas such as R&D and test marketing.

Because plans for strategic experiments must be revised often, they need to be vastly simplified. If fully detailed plans were revised monthly or quarterly, little time would be left for getting any work done. The level of rigor and detail that was standard practice at CW made it impractical for DMPS to revisit plans quickly.

Insufficient Emphasis on Trends. Although analysis of certain trends, especially market trends, is a common part of planning, analysis of a much wider range of trends can be important for experimental businesses.

To understand why, consider an analogy between managing a business and flying an airplane. Pilots are constantly engaged in the following iterative thought process: deciding how to shift controls and anticipating what will happen; scanning the instrument panel; comparing indications to expectations; and diagnosing unexpected outcomes before deciding again how to shift controls. This sequence is exactly analogous to the planning cycle (see figure 8-6).

Managing a mature business is analogous to flying a passenger jet at altitude. The situation is essentially static, with little movement on the instrument panel indicators and little need to move the controls. (In

FIGURE 8-6

Managing a business is similar to flying an airplane

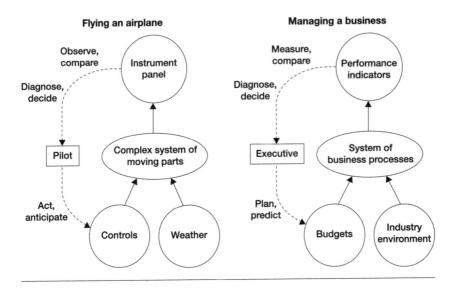

the case of business, the income statements look very similar from one year to the next. Of course, we are exaggerating to make a clear contrast: established businesses also face a certain degree of uncertainty and change.) This is *type 1 flying*. It can be best described as *monitoring and adjusting*.

Aviation is substantially more complex during takeoff and landing, which are dynamic situations. Most of the indicators on the instrument panel are in motion; however, the pilot understands the patterns of change, and the needed control adjustments are well established. This situation is analogous to building a new business that remains within a familiar business model—for example, a consumer products company launching a new product. Each month is different from the preceding one, but managers understand the dynamics fairly well based on experience. They know in advance how to sequence spending in various functions, and they understand early indicators of poor performance. Think of this as *type 2 flying*. It can best be described as *performing known routines*.

The most talented military aviators are assigned duty as test pilots. They fly cutting-edge and little-understood aircraft. They take such aircraft through maneuvers much more dramatic and dynamic than simple takeoffs or landings. Think of this as *type 3 flying*. It can best be described as *experimenting and learning* (see table 8-1).

Type 3 flying is analogous to managing a strategic experiment. It is especially tough to diagnose differences between what was anticipated and what happened. First, conditions are changing quickly, so both current indications and trends are relevant. Second, the pilot must ask whether she performed the maneuver correctly *and* whether the aircraft actually works as it is supposed to. In type 1 and type 2 flying, the pilot can presume that the plane works well.

An important note: We do not mean to imply that it is always harder to manage strategic experiments than to guide mature businesses. In fact, no business challenge may be more grueling than squeezing an extra half-percent of margin out of a mature and highly competitive industry. We mean only to highlight specific challenges associated with planning.

In type 2 or type 3 management, observing a variety of trends becomes crucial. A measure at a single point in time cannot tell the entire story. Rates of change are often the most telling pieces of data.

When digital technologies advanced to the point that new digital instrumentation for aircraft was practical, the reaction from aviators was surprising to some. Pilots were accustomed to analog instrumentation, in which a moving pointer sweeps in a circle through a range of numbers (like hands on a traditional clock face). In some cases, digital displays improved accuracy and were welcomed. But there was a problem: digital displays removed an intuitive indication of *how quickly*

TABLE 8-1

Flying lessons: The increasing degree of difficulty

LEVEL 1	LEVEL 2	LEVEL 3
Flying at altitude *Monitoring and adjusting*	**Maneuvers;** **takeoff and landing** *Performing known routines*	**Test pilot** *Experimenting and learning*
Steady flying	Dynamic flying	Dynamic flying
Few movements of controls	Coordinated movements	Coordinated movements
Well-understood system	Well-understood system	Experimental system
Clear indicators	Clear indicators	Ambiguous indicators

FIGURE 8-7

Trends tell a more complete story than numbers alone

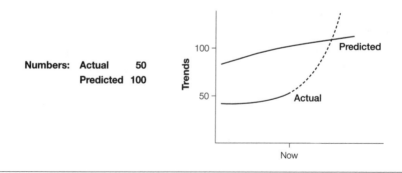

conditions were changing. During maneuvers such as takeoff and landing, a quick glance at an analog instrument gave more than just the current reading; it also gave pilots an intuitive feel for the rate of change, based on how quickly the dial was moving. Digital displays did not.

Similarly, when you're refining a production process for a new product, an indication that manufacturing yields are rising rapidly can be more important than a measured yield of 50 percent for a specific month. Comparing actual trends to predicted trends, as opposed to comparing single numbers, can lead to startlingly different conclusions: "Our performance is awful, only half what we hoped" may instead become "Our performance is only two months behind what we anticipated, and we are improving more quickly than we ever thought we would be able to" (see figure 8-7).

Trend analysis might have been particularly beneficial for DMPS during stage 3. Despite the "barely surviving" mind-set during this period, the DMPS managers made progress on a number of fronts. They began to understand their customers' buying process—in particular, they realized that the sales cycle was much longer than they had anticipated. They expanded their customer base substantially. Customers were satisfied, and none was lost, even as the business struggled through a demanding period of growth.

Because some positive momentum was developing, the changes in stage 4 were painful for the stage 3 leadership team. They had resolved some critical unknowns, and operational measures were showing positive trends. On this basis, they could have made a solid case that the business was starting to succeed. But it was difficult to make that case because the analytical templates emphasized numbers (particularly revenue) and profitability—and not trends. As a result, the stage 3 leadership team was never able to escape the residual dark shadow of the perceived debacle during stage 2.

Management made several positive changes in the shift from stage 3 to stage 4. But a more sophisticated approach to planning and learning would have allowed DMPS to consolidate more of the lessons learned from stage 3 before moving on.

Hidden Assumptions. When you're flying at level 3, it is crucial to constantly test assumptions about how the business works. Unfortunately, the most common analytical tool in business—the ubiquitous spreadsheet—does not facilitate the rigorous testing of assumptions.

The spreadsheet was the analytical tool of choice at CW. When DMPS went through a detailed reassessment of its business at the beginning of stage 4, it worked with consultants to build a detailed spreadsheet financial model. Built into this spreadsheet was a wide variety of assumptions about what needed to happen for the business to succeed.

Unfortunately, spreadsheets are poor tools for making assumptions explicit. When you open a spreadsheet, you see numbers. The assumptions are hidden, buried in equations with cryptic cell references. That is why models built with spreadsheets quickly lose their utility if they are not updated and maintained frequently. Otherwise, it is difficult to rediscover the assumptions that underlie the calculations. Instead of burying the logic in spreadsheets, it must be explicitly shared and communicated among the management team.

By their own admission, DMPS's finance team members allocated insufficient effort to revisiting the assumptions built into prior plans. Their extensive reliance on spreadsheet modeling made it too cumbersome to do so.

Discovery Driven Planning

The DMPS managers recognized that planning and learning were related, and for a time during stage 2 they implemented a new planning practice that they believed would help them learn from experience. The method is known as *discovery driven planning* (DDP).[5]

The central idea in DDP is that unknowns can be reduced to specific parameters—such as cost per sale, manufacturing cost per unit, and market price—that have a direct bearing on the income statement. These parameters are identified in advance, and then management teams focus on gathering evidence to firm up estimates of them. As estimates are refined, managers gain a clearer sense of whether the strategy will succeed or fail.

DDP, like theory-focused planning (TFP), is intended to improve planning when a higher level of uncertainty is present than mature businesses generally face. Both approaches are useful but are best used in different situations. The level of uncertainty determines which is the more useful approach.

The DDP approach is appropriate when the industry is established, the business model is well known, and the business uncertainties can be reduced to a set of operational parameters. TFP, by contrast, works when the industry is emerging, the business model is experimental, and the uncertainties are so large that the basic nature of the relationships between activities and outcomes is unknown.

New-product launches often can benefit from DDP, as can geographic expansions that alter key business parameters such as pricing or costs for certain activities. Disney's move to create Euro Disney, a theme park in France, is an example of a business situation in which DDP, had it been used, could have paid dividends.[6]

Strategic experiments face even higher levels of uncertainty. The unknowns cannot be reduced to specific, measurable parameters; they are more fundamental. Cause-and-effect relationships are merely hypotheses. For example, NYTD did not have any idea, at the outset, to what extent its investment in collecting demographic information from readers would enable it to charge advertisers higher prices (and that still remains unclear). And DMPS, at the outset, could not know to what extent enhancements to its services offerings would attract more customers.

When these types of uncertainties exist, it is not possible even to identify the parameters called for by DDP. When the DMPS team tried the DDP approach, they ended up with an extensive list—of possible parameters. As a result, the plans were too cumbersome to manage, and DMPS abandoned the DDP approach.

The Venture Capital Model

The DMPS team implemented one additional planning approach. In stage 4, following an in-depth review of strategy by an outside management consulting firm, DMPS again built a highly detailed plan. But to simplify evaluation and to provide clear criteria for additional investment, DMPS identified singular milestones. The most important of these was the attainment of ten "showcase accounts"—clients that purchased a full range of services. Attaining the milestones was a prerequisite for continued investment.

This practice mimics the approach taken by venture capitalists. But venture capitalists are too busy to be deeply involved in the management of each venture they invest in. They have a portfolio of businesses to keep up with, and they must also maintain relationships with their investors. Ventures are chosen based on the attractiveness of the market and of the team proposing them, and venture capitalists know that if they make enough investments on those criteria, they will come out ahead in the long run. They remain involved, but not closely enough to be immersed in planning and learning.

The venture capital model—singular milestones that must be met to win further funding—is not a planning approach at all. It is simply a technique used to limit losses from failures. It may be successful at that, but it is too simple an approach to support learning. After an experimental business is past a proof-of-concept, it must resolve several interrelated unknowns to demonstrate that it is viable. The venture capital approach is too one-dimensional to be a useful learning tool.

For example, if DMPS does not win its ten showcase accounts, what does that really mean? Any one of several elements of its approach to the market could have led to failure. Any one of several assumptions in its business plan might have been incorrect. A more comprehensive approach to planning is needed—one that focuses on resolving critical unknowns. Theory-focused planning is one such approach, and we discuss it next.

Chapter Nine

FINDING GOLD WITH
THEORY-FOCUSED PLANNING

IN A FLUID, fast-changing, uncertain environment, planning might seem fruitless. But planning is crucial for strategic experiments because it establishes the context for learning.[1] In past chapters, we explained why the conventional planning process is inappropriate. Discovery driven planning underestimates the magnitude of the uncertainties, and the venture capital approach is too simplistic. So what works?

Based on the discussion of learning disabilities, you know some of the characteristics of a desirable planning approach. It must be simple enough that managers can iterate through the planning cycle, reassessing theories and predictions, as often as monthly. And it must focus on trends.[2]

But there is more. In chapter 8 we introduced a comparison between flying and managing. The task of managing a strategic experiment was likened to test-piloting an experimental aircraft. But managing a strategic experiment is even more difficult, in two important ways. First, flying is often an individual activity, but businesses are managed by teams. Second, feedback in flying is immediate. In management, feedback is delayed by weeks, months, quarters, or even years.

For this reason, leaders of strategic experiments must do more than simply make predictions. They must share them with colleagues and retain them until results are available. At that point, leaders must reexamine their predictions and underlying theories.

It is not easy to clearly articulate theories and predictions. Nor is it easy for an individual to record theories and predictions in a way that allows them to be understood many weeks later. These skills are crucial. Without them, you can't have a healthy discussion of business results. Each team member has his own theory about actions and outcomes, and as a result each member interprets results differently. If you can't clearly discuss theories and predictions, you'll find it impossible to reconcile them. Self-interest, power, and influence carry the day, and learning opportunities are lost.

Several years ago we developed a planning approach and supporting set of tools that meet all the foregoing criteria. *Theory-focused planning* (TFP) may seem difficult on your first read through this chapter. Each of the steps will feel new, at least in the context of planning. And, our recommendations are more detailed here than elsewhere in the book. Although we provide an illustration of each step, you may find it best to read this chapter once quickly, to understand the general concepts (pay particular attention to the end of the chapter, starting with the section "Departures from Conventional Planning") and then read it again more carefully when you are ready to apply TFP in your own company. Though the detail is heavy, the steps are not complex, and TFP as a whole is straightforward. In fact, the entire planning process can be completed with pencil and paper. You can finish a reasonable plan for an actual experimental business in less than one day.

We created a business simulation as a testing ground for TFP.[3] The simulation is based loosely on the experience of New York Times Digital (see chapter 4), but we simplified the scenario to accommodate time constraints for the executives participating in the exercise. We have run the simulation with hundreds of executives from dozens of organizations. Participants manage the strategic experiment through a virtual three-year period. They begin with a struggling start-up, seek rapid growth in the middle of the simulation, and target profitability toward the end.

Participants always run the simulation once with no help—that is, with no discussion of planning techniques, old or new. They naturally apply the planning mind-set they are accustomed to using in their own organizations. Not once has a team succeeded in achieving profitability on this first attempt.

After the first failure, participants spend time devising a theory-focused plan. The results are remarkable: on the second attempt, the majority of the teams succeed.

TFP's value lies in its ability to create open and candid discussion about the future of a strategic experiment—discussion that is grounded, as it must be, in theories, assumptions, predictions, and outcomes.

Senior executives play a critical oversight role. TFP cannot work if leaders of strategic experiments perceive that they will be held accountable for performance against plan. When they do, they are likely to cling to failing plans and to hide bad news. Instead, senior executives must hold the leaders accountable for learning; they must judge the leaders' speed, rigor, and discipline in following the TFP process. After describing TFP, we offer specific questions to guide this evaluation.

Overview of Theory-Focused Planning

There are two aspects to theory-focused planning: building a theory and testing it. You must construct your theories with testing in mind. Rapid learning is possible only when you can break your theories into several parts and test each one individually. Also, for theories to be useful, they must predict measurable quantities. One purpose of building the theory is to identify the metrics you will use in measuring the performance of the new business.

With these criteria in mind, the TFP process proceeds through eight steps. In the first six, managers build the theory. In the last two, they test and revise it.

1. *Describe how the business works*: What actions will lead to success? How?

2. *Identify metrics*: What can we measure?

3. *Establish goals*: What constitutes success, on multiple dimensions?

4. *Create spending guidelines*: How much do we need to spend, and when, to achieve success?

5. *Predict performance*: Given the budget we have established, what results do we expect?

6. *Identify critical unknowns*: What assumptions have we made that could either make or break the business? How can we test these assumptions?

7. *Analyze disparities between predictions and outcomes*: What evidence have we gathered? Can we validate or invalidate portions of our theory? Can we resolve any critical unknowns?

8. *Revise the plan*: Based on lessons learned, do we need to change our plan? If so, how?

Step 1: Describe How the Business Works

To start, management teams must create a shared understanding of how the strategic experiment is expected to work. A useful approach has two steps: tell a cause-and-effect story about actions and outcomes, and then estimate how long it will take to get from action to outcome.

Cause-and-Effect Stories

A simple tool for communicating cause-and-effect stories is the *influence diagram* (also called *bubble-and-arrow* diagrams). The concept is straightforward: by showing an arrow leading from an action to an outcome, the diagram implies a causal connection between them. The influence diagram in figure 9-1 communicates that action A causes outcome B.

The influence diagram can be taken one step further to convey *subsequent outcomes*. For example, in figure 9-1, action A causes outcome B, which subsequently causes outcome C. Influence diagrams show *chains of causality* from action to ultimate outcome.

In a theory for a strategic experiment, the actions are usually spending decisions (major budget items), and the ultimate outcome is financial, such as revenue. For example, figure 9-1 suggests that advertising expenditures will lead to potential customers trying a new product, and that will lead to continued use by some and then to revenues—the A-B-C-D chain.

Describing chains of causality for strategic experiments can involve some guesswork. It is a good practice to make a note of your assumptions. Include notes such as, "We assume that advertising is the best way to generate trial use, but it could be that our customers are not particularly responsive to advertising. It could be that trial use is more a function of simply getting our product into the best distribution channels." The more explicit you can be about your assumptions and possible alternatives, the better. Ultimately, you will revisit these assumptions when you analyze disparities between predictions and outcomes.

FIGURE 9-1

Influence diagrams convey cause and effect

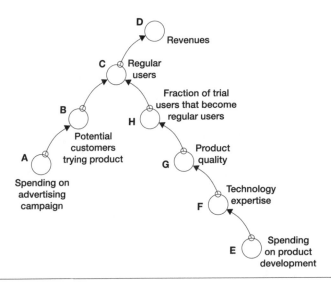

Usually, chains of causality are not isolated. There are interactions with other chains. In figure 9-1, the product development team certainly has a great deal to do with the success of converting trial use of the new product to ongoing use of it. The impact of its actions is described by the E-F-G-H-C chain.

Getting started can be the hardest part of creating a cause-and-effect diagram. Here are three tips. First, it helps to focus on one function (such as marketing or product development) at a time and tell simple stories about how that spending contributes to revenues. Second, at this stage, do not constrain your thinking by eliminating quantities that are not directly measurable; you will deal with measurement in the next step.

Third, it helps to recognize that many causal chains follow the same generic pattern. Starting with major spending decisions, they pass through one or more measures of a NewCo *competence* or *asset*, through one or more measures of a NewCo *core process*, and through one or more measures of NewCo's *market*, before ending with a financial outcome (see figure 9-2). This is the sequence in the product development chain, E-F-G-H-C-D, in figure 9-1. Some causal chains follow only a portion of this pattern. For example, marketing spending may be linked

FIGURE 9-2

A common pattern for causal chains

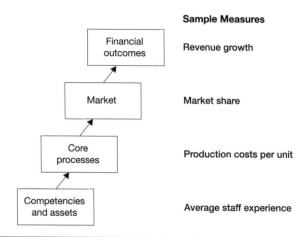

At minimum, the influence diagram should capture the *critical unknowns*: elements of the theory of your business that, if incorrect, could radically alter or break it. Even before you start planning, you likely have a strong intuition about what these critical unknowns are. You will reassess them in step 6.

directly to market outcomes and then financial outcomes, without explicit identification of competence or core process outcomes.

Influence diagrams can grow excessively large. To avoid this, capture in the diagram only the most important elements of how the business is expected to work. Still, for the diagram to be useful, it is best to add a few extra cause-and-effect links that capture important elements of competitor behavior. In addition, if business decisions other than spending play a crucial role, you should add them. The pricing decision is one common example.

At minimum, the influence diagram should capture the *critical unknowns*: elements of the theory of your business that, if incorrect, could radically alter or break it. Even before you start planning, you likely have a strong intuition about what these critical unknowns are. You will reassess them in step 6.

Illustration: The Island Post *Online*

The scenario we created for the simulation begins with a global media conglomerate acquiring a newspaper property, the *Island Post*. The newspaper is located on an isolated island nation, where it competes with one other newspaper. Both competitors operate news Web sites, but both are losing money. However, the island has invested heavily in creating a world-class wireless infrastructure, and the proliferation of wireless, portable Internet devices is expected to have a profound impact on the growth potential of these businesses.

In fact, market research firms estimate that revenues could grow by a factor of 10 over the next three years, for two reasons: advertisers will adapt to the potential of online advertising, and consumer usage will explode as it becomes increasingly convenient to access the Web sites at any time from any place. The challenge for the *Island Post Online* is to make the right investments at the right time to capture this opportunity.[4]

Figure 9-3 shows the influence diagram for the *Island Post Online*. At first, the diagram is overwhelming. When you create such a diagram, it is best to break the process into smaller steps. Each functional team can work independently, and then you can combine their diagrams to create a diagram for the entire business. Also, many people find that it is easier to first verbally describe a theory of how actions lead to positive outcomes and then convert that description to an influence diagram.

For example, the *Island Post Online* is organized into five functions— content creation, operations, market research, marketing, and sales—and each represents one of five major budget categories. Each function head might describe her role in contributing to success and create partial influence diagrams:

- **Content creation**: "Our team of journalists and programmers maintains the content on the Web site. With any remaining free time, we program new features that market research indicates our readers or advertisers will value" (chain A-B-C-D in figure 9-3).

- **Operations**: "We keep the site's technology infrastructure running smoothly. We want to ensure we build capacity ahead of demand. If the site is overloaded, users have long waits for each page to download, and perceptions of quality go down" (E-F-G-H and L-G).

- **Market research**: "We identify features that users want and turn these ideas over to the content creation team to add to the site" (I-J-C-H).

- **Marketing**: "We ensure that customers and potential customers are aware of our great features, bringing additional traffic to the site" (H-L and K-L).

- **Sales**: "We try to convert each page on the site into revenue by selling the advertising space available on it" (L-N-O and M-N).

FIGURE 9-3

The influence diagram for the *Island Post Online*

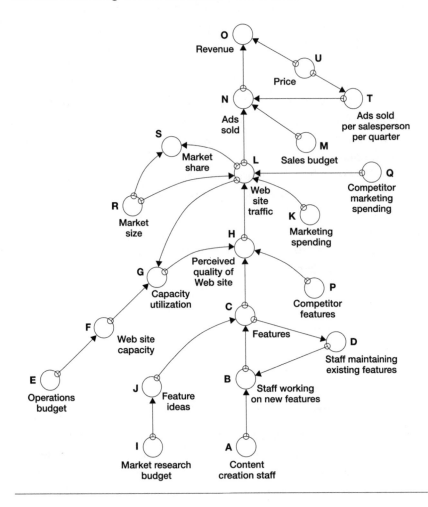

Typically, the functional diagrams will have overlaps. Thus, it's straightforward to combine them into a single, shared, cause-and-effect story about how the strategic experiment is expected to work.

A few additions to the diagram capture competitor behavior (P-H and Q-L) and the pricing decision (U-O). Management teams in real-world strategic experiments can spend hours debating possible additional causal relationships that could be added, but keep in mind that a trade-off exists between accuracy and usefulness. In assessing how detailed the diagram should be, managers must consider how far they can go before it becomes more confusing than enlightening. The *Island Post Online* influence diagram is close to the practical limit.

How Long Does It Take?

We now have a theory, and we will eventually use it to make predictions. This will take several steps. We cannot predict until we have a plan of action, which in TFP takes the form of a set of spending guidelines. We cannot establish spending guidelines unless we have a set of goals. And we cannot determine reasonable goals without first giving some thought to what is feasible over what time frames.

We need to enhance our story with basic hypotheses about the time periods between cause and effect. In other words, if an action is taken, what will be the *trend* in the outcome? How will it change over time? As discussed in chapter 8, often the trend in an outcome is a more valuable piece of information than the outcome itself.

TFP requires a great deal of discussion of trends. The ideal tool to support this discussion is the *qualitative trend graph*, which has an outcome on the y-axis, and time on the x-axis. At first, qualitative trend graphs can be intimidating, especially if you already are nervous about making predictions. After all, in drawing a trend, you are, in effect, making many predictions at many points in time. However, predictions for strategic experiments do not require nearly the same level of accuracy as needed in mature businesses.

For example, in a typical strategic experiment, market research may suggest that the market could grow tenfold. In reality, it could be twofold or twenty-fold. Typically, you label the y-axis with a multiple of a current value or a benchmark value (2×, 5×, 10×, and so on). On the x-axis, getting the time units correct (months, quarters, or years) is sufficient. These graphs are *qualitative* trend graphs; what is important is not the accuracy of the prediction but rather the *shape* of the trend. Many shapes are possible, as shown in figure 9-4.

To develop basic hypotheses about the time between cause and effect, ask the following question for each function: if the function dramatically increased its budget (say, doubled it) and everything else remained constant, what would happen over time? The result is a series of *isolated response trend graphs*.

In the real world, of course, not everything else remains constant. Your purpose here is simply to think about time periods associated with

FIGURE 9-4

The shape of the trend graph is important

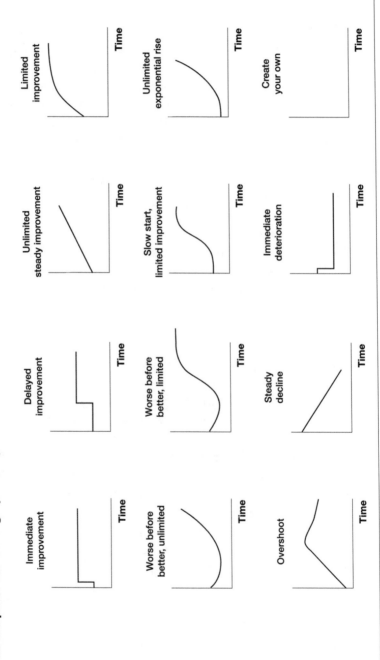

cause and effect. In doing so you will gain intuition that is invaluable later, when you will make predictions for the experiment as a whole, all factors considered.

As an example of how isolated response trend graphs enhance influence diagrams, consider figure 9-5. This partial theory could apply to many service businesses, including CW's DMPS business (described in chapter 8). The influence diagram suggests that as investment in the training of service-delivery personnel increases, their knowledge expands. This subsequently causes an improvement in service quality, which in turn causes an increase in market share and in revenues.

Now consider the following: what would happen if the investment in training was doubled (and nothing else changed)? The trend graphs in figure 9-5 show one possible hypothesis: the increase in training intensity would increase knowledge (the knowledge level trend chart). But the rate of increase would slow, eventually leveling off. The logic for this prediction could be that there is a limit to what can be taught in the classroom, or that eventually gains in the classroom are offset by turnover in the workforce. Other explanations might also be relevant. It is worthwhile for planners to document both the trend and the underlying logic.

FIGURE 9-5

Example of isolated response trends

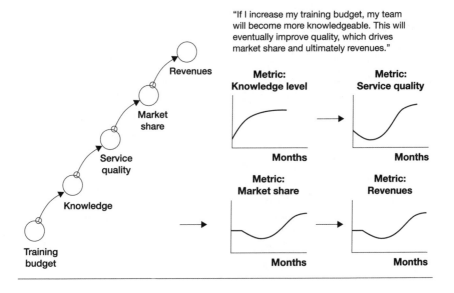

The trend prediction for service quality is interesting; it shows that service quality declines before it starts to improve (the service quality trend chart). Again, there is more than one possible line of reasoning for this prediction. It could be that requiring service personnel to spend more time in the classroom would mean less time spent with clients, and that could cause an initial decline in quality. Or perhaps in trying to apply the classroom lessons, service personnel initially make mistakes, and quality drops. Over time, they become more proficient, and quality rises.

The predictions for market share and revenues are similar, except that the trend is delayed (the flat initial segment in both charts). The thinking here is that it takes a few months for the market to recognize changes in quality.

Illustration: The Island Post Online

Figure 9-6 shows the isolated trend graphs for the *Island Post Online*. Again, it is often easier to start with verbal descriptions of predicted trends and then sketch the trend. In the simulation, here are likely descriptions of isolated responses:

- *Content creation*: "New hires take some time to train. During this time we will be less productive. After that, features will be added quickly, but the rate of increase will decline as it takes more effort just to maintain the new features."

- *Operations*: "A decision to increase Web site capacity would lead to a one-time, rapid increase in the quality of the site (at some point after we made the decision—the process of adding capacity takes time) because it would reduce wait time for downloading pages."

- *Market research*: "With increasing spending we would generate new feature ideas faster. But it takes time for market research insights to accumulate and give clear pointers to features that users want. And eventually, we will exhaust all possible ideas for features that customers could want."

- *Marketing*: "Over time, increased marketing will drive additional users to our site. But eventually, it will no longer be able to attract additional users. The user base will stabilize at a higher level."

- *Sales*: "With a larger sales force, we will quickly be able to sell more ads, up to the point that we are sold out."[5]

FIGURE 9-6

Isolated response trend graphs

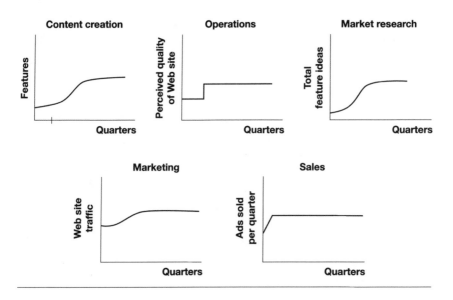

It is a good practice to retain both the trend graphs and the verbal descriptions. The latter often contain the logic underlying the trend, and this is part of what you will test.

Step 2: Identify Metrics

Recently, a great deal of interest has developed in identifying measures of innovation. However, it is not possible to identify a general set of measures for strategic innovation. Each strategic experiment is unique. Each will need a set of measures that are customized to the business model.

Measures are important because many of the causal relationships in an influence diagram are merely unproven hypotheses. To learn, you must gather evidence to confirm or disconfirm the relationships.

At this point, the influence diagram likely has some outcomes that are quantifiable and readily measured, such as customer satisfaction. There may be others, such as technical expertise, that require a more qualitative assessment. Both kinds of measures can be useful. It may not seem scientific to include qualitative measures, but exact measures are less important than trends, and trends are often clear even on the basis of qualitative judgment. Not only that, but who would argue that technical expertise is not a crucial success factor and thus a crucial part of the story about how a business is expected to work?

Still, wherever you can identify a quantitative measure to enhance or even substitute for a qualitative one, it is desirable. For example, in figure 9-1, the measure of "fraction of trial users that become regular users" is similar to "product quality," but it is more valuable because it can be more precisely quantified.

You must try to identify measurable quantities near the bottom of each causal chain, close to each budget category and far from revenues. For example, features and perceived Web site quality are leading indicators for the *Island Post Online*. These measures are important because of time delays between actions and outcomes. The closer an item is to the bottom of the chain, the quicker you will have evidence that can validate portions of the theory.

This step is completed when you have added a comprehensive but practical set of measures to the influence diagram. This should not entail adding entirely new cause-and-effect chains. When the diagram is complete, there should be at least one measure in each of the four categories: asset or competence measures, core process measures, market measures, and financial measures (see figure 9-2).[6]

Illustration: The Island Post Online

The influence diagram for the *Island Post Online* now contains many quantifiable measures, including site traffic, capacity utilization, and advertisements sold. A few, such as features, require qualitative judgment.

We have added a few measures (see figure 9-3). Market size (R) and market share (L-S and R-S) give us an improved assessment of progress compared to the competition. Advertisements sold per salesperson per quarter (U-T and T-N) is important because the business must markedly reduce the cost per ad sold in order to reach profitability. Whether this can be achieved is a critical unknown.

Step 3: Establish Goals

We can now move forward to establishing *goals*, or our best guesses about what is possible under an optimistic yet realistic scenario. The

FIGURE 9-7

A comparative goal trend graph

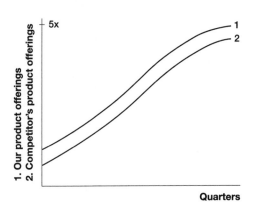

isolated trend graphs shape our intuition in determining goals, as do reasonable assumptions about the competition. For example, you might assume that the competition has capabilities very similar to your own and is actively considering the same opportunity.

Long-term financial goals are not the focus here. The objective at this stage is to set shorter-term success criteria for each function—early signals that the business is succeeding. The goals should seem intuitively realistic, all factors considered. However, we can amend our goals later, after a budget is in place.

The most sensible tool to use in describing goals is the qualitative trend graph. Each major budget category should be directly linked with at least one important goal trend.

Goal trends are sometimes best expressed as *comparisons*. For example, a start-up might make it a goal to have more product offerings in the market at all times than does the competition. The trend graph should show both "our product offerings" and "competitor's product offerings" (see figure 9-7).

In addition, some generic goal trends apply to almost all start-ups, such as an S-curve for market growth and a worse-before-better profile for profitability (see figure 9-8). These trends should also be discussed. What is a reasonable multiple for market growth? Over what time period? To what extent can we endure losses? Over what time period?

FIGURE 9-8

Generic trend graphs for start-ups

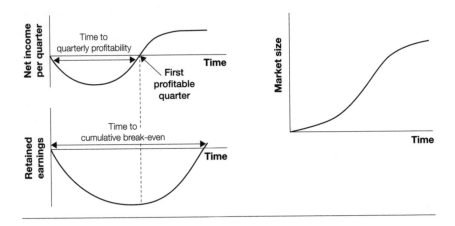

Illustration: The Island Post Online

Here are verbal descriptions of goals for the *Island Post Online*:

- **Content creation**: "We want to steadily increase the features on our site until customers no longer find additional features valuable. And we want to stay ahead of the competition in terms of features."

- **Operations**: "We want to build capacity ahead of traffic on our site by a comfortable margin so that the quality of our site is never diminished."

- **Market research**: "We want to keep content creation busy by always having a few new feature ideas for their programmers to work on."

- **Marketing**: "We want to build and sustain a large share of the market."

- **Sales**: "We always want to keep the ad space on the site sold out."

These descriptions translate to the goal trends in figure 9-9. But what spending will be required to achieve these goals? This is the question we turn to next.

FIGURE 9-9

Goal trend graphs for the *Island Post Online*

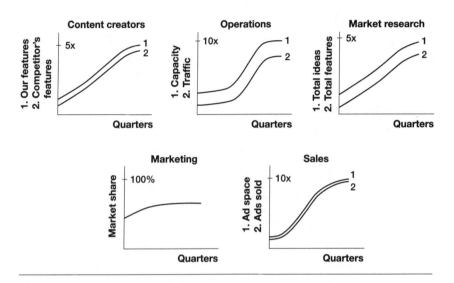

Step 4: Create Spending Guidelines

Managers in mature businesses become accustomed to thinking incrementally about budgeting. The budget for the prior period is the primary benchmark for defining the budget for the next period. In strategic experiments, however, you should *not* use the prior period's budget as a benchmark. You must sequence major budget priorities as part of an overall plan. Some budgets may be scaled up much sooner than others.

In strategic experiments the key to creating the appropriate mind-set for budgeting is to shift from asking, "How much different from last time?" to "How much will we need to spend in the future, and how quickly should we build up to that level?" And then, "How much of the increase should come this quarter? This year? Next year? What is the spending pattern over time?" In other words, just as when you're establishing goals, you should focus on qualitative trends and not on numbers.

Start by Considering Total Spending

It is easiest to start by considering the budget in its entirety rather than each budget category individually. Start with an estimate of the size of the total budget in the future—the day the business reaches profitability. This estimate can be based on back-of-the-envelope calculations. For example, if the market is ultimately expected to reach $150 million and you anticipate having about a one-third share, then the total budget will be in the neighborhood of $50 million on the day you reach profitability. The question is, how quickly do you increase spending to that level?

The most aggressive approach is to immediately increase the budget to the expected future state and hope for revenue growth. The risk is that if the anticipated market does not materialize, the entire investment is lost. A second approach is to be patient and wait for conclusive proof that market growth is there, and then start spending. The risk here is that if a competitor captures the market well ahead of you, it may be difficult to win it back.

Usually the best answer lies in the middle: deliberately scaling up the budget as unknowns are resolved and as confidence in the emerging market increases. Figure 9-10 illustrates the options. It can be fruitful to discuss the pros and cons of investing a bit ahead of the market or a bit behind. You must weigh the advantages of being first to market against the risk of investing heavily in an uncertain project that fails.[7]

FIGURE 9-10

Options for timing the increase in the total budget

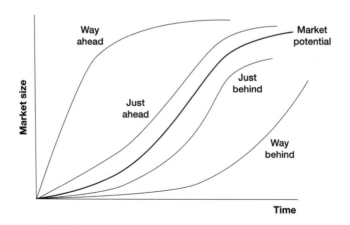

Apply the Same Process to Each Function

For each budget category, the approach is similar. Estimate the approximate level of spending at a distant point in the future, such as the estimated date the business becomes profitable. Then establish the trend in spending from today to that future point. Will the increase parallel overall spending growth? Be ahead of overall spending growth? Behind? Sketch a comparative trend graph that shows an individual spending trend against the total budget trend. Initially, this requires a great deal of guesswork. No matter; you can update these numbers frequently as you learn more.

You should refine spending guidelines by addressing two additional questions. First, how should you sequence the scale-up of spending in the various functions? That is, which functions *lead* or *lag* other functions, and why? For example, marketers often feel that they need to know at least something about a product before they begin marketing. Therefore, marketing spending often lags product development spending (excluding market research spending, which usually leads product development spending). Second, are there measures that would alert you that you are increasing spending too slowly or too quickly? Often, you can take such measures directly from the influence diagram.

A Method for Estimating Future Spending

Perhaps the trickiest aspect of this step is estimating the necessary level of spending in each function at the point of profitability. As soon as the strategic experiment has been generating revenues for a few months, you can simplify estimating by using a method based on the concept of economies of scale.

Early on, NewCo is losing money. If it is to reach profitability, revenues must grow more quickly than expenses. Therefore, each function must find ways to support additional business without expanding expenses in proportion. This can happen, for example, when salespeople build solid relationships with regular customers; or when marketers succeed in building a new brand and then need only sustain it; or as service staff learn their jobs and become more efficient.

Whether a strategic experiment is on a path to profitability depends on the extent to which each department can achieve these economies of scale. The accuracy of such estimates will of course be suspect early in the life of a new business, but gradually they will get better.

A convenient format for the analysis of future profitability is a simple table that compares the current income statement (with all figures given as a percentage of revenues) to a predicted future income statement. You assume a certain multiple for revenue growth—say, 10×—and then each department estimates, as well as it can, the growth required to support that much higher level of revenues.

For example, the simulation scenario starts with the strategic experiment operating at a −63% operating margin. Each department has come up with an estimate of the multiple by which it would have to increase its own budget to sustain a business ten times as large. The math is then straightforward. To project the future budget for each function as a percentage of revenues, you multiply the current level by the estimated cost multiple and then divide by 10 (the revenue multiple). Based on the estimates and this calculation, the business should achieve profitability—in fact, an operating margin of 15% (see table 9-1).

Illustration: The Island Post Online

Spending guidelines as established by the preceding questions should be simple rules that help managers determine how quickly to scale up budgets. For example, the operating guidelines for the *Island Post Online* might look something like this:

- *Content creation*: "We must build a large staff of content creators quickly. We must scale up well in advance of the market and must consider the delays associated with hiring and training new people, so that we have a high-quality product ready as the market materializes. We should lag only the market research budget, because we are dependent on market research for ideas for new features. We know we are investing too slowly if we have good feature ideas but no free time to add them to the site, or if the competitor is adding features more quickly than we are. We are investing too quickly if we have idle programmers."

- *Operations*: "We must maintain capacity ahead of actual use of our site. Actual use will be driven by solid features and good marketing. Therefore, our spending can lag these categories—but not by much, because it takes time to add capacity. We are scaling up too quickly if our capacity utilization drops very low, and too slowly if our site is constantly overloaded."

TABLE 9-1

Projection of future profitability

Cost category	Current, as % of revenues	Growth in this cost category, if revenues went up10×	Projected, as % of revenues
Content creation	59%	5×	29%
Operations	45%	8×	36%
Marketing	15%	5×	7%
Market research	2%	5×	1%
Sales	42%	3×	12%
Total expense	163%		85%
Operating margin	−63%		15%

- *Marketing*: "As the content creators build new features, we must make customers and potential customers aware of them. Our spending should lag that of content creation, building up in parallel with the market. We know we are spending too much if increases in spending have no noticeable impact on market share. If we appear to be spending less than the competition on marketing, we are losing share, and at the same time believe our product is of higher quality, we are likely spending too little."

- *Market research*: "Our spending must scale up first. We are the smallest cost category, so the risk of scaling up is small. We must produce feature ideas for the content creators to program. We are spending too much if content creation has a large backlog of unprogrammed feature ideas, and too little if we are not coming up with ideas even as the competitor adds features."

- *Sales*: "We need to add salespeople only as traffic on the Web site increases and we therefore have more opportunities to sell ads. We can scale up last. We know we are increasing the budget too slowly if we are unable to sell all available ad space, and too quickly if we are sold out and the salespeople have free time on their hands."

A final word about spending guidelines: the cues for signaling that the investment is scaling up too slowly may come too late to be useful. For example, if the *Island Post Online* falls too far behind the competition in the number of features on its Web site, catching up may be difficult. It takes time to hire and train new programmers, and training the rookies distracts the pros. The rate at which features can be added is limited by this training process.

When such a possibility exists, there is more justification for investing early. This action is risky; it entails greater investment before we have any certainty of a return. But this risk must be balanced with the risk of falling too far behind the market.

Step 5: Predict Performance

Now that you have spending guidelines, you can generate a complete set of performance predictions. Draw a qualitative trend graph for each measurable quantity on the influence diagram. These predictions will serve as the basis for ongoing learning.

The easiest way to approach this task is to start with each budget category and move up the influence diagram one measure at a time, making a trend graph prediction for each. The process becomes more challenging when there are multiple influencers of a single outcome measure. The intuition that you have built by predicting isolated response trends comes into play here. Your judgment will lead to reasonable predictions. Remember that the predictions are usually wrong early in the life of a strategic experiment, and they improve as you gain experience.

In working through this process, you will revisit your goal trend graphs. Given the specific spending guidelines you have developed, you may need to revise some goals.

Illustration: The Island Post Online

Figure 9-11 shows a partial example. At the top of the diagram are two spending guidelines—for market research and for content creators—consistent with the foregoing descriptions.

Predicting feature ideas is straightforward because only one budget item influences the measure. The prediction for feature ideas shows a delay of perhaps one quarter before reaching a steady rate of new idea generation. Predicting features, as opposed to feature ideas, is a bit

FIGURE 9-11

Predictions require combining trends

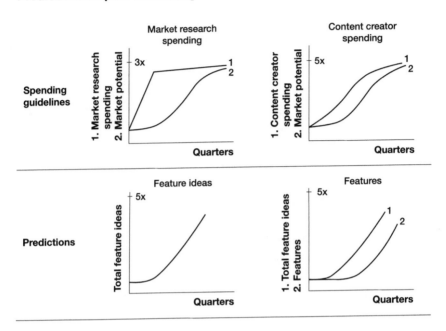

more complex. It depends both on market research and on the content creators. The addition of new features involves a longer delay, as long as two quarters, because the productivity of the content creation staff drops when rookies are hired and trained. After that, the number of features rises, but it can never rise any higher than feature ideas, regardless of the investment in content creators.

The delay before new features begin to show up on the Web site affects all subsequent predictions, and this leads to the revision of previously established goals. For example, the marketing team set a goal of immediately starting to have an impact on market share (review figure 9-9). The team's spending guideline, however, calls for a strategy of focusing spending on making customers aware of new features. This means that they will have to wait until features are actually added to the site before increasing marketing spending. It would be more sensible, therefore, to predict a steady market share for a few months, until features are ready, and *then* a steady increase in market share as marketing spending increases.

Step 6: Identify Critical Unknowns

At this point, we have a complete theory and a complete set of predictions. But we have made many assumptions—the critical unknowns—along the way. Some of these, if incorrect, could dramatically alter the course of the strategic experiment, even leading to long delays or abandonment. As a last step in planning, you should identify the critical unknowns. Another way of thinking about them is simply to ask the question, what can go wrong?

It's easiest to identify those critical unknowns that relate directly to whether the business will achieve profitability. As new information becomes available, you must constantly reassess the path to profitability. If you made an analysis of economies of scale, you must frequently review the probability of achieving those economies. Other critical unknowns include whether the causal relationships in the influence diagram are accurate, how the competition will behave, and how quickly the market will develop. Recall Hasbro Interactive's expansion plans (chapter 7), which included unknowns in each of these categories.

In addition, you should look back at your influence diagrams and predictions and ask, what will be the earliest indication that can resolve each critical unknown? How can I be sure that I am aware, as soon as possible, that the assumptions I have made are clearly right or wrong?

Plans for strategic experiments should include a table that lists critical unknowns and identifies how each will be resolved. Limit it to the *critical* ones, only one or two per major budget category.

Illustration: The Island Post Online

Table 9-2 shows critical unknowns for each of the five major budget categories, along with the measures that can be used to resolve them.

Using TFP, you now have a complete plan for a strategic experiment. The business is off and running.

Step 7: Analyze Disparities Between Predictions and Outcomes

Now the planning focus shifts from building theory to testing it. The planning cycle should be as rapid as is needed to let you keep up with new information. Emerging industries move at different speeds, but in

TABLE 9-2

Critical unknowns

Category	Critical unknown	Measure to resolve unknown
Content creation	1. How quickly will staffing requirements for content creators grow as market grows? 2. How quickly will the competitor add features to its Web site?	1. Staff required to maintain Web site 2. Competitor features
Operations	3. How long can download times become before perceived quality suffers?	3. Perceived quality of Web site (survey based) during busy times
Market research	4. Can market research actually identify solid feature ideas?	4. Perceived quality of Web site (survey based)
Marketing	5. Does marketing spending have a significant impact on traffic on the Web site, or do people naturally go to the site published under the same brand as the newspaper that they read? 6. How aggressively will the competition market its site? 7. How rapidly will market grow?	5. Web site traffic (especially following concentrated marketing campaigns) 6. Estimate of competitor marketing spending 7. Market size, market forecasts
Sales	8. Will sales force become more productive? Will advertisers buy larger ad packages? 9. How will advertising prices evolve?	8. Ad space sold per salesperson per quarter 9. Market rates for online ad space

almost all cases you will need at least quarterly updates. In some industries, monthly updates can be worthwhile, even if the level of detail is curtailed. The planning cycle and the learning cycle are the same. This means that in fast-moving industries, a management team's learning rate can be twelve times as fast if it operates on a monthly cycle rather than on an annual one.

The comparison between predictions and outcomes is a comparison of trends. This means that you must retain historical data from one period to the next. In our research, we looked at numerous plans that *only* looked forward. Learning from experience in a dynamic environment requires looking backward as well as forward.

When you observe disparities between predicted trends and actual trends, again one of two conclusions is possible: either the prediction was unrealistic, or the management team underperformed. You must consider both, recognizing that in strategic experiments the prediction is more often wrong.

Careful discussion of predictions and outcomes drives the learning process. Consider the comparison, shown in figure 9-12, between predicted and actual perceived quality. One of the critical unknowns for the *Island Post Online* is whether addition of researched features to the Web site would increase customer perceptions of quality. The analysis in figure 9-12 shows that so far, no evidence indicates that it does. Why? There are several possibilities.

- Not enough users have yet noticed and tried the new features.

- The features require a new technology, such as an Internet-enabled cellular phone, that is being adopted by the market more slowly than anticipated.

- Users have noticed the new features but have not yet used them long enough to get full value from them.

- The features will never be valued by customers. The theorized causal relationship between features and quality does not actually exist.

This is the type of questioning that leads directly to learning. In any given quarter, it may not be possible to find definitive answers. But based on new information since the preceding review, you should be

FIGURE 9-12

Possible futures to discuss

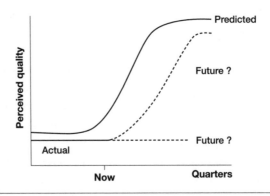

able to ask more specific questions and reassess what is known and what remains unknown.

Multiple interpretations of the analysis will be possible. Thus, it is critical to remain aware of how self-interest can shape interpretations of past experience. To learn, you must conduct your analysis in a rigorous, honest, transparent, candid, and emotionally detached fashion.

Your focus should be on the critical unknowns. Have they been resolved in some way, or is more time needed for additional evidence to accumulate? You should document the lessons learned, and classify them as either tentative or solid, so that knowledge accumulates from one period to the next. Tentative lessons may later become solid, or they may be reevaluated.[8]

For the *Island Post Online*, some possible conclusions about critical unknowns include:

- We are able to quickly increase Web site traffic with marketing spending.

- Market research does not appear to be any more effective than the intuition of the content creation staff in identifying features that customers want.

- Readers are very sensitive to lengthy download times.

Step 8: Revise the Plan

When you learn a lesson that calls the theory or the plan into question, it is time to revise. The new plan may involve new initiatives and may require testing different causal linkages. Therefore, you should repeat the entire sequence of steps.

1. Update the theory of the business.

2. Reassess the measures.

3. Reconsider the goals.

4. Reevaluate the spending guidelines. Again, this starts with considering the budget as a whole. As you analyze the lessons learned, you sharpen your intuition about risks and returns. Based on this intuition plus any new information, leaders can decide how ready they are to step on the accelerator—that is,

increase the total spending over the preceding planning period. Then you may need to reassess the spending guidelines for each function based on the lessons learned.

5. Update your predictions. Changing a prediction should not be a casual process. You should have a specific reason for doing so, such as an assumption that has proved false or spending guidelines that have been altered. You should document the reasons and retain them for the next cycle.

6. Update the list of critical unknowns. Unknowns that have been resolved can be removed from the list. If new unknowns have become apparent, you can add them.

Now the plan is once again complete, and the process continues with additional testing and revising.

Figure 9-13 summarizes theory-focused planning.

Departures from Conventional Planning

The planning recommendations outlined in this chapter are radical. To fully grasp their weight and to understand TFP in a nutshell, consider the following seven characteristics of TFP, each distinctly different from conventional practice.[9]

- *Predictions are revisable*: In conventional planning processes, predictions are fixed for one year at a time. But the focus in strategic experiments must be on learning—specifically, learning to more accurately predict the outcomes from experimental business activities. This focus requires that you revise predictions as you gain more information and learn.

- *Plans emphasize critical unknowns*: Conventional plans incorporate a lot of detail, but such detail is unrealistic for a strategic experiment. Too much is unknown. The relevant lessons are not in the details but rather in the handful of critical unknowns, and you should focus on them during each review of business performance.

- *The theories underlying the predictions are explicit*: The theory underlying the predictions is more important than the predictions themselves. In mature businesses, the guiding theory is that the past serves as a reliable guide to the future. But that mind-set has

FIGURE 9-13

A summary of theory-focused planning

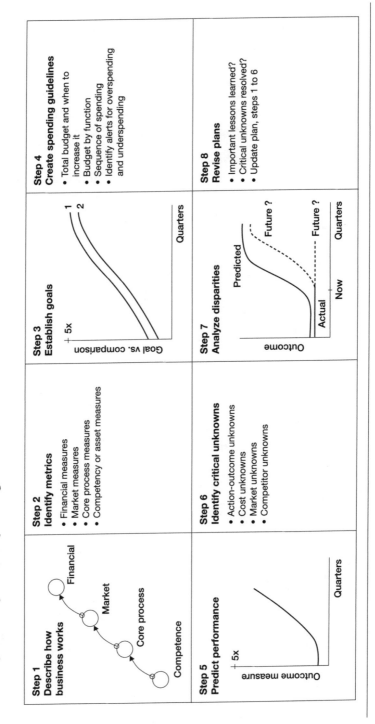

no relevance to strategic experiments. The influence diagram clarifies the logic behind predictions. Both theory and prediction must be explicitly made, shared, retained, and later revisited.

- *Predictions are of trends*: Conventional plans make only modest use of trends. In contrast, plans for strategic experiments should extensively compare predicted trends versus actual trends. You should make predictions in the form of qualitative trend graphs.

- *Performance reviews include history*: Conventional plans often include outcomes only from the most recent period. In TFP you compare trend predictions to trend outcomes, and this might require retaining more history than is customary.

- *Revisions are frequent*: The rate of learning is limited by the rate of iteration through the planning cycle. Annual iteration is inadequate. To enable rapid iteration, plans for strategic experiments must be much simpler than those of mature, established businesses.

- *Plans emphasize leading indicators*: Conventional planning in many corporations has begun to at least include indicators other than financials. In strategic experiments, plans should *focus* on leading indicators—the operational measures closest to the bottom of the influence diagrams. These measures will give the earliest indications that a plan is working or failing.

Table 9-3 summarizes these differences.

TABLE 9-3

Planning in two environments

Proven and mature business	New and unproven business
Accountable for results	Accountable for learning
Details	Critical unknowns
Predictions	Underlying logic
Numbers	Trends
Forward-looking	Forward-looking and historical
Annual cycle	Monthly or quarterly
Financial measures	Leading indicators

Because these differences are stark, it is highly advisable to create a planning process for strategic experiments that is isolated from the planning process for the rest of the corporation. For example, TFP could be the responsibility of a special committee, a *high-growth council*, that is charged with maintaining a strong learning discipline within all strategic experiments.

Of course, you will still need to include strategic experiments in the normal planning process for some purposes, such as capital planning for the corporation as a whole. However, the core planning activities—developing specific operational plans and reviewing results—should be managed on a parallel track, completely separate from the mainstream planning process.

Holding Managers Accountable for Learning

The senior management team must be involved in theory-focused planning. Only through close monitoring can they feel secure that the team leading the strategic experiment is doing everything it can to learn and adjust as quickly as possible. Close involvement also brings experienced judgment into the critical step of evaluating lessons learned.

After a theory-focused plan has been completed, at the launch of the business, the senior executive team should evaluate the following:

- Do we have a reasonable cause-and-effect story about how this business can succeed? Are the delays that we anticipate between action and outcome realistic? (Time from action to outcome is almost always underestimated.)

- Have we identified sufficient quantitative or qualitative measures to enable us to gather evidence to test our plan as quickly as possible?

- Do our spending plans make sense? Are our predictions consistent with our cause-and-effect story?

- Has the team identified the most critical unknowns? How does it plan to resolve them?

In the testing phase, a different set of questions is appropriate:

- Did we retain our original cause-and-effect story, spending plans, and predictions? Do we still understand them?

- Have we gathered the right data to test our predictions?

- How quickly are we revisiting the predictions?

- Are we comparing outcomes to predictions rigorously and dispassionately?

Finally, whenever NewCo's leader proposes a significant change in direction, there are important questions to be asked:

- What inspired this change in direction?

- Is there a specific lesson learned that is supported by an analysis of disparities between predictions and outcomes?

- Do we have a clear cause-and-effect story that shows how the new initiative is expected to lead to positive results, and over what time period?

- Have we made reasonable predictions based on the new theory and our new spending plans?

With this rigorous oversight, TFP is much more likely to be implemented effectively. Learning is faster. And the strategic experiment has the best chance of quickly zeroing in on a workable business model.

Using These Tools in Other Contexts

We created the tools described in this chapter to help overcome the numerous learning disabilities that handicap strategic experiments. However, the tools also have value in proven businesses.

First, the influence diagram is a clear way to communicate an understanding of how a business works as a whole. It can help employees who are specialized in one function to have a clearer understanding of how their actions affect other departments.

Second, mature businesses also change in uncertain and unpredictable ways. The influence diagram, by making explicit a theory of business, can lead to clear discussions of how the business is changing. For example, executives may theorize that customers are becoming less interested in finding the lowest price and more interested in receiving higher-quality service. When theories about how a business might be changing are explicitly communicated, a management team can devise experiments to test the theory. It may be that only one causal relationship is being tested, as opposed to an entire business model. Trend predictions are appropriate in this context.

Finally, mature business operations have dynamic aspects. New-product launches within an established business model—for example, a software company releasing a new version of an application—are the most obvious example. Influence diagrams and trend graphs can help guide the evaluation of product launches as they proceed. Based on experience launching similar products, however, there should be less uncertainty. Trends should be more predictable, and standards for performance more clear.

Assessing the Intensity of the Learning Challenge

As was true of the forgetting and borrowing challenges, the learning challenge is always demanding for strategic experiments. Still, some strategic experiments present more difficult learning challenges than others.

The two factors that determine the degree of difficulty are the range of the critical unknowns and the presence of factors that intensify the learning challenge. It is worthwhile to assess the degree of difficulty of learning by using figure 9-14 and table 9-4. They guide senior executives in anticipating how much time they should dedicate to supervising TFP and how best to direct their efforts.

FIGURE 9-14

Intensity of the learning challenge

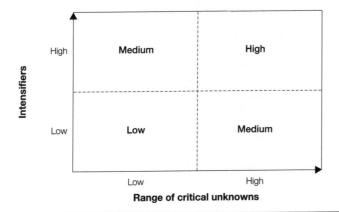

In chapter 10 we present the dramatic story of a successful strategic experiment that illustrates the principles we've presented throughout this book.

TABLE 9-4

Assessing the intensity of the learning challenge

This table is used in conjunction with figure 9-14 to assess the intensity of the learning challenge.

	Do you agree with these statements? (1 = strongly disagree, 7 = strongly agree, or NA)	**Rating (1–7)**
Range of critical unknowns	1. There are uncertainties related to the technologies that are enabling the new market, such as how quickly they will develop or how standards will evolve.	
	2. There are a number of competitive entries, from multiple industries, with differing strengths.	
	3. It is not clear what customers value, how quickly they will actually purchase and use the products offered, or how much they will pay.	
	4. The internal capabilities required to address the market opportunity are evolving. It is not clear that we can develop processes that allow us to offer new products or services at the prices customers will pay.	
	Calculate the average rating (excluding NAs) to determine the range of critical unknowns. On the horizontal axis of figure 9-14, a score of 4 defines the midpoint between "low" and "high."	
Intensifiers of the learning challenge	1. There is a strong perception that NewCo is in a tremendous rush to get to market first and therefore has little time for planning.	
	2. The company has a tradition of very detailed and exact planning.	
	3. The company has a history of insisting on common planning approaches for every business unit.	
	4. The nature of the experiment demands large one-time commitments rather than a series of small investments, and thus has little opportunity to change direction.	
	5. Data on NewCo's performance (other than financials) is difficult to gather, will not be available for long periods of time, or is highly ambiguous.	
	6. The company strongly penalizes managers for failing to make their numbers.	
	7. There are one or more measures of business performance that are viewed as important throughout the company but do not apply to NewCo.	
	Calculate the average rating (excluding NAs) to determine the magnitude of the intensifiers of the learning challenge. On the horizontal axis of figure 9-14, a score of 4 defines the midpoint between "low" and "high."	

Chapter Ten

The Ten Rules Explained

R AY STATA, founder of Analog Devices, Inc. (ADI), had no short-age of ambition. Between 1965 and 1990, he built his semiconductor design and manufacturing operation into one of the most respected companies in the Boston area.

But that was not enough. He wanted to build a truly great company, and he was prepared to take a huge risk on a new technology. His story is one of the most dramatic that we studied—one with a promising beginning, more than one near-death experience, gutsy risk taking, miraculous breakthroughs, and, ultimately, profitability. It's an ideal demonstration of the ten rules for strategic innovators. Rules 1 and 10 are general rules, rules 2 through 4 relate to the whys of forgetting, borrowing, and learning, and rules 5 though 9 relate to the hows.

Hitting Limits to Growth

In 1990, ADI was not a competitor in the fastest-growing and perhaps the most glamorous segment of the semiconductor industry: computer microprocessors. Companies such as Intel seemed to have the brightest futures. Its products were the central engines driving the PC revolution that would forever change how the world worked and lived.

Microprocessors operate in the abstract world of mathematics, instantaneously manipulating millions of 1s and 0s to perform complex calculations. But these digital devices, the heart of the computer world, need help to interact with the analog world of human beings.

ADI's specialty—analog semiconductor products—converted analog signals to digital and vice versa. They amplified and processed analog signals and regulated electrical flows in computers and communications devices as well as in military and industrial applications, particularly in instrumentation systems.

From its founding through the mid-1980s, ADI enjoyed double-digit growth. However, toward the end of the decade, ADI's markets appeared to be maturing. Growth rates dropped below 10 percent. How would ADI take its next discontinuous leap in growth, from a few hundred million dollars in annual revenues to a few billion? Certainly it would not happen through ADI's existing business model. Most of its products were custom designed and therefore engineering labor intensive. Even if demand continued to rise, growth would soon be limited by the unavailability of electrical engineers.

Every organization reaches a natural limit to its growth, and ADI had hit its own ceiling. Stata was ready to explore new territory, find ADI's next platform for growth, and take his company to the next level. Unforeseeable industry changes would inevitably threaten ADI's core business, so he also wanted to protect the company's future by staying ahead of the curve. "The primary job of the CEO . . . is to be an encouraging sponsor of those who see the future," said Stata. "It's all about detecting and managing the points of inflection. One can always do that with greater wisdom in hindsight, of course. But nonetheless there needs to be sensitivity to the fact that everything has a life, and you always have to be looking beyond that life."[1]

MEMS: A Promising New Technology

In the late 1980s, Richie Payne, one of ADI's most talented engineers, was chasing possibilities for a new technology that he and a few colleagues had been experimenting with. These new semiconductor chips, called microelectromechanical systems (MEMS), looked much like other chips, but MEMS were unique in that they had microscopic moving parts.

MEMS had many potential applications, the most important of which was to sense acceleration. In automobiles, MEMS devices could trigger air bags, replacing a ball-and-tube design that was heavier, less reliable, and more costly by a factor of 10.[2] Other possible applications ranged from video games to advanced optical telecommunications switches. After the technology advanced, additional applications would likely develop. Payne believed that by mastering MEMS technology ADI could build a platform for rapid growth for years to come.

ADI had developed an effective system, the ADI Fellows Program, for culling great business ideas from its talented technologists. Stata explained, "I think companies get in trouble because there is too much power in the management structure. They don't make it clear that management has a role, but they are not the end of the world . . . they are just part of the puzzle. There are others who are just as important or maybe even more important."[3]

The ADI Fellows, fewer than one percent of the engineering staff, had a direct line to the CEO and the board. "Customers want you to continue doing what you are doing, if you are doing it well, and of course the managers running successful businesses within the company just want more and more resources to serve their customers," Stata said. "Taking resources away from successful businesses and devoting them to high-risk experiments is anathema to business unit managers . . . it can only be done at the top of the company."[4]

ADI tolerated engineers spending perhaps 10 percent of their time pursuing their ideas, even if the ideas did not lead directly to revenues. ADI also encouraged interaction both inside and outside the company, knowing that it accelerated the rate at which ideas evolved and ripened.

After Payne and his colleagues demonstrated the viability of MEMS technology, ADI committed a formal budget to the project. Payne would lead the experimental business. Initial research showed that although the automotive market was growing at only a few percent per year, the market for automotive sensors was growing at more than 20 percent per year. Payne drafted a business plan that focused on the market for crash sensors for automotive air bags.

As effective as the Fellows system was, it only generated ideas. To succeed in converting breakthrough ideas to breakthrough growth, ADI would have to forget, borrow, and learn.

Rule 1: *In all great innovation stories, the great idea is only Chapter 1.* Building breakthrough businesses requires forgetting, borrowing, and learning. These central challenges demand more than just a talented and ambitious leader; they require leveraging the power of organizational DNA.

The Forgetting Challenge

The MEMS business model had some similarities to the typical ADI business. The product was a semiconductor component, and the customers were manufacturers of larger systems of which ADI's product was only one small part. The potential competition was similar—namely, other semiconductor manufacturers that developed and sold analog components.

Despite these similarities, the MEMS division faced a significant forgetting challenge:

- The automakers were an unfamiliar customer and had developed extraordinary levels of sophistication in supply chain management.

- Because MEMS devices would serve an automotive safety application, ADI would face demands for quality and precise delivery times that exceeded its already high standards.

- ADI's market was horizontal (its products cut across industries), but MEMS was vertical (it served a single industry).

- The cost structure differed in that MEMS would sell only a few crash sensor designs in high volumes, whereas ADI's product catalog included thousands of low-volume products.

- Most ADI products were based on proven technology, and manufacturing costs were predictable. MEMS was a new technology, and costs would prove difficult to project.

- ADI had developed strong systems for ensuring accountability to plans, including confrontational performance reviews. This practice is inappropriate for strategic experiments.

The ADI management team understood—and explicitly discussed—these differences. Nonetheless, ADI executives struggled to forget because ADI's business model was consistent across thousands of products. They even used the term *ADI business model* when referring to the set of assumptions about ADI's customers and products, appropriate spending levels, and appropriate indicators to use in judging business performance. The existence of a single, proven business model intensified the forgetting challenge. As you will see, assumptions about the business model can be stubbornly pervasive.

Rule 2: *Sources of organizational memory are powerful.* Organizations naturally cling to CoreCo's orthodoxy, even when moving into new environments. But NewCo needs to operate in fundamentally different ways.

The Borrowing Challenge

The MEMS venture did not face an overwhelming borrowing challenge. However, ADI had two assets that MEMS could not live without: semiconductor manufacturing expertise and plant capacity. The MEMS business therefore needed access to ADI's large manufacturing facility in Wilmington, Massachusetts. More than nine thousand products were manufactured at the facility, accounting for two-thirds of ADI's total business. The facility's staff was deep in technology expertise and manufacturing know-how.

This advantage was not trivial. Semiconductor plants are tremendously expensive, and the manufacturing process is complex, involving hundreds of computer-controlled production steps. The ability of the MEMS division to set up manufacturing operations at the Wilmington facility was an advantage that no independent start-up could match.

Although the need for links between CoreCo and NewCo was limited, certain factors—especially capital constraints—would intensify tensions. Relative to ADI's operating profits, MEMS would need a great deal of financing to reach profitability.

Rule 3: *Large, established companies can beat start-ups* if they can succeed in leveraging their enormous assets and capabilities.

The Learning Challenge

MEMS faced a difficult but not impossible learning challenge. The business plan contained three critical unknowns:

- Would the automakers bet on a new crash-sensing technology?

- After MEMS mastered the manufacturing process, how cheaply could it produce a single sensor?

- To what extent would other markets for MEMS devices develop?

Several of the strategic experiments we studied faced a longer list of make-or-break unknowns. But the MEMS division's learning challenge was intensified because the business required big, one-time bets, such as signing large contracts with automakers. Moreover, feedback would be slow. It would take several years to perfect the MEMS manufacturing process and accurately assess the profit potential of the business.

Rule 4: *Strategic experiments face critical unknowns.* No amount of research can resolve these unknowns before the business is launched. Therefore, success depends more on an ability to experiment and learn than on the initial strategy.

In summary, MEMS faced moderately difficult challenges on all three dimensions: forgetting, borrowing, and learning (see figure 10-1). For guidelines on assessing the intensity of each of the three challenges, we suggest you review the frameworks at the ends of chapters 3, 5, and 9. Your assessments should play a role when you evaluate ideas for strategic experiments. If you have two opportunities with roughly equal market potential, the one with a lower organizational degree of difficulty is preferable.

FIGURE 10-1

MEMS faced a moderately difficult challenge on all three dimensions: forgetting, borrowing, and learning

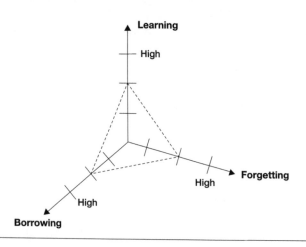

The First Years of the MEMS Business

In 1989, ADI's senior management team created a formal budget for Payne and the MEMS project and assigned the project to one of ADI's business units. Payne reported to a general manager whose business included the Wilmington plant. This arrangement enabled the borrowing that the MEMS division needed, and MEMS engineers were able to prove manufacturability.

Soon, Payne had grabbed the attention of the automakers by quoting aggressively low per-unit prices for MEMS devices. He offered to sell MEMS at a loss. However, based on his extensive experience with other new semiconductor products, Payne anticipated that manufacturing costs would drop dramatically as the company gained experience. At the prices he was quoting, Payne expected MEMS to be profitable by 1995.

MEMS signed its first contract in 1991. The first critical unknown was resolved, at least tentatively: the automakers were interested. But not everything was perfect for MEMS. Although it was succeeding at borrowing and had made progress in learning, it was struggling to forget. This struggle is described in the next three sections.

Adapting to New Levels of Uncertainty

The general manager to whom Payne reported had interests other than MEMS most immediately at heart. Because the manager faced a personal evaluation based on financial results relative to targets, he had a natural interest in restraining spending on MEMS so that he could dedicate as many resources as possible to existing customers and their current needs. He wanted to improve profitability in the current year. Instead, Payne wanted only to consume more and more resources even though MEMS had yet to earn any revenues.

NewCo's reporting structure has a critical influence on how the competition for resources plays out. NewCo should always report to someone high enough in the organization to take long-term risks. Often, this is a counterintuitive choice for a corporation, because it may result in the general manager of NewCo appearing to be a peer of a general manager in charge of far more resources and many more people. But if the reporting relationship is set any lower, the needs of NewCo are squeezed out to meet the shorter-term needs of a proven business.

Fortunately, Jerry Fishman, the COO, believed that the MEMS technology could lead to extraordinary products that could not easily be commoditized. So he responded when Payne sought his help to overcome the unwillingness of his boss to support MEMS. Fishman ensured that MEMS received the resources it needed. Had Payne not been willing to go over his boss's head or had Fishman not responded, MEMS might never have made its first delivery.

In 1992, as part of a reorganization, ADI shifted MEMS to a newly created division. Frank Weigold, a new hire from outside ADI, was named general manager. Fishman had taken advantage of an unexpected opportunity to hire Weigold, who had built a reputation at his prior company as a successful troubleshooter and broadly skilled general manager.

Wanting to take full advantage of Weigold's capabilities, ADI assigned him a mix of businesses in various stages. He was given wide latitude. Options for each business ranged from substantially increasing investment to selling or suspending operations.

The increased latitude was promising for MEMS. No longer would its general manager be concerned chiefly with the negative impact that MEMS would have on the near-term profits of an existing unit. In the new arrangement, MEMS would be evaluated independently.

Like the selection of an organizational structure, however, the selection of a leader for a strategic experiment has powerful implications. MEMS would continue to struggle to forget, because most of Weigold's past successes involved returning troubled but established business units to profitability. For this reason, he was a questionable choice to lead MEMS. The demands of general management vary dramatically over the course of a business life cycle, from start-up to growth to maturity to decline. It is a rare general manager who can be effective at all parts of the life cycle, but that, in effect, was what Weigold was asked to do. His skills and biases were more fitting for a turnaround than for a start-up.

Weigold became uncomfortable when he saw that profitability for the MEMS venture was several years away, and uncertain even then. His instinctive drive for near-term profitability was in some ways healthy, but, left unchecked, it would have sunk MEMS.

Adapting to the Need for New Competencies

Soon the MEMS team, after a lengthy and costly sales effort, was on the cusp of signing its second contract—this one with a much bigger automaker, a company that was well known for brutal negotiations with suppliers. Evaluating what appeared to be the best possible deal, Weigold leaned toward foregoing the opportunity, again because of concerns about profitability. But under intense pressure from his colleagues, Weigold accepted the deal. Now the first critical unknown was resolved: there was no doubt that MEMS technology was at the heart of future air bag systems.

In the deal, however, ADI was locked in to a long-term, fixed-price contract. This type of contract may have been the norm in other ADI business lines, but for MEMS it led to a serious risk. Manufacturing costs were still much greater than the quoted price. If MEMS could not get costs down as anticipated, it would be stuck in a losing contract. We speculate that ADI would have avoided this situation if it had built a sales team composed of outsiders experienced in negotiations with automakers. MEMS leaders other than Weigold, in their excitement to sign the deal, likely underestimated the strength of their negotiating position.

Adapting to a New Value Proposition

In the early months of the deal, ADI struggled to meet the automaker's quality requirements. The situation soon became a crisis. ADI had always had a strong reputation for quality, but MEMS devices were being used in an automotive safety application, and quality standards were higher than they were for most ADI customers. To keep the program on solid footing, MEMS reps were forced to make weekly visits to the automakers and explain in detail what the quality problems were and how they were being fixed. The MEMS business might have anticipated and avoided this crisis if it had created MEMS with a separate organizational DNA—in particular, if it had hired outsiders with automotive experience.

ADI replicated its DNA when it created the MEMS division. Most critically, MEMS made few outside hires, and MEMS reported to a mature business unit. As a result, MEMS was initially unable to forget.

Rule 5: *The NewCo organization must be built from scratch*, with new choices in staffing, structure, systems, and culture. This is the only way to defeat the powerful forces of institutional memory. Conversational awareness of the differences between NewCo and CoreCo business models does not suffice.

Heightened Tensions

A bigger crisis would come in 1995. Sales of air bag crash sensors were rising rapidly, but each unit was still being sold at a loss. Profitability was a long way off.

"Jerry, come on. You've always been the voice of reason! Quit giving money to divisions who have never made a profit!" This angry retort from a colleague of Fishman's was a direct result of Fishman's continuing support of MEMS. He had overcome even more vocal resistance in the past, at one point being booed while explaining why MEMS needed further support.[5]

Because strategic experiments are usually funded from operating earnings, it should be no surprise that a decline in the core business can make it difficult to sustain funding. What is less obvious is that unexpected success in the core business can also make it difficult. Whereas a downturn in the core business reduces the total resources available, an upturn increases competition for resources as the core business needs additional capital to support its own growth. MEMS was experiencing the latter.

In addition to conflicts over capital, an immediate point of pain existed at the Wilmington facility. When MEMS was assigned to the facility, it looked as though Wilmington would have excess capacity for years to come. But renewed growth in the core business had pushed Wilmington to its capacity sooner than anticipated. Production starts were coveted, and representatives from each business unit actively competed at weekly production planning meetings. Arguments were heated.

Close integration had enabled MEMS to borrow easily at first, but now MEMS and ADI were wrangling. ADI had not assigned a senior executive to manage this type of tension. Instead, the company reacted as problems arose.

Some ADI managers threatened to quit, so firmly did they believe that the company was wrongly putting the needs of MEMS over those of the core business. In retrospect, Fishman himself, who became CEO in 1996 (Stata kept the title of chair), would wonder how close MEMS came to inflicting irreparable damage on ADI's core business. The tensions were disruptive, and they hindered learning.

Competing for production starts in Wilmington, CoreCo managers judged MEMS by their own business standards. They pressured MEMS leaders to defend their new business on the basis of gross margins, a common measure for judging product line performance within ADI.

For MEMS, gross margins were negative. Although MEMS's costs were improving, it could never win the gross margin battle because the MEMS cost structure differed fundamentally from ADI's. MEMS products sold in higher volumes and needed less custom design work. Consequently, sales, marketing, and product development expenses as a percentage of revenues were *lower* for MEMS than for other ADI products. Therefore, it was theoretically possible, even likely, that MEMS operating margins could be higher even with lower gross margins.

Politically, however, this reality did not make comparisons of gross margins any less influential. Gross margins were immediately available, and they were factual. Other performance indicators for MEMS relied on forward-looking projections and were regarded skeptically. In addition, gross margin as a reliable predictor of economic performance was deeply embedded in ADI's culture. Ultimately, however, the focus on gross margins distracted MEMS from what mattered: resolving critical unknowns in the business plan.

In the end, the demanding nature of serving the automotive industry saved the day for MEMS. Automakers did not tolerate supply disruptions because assembly-line shutdowns were expensive. Fishman and others feared that delaying shipments would lose ADI's biggest MEMS customer, and that would kill the business. With Fishman's support, the MEMS division continued to borrow capacity from the Wilmington plant.

> Rule 6: *Managing tensions is job one for senior management.* The health of the links between NewCo and CoreCo deteriorates easily. There are several natural sources of tension, driven by dynamic forces— particularly the changing demand for and supply of capital within the organization.

> Rule 7: *NewCo needs its own planning process.* CoreCo's norms for evaluating business performance will disrupt NewCo's learning.

Manipulation of Gross Margin

Being taken to task on gross margin changed the behavior of the MEMS team in a way that further harmed its ability to learn. From its inception, the MEMS division looked for opportunities outside the automotive industry. The original business plan predicted that nonautomotive revenue would be roughly twice that of automotive revenue.[6] But nonautomotive markets never developed as expected. In fact, MEMS had gained no significant nonautomotive revenues by 1995.

Nonetheless, the MEMS team continued to project significant nonautomotive revenues. Why? It was because the managers anticipated that gross margins in nonautomotive markets would be substantially higher than those in automotive markets. Therefore, by continuing to project rapidly growing nonautomotive revenues, the MEMS division could project an *average* divisional gross margin that met ADI standards and thereby compete more effectively for resources.

In effect, the focus on gross margin delayed learning. Nonautomotive revenues were still immaterial several years later.

Rule 8: *Interest, influence, internal competition, and politics disrupt learning.* To ensure learning, you must take a disciplined, detached, and analytical approach to making predictions and interpreting differences between predictions and outcomes.

The View from the CEO's Office

As ADI's COO, Fishman had strongly advocated for MEMS. When promoted to CEO in 1996, however, he immediately faced new pressures that encumbered his advocacy. Now he bore a public responsibility to investors for the bottom line—a bottom line significantly dented by MEMS as its losses continued to grow. Losses were significant enough for investors to notice, and there seemed to be no good strategy for communicating MEMS activities to Wall Street analysts.

As Fishman's enthusiasm for MEMS waned, Stata, as board chair, picked up the role as the key advocate. MEMS had several strikes against it: it was already one year beyond its original projected date of profitability, it had missed its targets every year, and its losses were still mounting (because sales were rising and prices were below cost; see figure 10-2). Nonetheless, Stata became more attracted to the technology.

Because the MEMS business had missed cost targets consistently, MEMS engineers endured much criticism. ADI had proven its ability to hit the same targets with many other products. But the criticism was

FIGURE 10-2

Revenues and operating profits for the MEMS venture

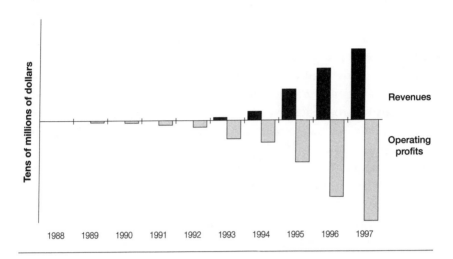

unfair because the company had never met a manufacturing challenge quite like MEMS. In companies with strong performance cultures, New-Co's predictions commonly become rigid, and this disables learning.

Stata viewed the performance of the MEMS division differently. Rather than focus on performance against forecast or on ADI's traditional financial measures, he concentrated on the most critical unknown: could MEMS reduce manufacturing costs to levels comparable with those of other ADI product lines? Was there any evidence of that possibility? After studying the MEMS manufacturing processes, he saw that MEMS was making progress. He believed that profitability *was* possible.

As the new venture struggled in Wilmington and losses continued to mount, Stata continued his advocacy. Stata and Fishman had many vocal confrontations. Fishman grew more concerned that MEMS might never earn a profit, and he persistently asked, "How much more time? How much more money?" At the end of one such confrontation, Fishman challenged Stata directly: "If you think MEMS is such a great business, why don't you go run it yourself?"[7]

Much to Fishman's surprise, Stata called his bluff. He had been looking for a new challenge since stepping down as CEO. He accepted the dual role of board chair and general manager of the MEMS business, now reconstituted as an independent division.

Taking a major risk, Stata invested nearly $100 million in refurbishing and reequipping a building in Cambridge, Massachusetts, that had once been an integrated-circuit facility for Polaroid. Stata saw that the MEMS team needed an environment in which accountability was to learning and not numbers, and it required a focused learning effort in a more ideal learning environment. The Wilmington facility, with its thousands of products and operating at full capacity, had become too chaotic. Borrowing was less necessary than in MEMS's early years, and capacity was scarce.

Now MEMS had a distinct organizational DNA and could forget more fully and freely. It no longer borrowed capacity, but, by maintaining relationships with the Wilmington plant, it still borrowed expertise. It had an entrepreneurial leader in Stata, ADI's original founder, and it "reported" directly to the chair of the board, who could evaluate whether risks on the strategic experiment were sensible for ADI's long-term health. (In larger companies, the board or CEO need not directly oversee new ventures.) MEMS could both forget and borrow. Still, it remained unprofitable.

As general manager of MEMS, Stata represented his division at business performance reviews alongside other division managers. The atmosphere in these meetings was tense and confrontational. The other business heads had significant personal wealth tied up in ADI stock options, and they treated Stata as they would any other business head, even though he chaired the board. They demanded justification for continued losses. (MEMS reported record losses in 1997.)

Soon, Stata moved to isolate discussion of his unit's business performance from discussions of other divisions' performance. He chose not to attend the meetings, in part to give Fishman the chance to run the company without such direct participation from the outgoing chief executive. The action was fitting. Discussion of the performance of new divisions and established divisions does not belong in the same room at the same time.

> Rule 9: *Hold NewCo accountable for learning and not results.* You can achieve accountability for learning by insisting on a disciplined learning process. Accountability for results against plan, while simpler to practice, is counterproductive.

Achieving Profitability

Stata managed MEMS with a singular focus on reducing costs. In the new, independent manufacturing facility, Stata assembled a dedicated team to solve problems as soon as they arose. One overwhelming problem occurred after another, but the division never missed a delivery. One manufacturing leader recalled, "People were willing to endure the pressures because this was an unusual job and an unusual technology. This is the kind of life experience that you don't get every day. I used to tell people when things got particularly tough, 'Look, I know your life is difficult now. You have more crises on your hands every day. But ten years from now you are going to look back and appreciate the uniqueness and excitement of what we are trying to do.'"[8]

During a downturn in ADI's core markets in 1998, the MEMS division faced even greater pressures. MEMS losses were negating most of ADI's profits.[9] With the rest of ADI, the MEMS division endured budget cuts. Nonetheless, MEMS' manufacturing costs-per-unit steadily improved. By 1999, MEMS had demonstrated that it was on a clear path to profitability. It had resolved a critical unknown: MEMS could manufacture at costs comparable to those of other ADI products.

Stata was ready to relinquish control, so he asked Weigold, with his different management style, to return. Under Weigold's leadership, MEMS reached profitability. By 2002, revenues neared $100 million, still almost entirely from automotive contracts.

The final critical unknown—whether other MEMS markets would develop—remained unresolved, but Stata believed that new major growth markets for products based on MEMS were coming soon. ADI's panel discussions about MEMS at scientific conferences were standing room only, as engineers pondered the possibilities.

With technical supremacy built over fifteen years, ADI was perfectly positioned to capitalize on any new MEMS market. Stata had his growth platform, and so the venture's full payoff would soon be clear to everyone.[10]

A Final Note

ADI faced another alluring investment opportunity when a few MEMS engineers toyed with a new technique for measuring acceleration, one based on a thermochemical reaction rather than mechanical movement.

At the time, Stata and Fishman felt that ADI could not finance another high-risk venture.

Interestingly, much resistance to the project came from within the MEMS division, because the new technology could compete directly with MEMS. Fishman reflected, "The entrepreneur, when trying to protect his own jewels, can easily become the bureaucratic control freak—the non-supporter of innovation. Any time you move on, the incumbent complains bitterly."[11]

Suppose ADI had wanted to pursue the technology. It would have created a new business unit, and it would have faced the three central challenges: forgetting, borrowing, and learning. It would have needed to forget part of what made MEMS successful, borrow some of its resources, and learn by resolving critical unknowns.

MEMS was still young, but barriers to breakthrough growth were arising. Even among entrepreneurs, the desire to protect a known success is powerful. And the urge to protect only gathers force as companies transition through the business life cycle from launch, to viability, to growth, to maturity, and to decline.

> Rule 10: *Companies can build a capacity for breakthrough growth through strategic innovation.* Skills in forgetting, borrowing, and learning are the foundation. Managers must start building these organizational skills early in a company's life.

The MEMS division somehow survived several live-or-die episodes. Such is the nature of strategic innovation. There is potential for a huge win, but with great potential comes great uncertainty. The corporation can increase the odds by lending NewCo its tremendous assets, but the corporation also can easily get in the way.

Leading a strategic experiment may be general management's triple-flip-with-a-quadruple-twist, but it is well within reach when you design NewCo so that it can forget, borrow, and learn.

NOTES

Preface

1. The case histories that appear in this book are abridged, and the factual information is laced with our own analysis. The complete, "just the facts" versions of the case histories, intended for use in MBA classrooms, are available on the Center for Global Leadership Web site: http://www.tuck.dartmouth.edu/cgl.

2. We published our own article on the topic: "Not All Profits Are Equal," *Across the Board*, September 2002, 43–48.

Introduction

1. Clayton Christensen has popularized the notion of a *disruptive* innovation. See Clayton M. Christensen, *The Innovator's Dilemma* (Boston: Harvard Business School Press, 1997). We view disruptive innovation as a subset of strategic innovation. According to Christensen, a disruptive innovation typically is not attractive to mainstream customers at the time of introduction, because it offers inferior performance on the attribute that these customers value most. At the same time, there is an emerging market segment that places little or no value on this attribute. These customers value a different attribute delivered by the disruptive innovation. Over time, its performance on the attribute valued by mainstream customers rises to a level that satisfies them. Thus, incumbents may at first ignore the new technology and the emerging market; it is irrelevant to their customers. But eventually, it satisfies their customers, thereby disrupting their core business. Similarly, strategic innovations depart from proven business models. But they differ from disruptive innovations along a number of dimensions: they may offer superior or inferior performance on attributes that mainstream customers value; they may be targeted at mainstream customers or a new niche customer segment; and they may or may not threaten the core business.

2. See Vijay Govindarajan and Anil Gupta, *The Quest for Global Dominance* (New York: Jossey Bass, 2001), especially chapter 8, "Changing the Rules of the Global Game."

3. When change is nonlinear it is subject to unanticipated, sudden accelerations. It's difficult to adapt to such change without a fundamental change in strategy. For

vivid descriptions of the nature and impact of nonlinear change in the economic environment, see C. K. Prahalad and Jan P. Oosterveld, "Transforming International Governance: The Challenge for Multinationals," *Sloan Management Review* (Spring 1999): 31–39, and Richard D'Aveni, *Hypercompetition* (New York: The Free Press, 1995).

4. Fara Warner, "Detroit Muscle," *Fast Company*, Issue 59 (June 2002), 88–93; "GM Aims to Boost OnStar Exposure in Car Giveaway," *Wall Street Journal* 243, Issue 2 (January 4, 2004), B3; and Karen Lundegaard and Gregory L. White, "A Car Safety Net with Holes," *Wall Street Journal* 240, Issue 109 (December 3, 2002), D1.

5. Melanie Wells, "Kid Nabbing," *Forbes* 173, Issue 2 (February 2, 2004), 84–88.

6. Bruce Orwall, "No Late Fees: Disney to 'Beam' Rental Movies to Homes," *Wall Street Journal* 242, Issue 63 (September 29, 2003), B1.

7. Researchers have identified nonlinear changes as danger points for established corporations, particularly when their core competencies are threatened with obsolescence. See Michael L. Tushman and Philip Anderson, "Technological Discontinuities and Organizational Environments," *Administrative Science Quarterly* 31 (1986): 439–465.

8. Innovations are often the result of combinations of knowledge—new and old, internal and external, within and outside the industry. For analyses of the relative merits of investments in these different categories of knowledge, see Riitta Katila, "New Product Search Over Time: Past Ideas in Their Prime?" *Academy of Management Journal* 45 (2002): 995–1010, and Riitta Katila and Gautam Ahuja, "Something Old, Something New: A Longitudinal Study of Search Behavior and New Product Introduction," *Academy of Management Journal* 45 (2002): 1183–1194.

9. The authors use the labels "NewCo" and "CoreCo" as shorthand for "new business" and "core business" to characterize the nature of the businesses discussed in the book. Any similarity to real corporations bearing those two names is coincidental and unintentional.

10. Our classification does not conflict with other treatises on innovation types. Refer to Hubert Gatignon, Michael L. Tushman, Wendy Smith, and Philip Anderson, "A Structural Approach to Assessing Innovation: Construct Development of Innovation Locus, Type, and Characteristics," *Management Science* 48, Issue 9 (2002): 1103–1122. See also William J. Abernathy and Kim B. Clark, "Innovation: Mapping the Winds of Creative Destruction," *Research Policy* 14 (1985): 3–22.

11. See Vijay Govindarajan and Chris Trimble, "The Tortoise, the Hare, the Acrobat, and the Test Pilot: Designing Organizations for Four Different Types of Innovation," working paper, Tuck School of Business, Hanover, NH, November 2003. Other researchers have also noted the vast differences in management approaches to different types of innovation. See, for example, Kathleen M. Eisenhardt and Behnam N. Tabrizi, "Accelerating Adaptive Processes: Product Innovation in the Global Computer Industry," *Administrative Science Quarterly* 40 (1995): 84–110, for a description of the distinct differences in highly uncertain versus less uncertain product development activities. For a description of how excellence in managing continuous process improvement can inhibit other types of innovation, see Mary J. Benner and Michael L. Tushman, "Exploitation, Exploration, and Process Management: The Productivity Dilemma Revisited," *Academy of Management Review* 28 (2003): 238–256.

12. Daniel Kruger, "You Want Data with That? If Customers Are Always Right, How Come McDonald's Wasn't Listening to Them?" *Forbes*, March 29, 2004, 58.

13. Although strategic innovation seems a daunting challenge, researchers question the popular but unproven notion that start-up firms are better suited to testing experimental business models than established corporations. For example, see Rajesh K. Chandy and Gerard J. Tellis, "The Incumbent's Curse? Incumbency, Size, and Radical Product Innovation," *Journal of Marketing* (July 2000): 1–17.

14. For a thorough review of the effects of organizational aging on growth and innovation, see Jesper B. Sorensen and Toby E. Stuart, "Aging, Obsolescence, and Organizational Innovation," *Administrative Science Quarterly* 45 (2000): 81–112. In general, aging improves competence at incremental innovation but damages competence at radical innovation. For a study of the effects of age on performance, see Andrew D. Henderson, "Firm Strategy and Age Dependence: A Contingent View on the Liabilities of Newness, Adolescence, and Obsolescence," *Administrative Science Quarterly* 44 (1999): 281–314. According to the author, technology firms that pursue a strategy that depends on the adoption of particular industry standards face their greatest risks of failure during adolescence and not old age.

15. See David Harding and Sam Rovit, "The Mega-Merger Mouse Trap," *Wall Street Journal*, February 17, 2004, B2.

16. James Bandler, "Kodak Shifts Focus from Film, Betting Future on Digital Lines," *Wall Street Journal*, September 25, 2003, A1.

17. See, for example, C. K. Prahalad and Gary Hamel, *Competing for the Future* (Boston: Harvard Business School Press, 1994).

18. See James March, "Exploration and Exploitation in Organizational Learning," *Organization Science* 2/1 (February 1991): 71, and Mary Benner and Michael L. Tushman, "Exploitation, Exploration, and Process Management: The Productivity Dilemma Revisited," *Academy of Management Review* 28 (2003): 238–256, for viewpoints on why it is difficult to simultaneously explore new business models and exploit existing ones.

Chapter One

1. Even though ideas are only a starting point, the preponderance of research and recommendations on innovation has been on processes, techniques, and organizational designs that can generate and identify innovative ideas. See, for example, Jay R. Galbraith, "Designing the Innovative Organization," *Organizational Dynamics* (Winter 1982): 5–25; Peter Drucker, "The Discipline of Innovation," *Harvard Business Review* (May–June 1985): 67–72; Gary Hamel, "Bringing Silicon Valley Inside," *Harvard Business Review* (September–October 1999): 70–84; and W. Chan Kim and Renée Mauborgne, "Knowing a Winning Business Idea When You See One," *Harvard Business Review* (September 2000): 129–138.

2. The authors use the labels "NewCo" and "CoreCo" as shorthand for "new business" and "core business" to characterize the nature of the businesses discussed in the book. Any similarity to real corporations bearing those two names is coincidental and unintentional.

3. Researchers have identified many reasons organizations have difficulty managing strategic innovation. We discuss specific examples throughout the book; our goal is to increase the odds of success. For further discussion, see Clayton M. Christensen, *The Innovator's Dilemma* (Boston: Harvard Business School Press, 1997); James M. Utterback, *Mastering the Dynamics of Innovation* (Boston: Harvard Business

School Press, 1994); and Pankaj Ghemawat, "Marketing Incumbency and Techno-logical Inertia," *Marketing Science* 10 (1991): 161–171.

4. Gifford Pinchot, *Intrapreneuring: Why You Don't Have to Leave the Corporation to Become an Entrepreneur* (New York: HarperCollins, 1985), 22.

5. Researchers still believe that encouraging autonomous action on the part of individual employees and providing resources for individual pursuit of experimen-tal projects are the critical elements of innovative organizations. See, for example, Charles W. L. Hill and Frank T. Rothaermel, "The Performance of Incumbent Firms in the Face of Radical Technological Innovation," *Academy of Management Review* 28 (2003): 257–274. Our view is that these characteristics of organizations are important but insufficient to support *strategic* innovation beyond the earliest stages of generat-ing ideas and writing business plans. Further support for this argument can be found in Deborah Dougherty and Cynthia Hardy, "Sustained Product Innovation in Large, Mature Organizations: Overcoming Innovation-to-Organization Problems," *Acad-emy of Management Journal* 39 (1996): 1120–1153.

6. Linda A. Hill, Nancy Kamprath, and Melinda B. Conrad, "Joline Godfrey and the Polaroid Corporation," Case 9-492-037 (Boston: Harvard Business School, revised April 4, 2000).

7. For compelling support of this argument, see Amar Bhide, "Hustle as Strat-egy," *Harvard Business Review* (September–October 1986): 59–65.

8. The forgetting challenge, in a general context, has been examined by Bo L. T. Hedberg, "How Organizations Learn and Unlearn," in *Handbook of Organizational Design*, eds. Paul C. Nystrom and William H. Starbuck (Oxford: Oxford University Press, 1981).

9. This argument is consistent with the notions of a "complacency trap." The more a firm succeeds, the more likely it is that it will view success as a validation of the past. This results in organizational inertia. See, for example, Michael T. Hannan and John Freeman, "Structural Inertia and Organizational Change," *American Socio-logical Review* 49/2 (April 1984): 149–164; Mary Tripsas and Giovanni Gavetti, "Capabilities, Cognition and Inertia: Evidence from Digital Imaging," *Strategic Man-agement Journal* 21 (2000): 1147–1161; and Gautam Ahuja and Curba M. Lampert, "Entrepreneurship in the Large Corporation: A Longitudinal Study of How Estab-lished Firms Create Breakthrough Innovations," *Strategic Management Journal* 22 (2001): 521–543.

10. It can be particularly difficult to forget the existing customer. See Clayton Christensen and Joseph L. Bower, "Customer Power, Strategic Investment, and the Failure of Leading Firms," *Strategic Management Journal* 17 (1996): 197–218, for a discussion of how existing customers can wield extraordinary influence.

11. The need to borrow in another context—acquisitions—has been highlighted by Philippe C. Haspeslagh and David B. Jemison, *Managing Acquisitions* (New York: The Free Press, 1991).

12. For a discussion of the learning challenge in a general context, see Barbara Levitt and James G. March, "Organizational Learning," *Annual Review of Sociology* 14 (1988): 319–340.

13. The major categories of organizational DNA, or, alternatively, organizational design, have been defined in different ways by different authors. See, for example, the star model in Jay R. Galbraith, *Designing Organizations* (San Francisco: Jossey-Bass, 2002), and the 7S model in Thomas J. Peters and Robert H. Waterman Jr., *In Search of Excellence* (New York: Warner Books, 1984). Our purpose in using the four cate-

gories (structure, staff, systems, and culture) is to give the concept its most useful form for our inquiry into strategic innovation.

14. The current version of Johnson & Johnson's credo is available on its company web site at http://www.jnj.com/our_company/our_credo/.

15. Several researchers agree that it is necessary to create autonomous and independent business units, even corporate spin-offs, to pursue new and uncertain business models. See Robert A. Burgelman and Leonard R. Sayles, *Inside Corporate Innovation* (New York: The Free Press, 1986); Joseph L. Bower and Clayton Christensen, "Disruptive Technologies: Catching the Wave," *Harvard Business Review* (January–February 1995): 43–53; and Clayton Christensen and Michael Overdorf, "Meeting the Challenge of Disruptive Change," *Harvard Business Review* (March–April 2000): 67–76.

16. While acknowledging the benefits of isolating NewCo from CoreCo, several authors have suggested that leveraging existing corporate assets is also important. See, for example, Jonathan D. Day et al., "The Innovative Organization: Why New Ventures Need More Than a Room of Their Own," *The McKinsey Quarterly* 21 (April 2001): 20–31, and Constantinos Markides and Constantinos D. Charitou, "Competing with Dual Business Models: A Contingency Approach," *Academy of Management Executive* 18 (August 2004): 20–31. See also Marco Iansiti, F. Warren McFarlan, and George Westerman, "Leveraging the Incumbent's Advantage," *MIT Sloan Management Review* 44 (Summer 2003): 58–64, for a discussion of why it is important to consider the need to leverage corporate assets early in NewCo's life. Our objective is to describe *how* to succeed at simultaneously forgetting and borrowing.

17. The organizational design that we propose in this book is similar to Charles O'Reilly and Michael Tushman's notion of the *ambidextrous organization*. See Michael Tushman, Wendy Smith, Robert Wood, George Westerman, and Charles O'Reilly, "Innovation Streams and Ambidextrous Organizational Designs: On Building Dynamic Capabilities," working paper, Harvard Business School, Boston, 2004, and Michael Tushman and Charles O'Reilly, "The Ambidextrous Organization," *Harvard Business Review* (April 2004): 74–81. Both designs call for two distinct organizational DNAs, and both call for interaction between units. The designs differ in that the ambidextrous design minimizes operational integration (interaction between CoreCo and NewCo functions) and emphasizes strategic integration—that is, heavy interaction between NewCo and CoreCo at the level of general management. Our design has the opposite emphasis. It minimizes interaction between general managers because they have many natural conflicts of interest and because such interaction can transfer only some of the many possible CoreCo resources to NewCo. It could transfer some knowledge, for example, but even here, a direct connection at an operational level is usually simpler and more efficient than using the hierarchy. For NewCo to borrow fully from CoreCo, significant but selective interaction at the operational level is required. We identify opportunities for creating such links and elaborate on the roles of the senior management team in facilitating borrowing while maintaining sufficient organizational separation between NewCo and CoreCo.

18. An alternative view is that CoreCo must shift modes of organizing in rhythm with changes in the industry. This may be an alternative in high-velocity environments having short product life cycles. Such industries were not represented in our sample. See Shona Brown and Kathleen M. Eisenhardt, *Competing on the Edge: Strategy as Structured Chaos* (Boston: Harvard Business School Press, 1998).

19. An emerging area of interest for strategy scholars is *dynamic capabilities*: internal processes that enable organizations to create new capabilities and new sources of

competitive advantage. One example of a dynamic capability is the ability to build breakthrough businesses by implementing an organizational DNA that enables NewCo to forget, borrow, and learn. See Kathleen M. Eisenhardt and Jeffrey A. Martin, "Dynamic Capabilities: What Are They?" *Strategic Management Journal* 21 (2000): 1105–1121, and David J. Teece, Gary Pisano, and Amy Shuen, "Dynamic Capabilities and Strategic Management," *Strategic Management Journal* 18 (1997): 509–533.

20. Because strategic experiments have links to much bigger businesses and because cost allocations are always ambiguous, it can be hard to judge financial success objectively. NewCo cannot easily be sold. There is no IPO that enables early investors to cash out and quantify a rate of return.

Chapter Two

1. Existing customers can become extraordinarily influential within organizations. See Clayton Christensen and Joseph L. Bower, "Customer Power, Strategic Investment, and the Failure of Leading Firms," *Strategic Management Journal* 17 (1996): 197–218. When NewCo's customers are dramatically different from CoreCo's, isolation from this influence is crucial.

2. See Kenneth A. Merchant, *Rewarding Results: Motivating Profit Center Managers* (Boston: Harvard Business School Press, 1989). See also Joseph A. Maciariello and Calvin J. Kirby, *Management Control Systems: Using Adaptive Systems to Attain Control* (New York: Pearson Education, 1994).

3. Research supports the notion that NewCo needs a distinct DNA. Researchers have extensively analyzed sources of organizational memory, or organizational inertia, and have identified at least five: cognitive filters, competency traps, local search, preservation of power, and absorptive capacity. For an explanation of how cognitive filters based in historical experience affect the way managers perceive new problems and develop solutions, see Mary Tripsas and Giovanni Gavetti, "Capabilities, Cognition and Inertia: Evidence from Digital Imaging," *Strategic Management Journal* 21 (2000): 1147–1161. The article demonstrates how Polaroid's responses to the rise of digital imaging technologies were limited by tightly held beliefs about why its business model was successful in the analog world—beliefs that proved false in the new digital environment. For a discussion of competency traps—in which favorable performance with an inferior procedure encourages an organization to accumulate more experience with it at the expense of investing in new and potentially superior approaches—see Barbara Levitt and James G. March, "Organizational Learning," *Annual Review of Sociology* 14 (1988): 319–340. For an explanation of local search, in which managers naturally seek solutions primarily in the neighborhood of existing solutions with which they are familiar, see Toby E. Stuart and Joel M. Podolny, "Local Search and the Evolution of Technological Capabilities," *Strategic Management Journal* 17 (1996): 21–38. For an explanation of how executives preserve their political power by ensuring that their organizations pursue activities that require their expertise and resist initiatives that do not, see Jeffrey Pfeffer, *Power in Organizations* (Marshfield, MA: Pitman, 1981). For an explanation of absorptive capacity—that is, how organizations may struggle to absorb new knowledge where they have no prior related knowledge—see Wesley M. Cohen and Daniel A. Levinthal, "Absorptive Capacity: A New Perspective on Learning and Innovation," *Administrative Science Quarterly* 35 (1990): 128–152.

Chapter Three

1. At Corning's request, these and other names in this chapter are fictitious.

2. Organizations are limited in their ability to bring about fundamental change. So great are these limits that ecologists have challenged whether organizations can learn and adapt at all. See Michael T. Hannan and John Freeman, "The Population Ecology of Organizations," *The American Journal of Sociology* (March 1977): 929–964. These limits underscore the need to enable NewCo to establish a separate DNA. Other theorists have emphasized the need for a separate or loosely coupled division for pursuing innovative business models. See Charles W. L. Hill and Frank T. Rothaermel, "The Performance of Incumbent Firms in the Face of Radical Techno-logical Innovation," *Academy of Management Review* 28 (2003): 257–274, and chapter 8 in Clayton Christensen, *The Innovator's Dilemma* (Boston: Harvard Business School Press, 1997).

3. Empirical studies are consistent with these recommendations. For example, see Vijay Govindarajan and Praveen Kopalle, "How Incumbents Can Introduce Rad-ical and Disruptive Innovations: Theoretical and Empirical Analyses," working paper, Tuck School of Business at Dartmouth, Hanover, NH, 2004. This study of 138 business units in 19 *Fortune* 500 corporations found that long-term subjective incen-tives, an adhocracy culture, and the creation of separate organizational units promote disruptive innovation. These recommendations are also analogous to the findings from a study of two approaches to product development, each with a distinct organi-zational DNA. The key variable that determined the superior approach was the level of uncertainty. See Kathleen M. Eisenhardt and Behnam N. Tabrizi, "Accelerating Adaptive Processes: Product Innovation in the Global Computer Industry," *Adminis-trative Science Quarterly* 40 (1995): 84–110. Although these studies argue that stand-alone divisions are needed for developing radical innovations, prior research has not examined how to achieve sufficient independence, particularly in the context of stra-tegic innovation.

4. It is not easy to build a new competence within an established firm. It requires many personnel changes, new promotion paths that reward excellence in unfamiliar disciplines, and a shift in culture that celebrates the new disciplines. See Dorothy Leonard-Barton, "Core Capabilities and Core Rigidities: A Paradox in Managing New Product Development," *Strategic Management Journal* (Special Issue, Summer 1992): 111–125. Furthermore, new knowledge often depends on combining new knowledge from outside the firm with the firm's related knowledge. See Wesley M. Cohen and Daniel A. Levinthal, "Absorptive Capacity: A New Perspective on Learn-ing and Innovation," *Administrative Science Quarterly* 35 (1990): 128–152. This may require staffing NewCo with both insiders and outsiders or linking NewCo to Core-Co, a topic covered here in chapters 4 and 5.

5. Research has identified the willingness to cannibalize existing products or assets as a critical determinant of an organization's propensity for innovation. See, for example, Rajesh K. Chandy and Gerard J. Tellis, "Organizing for Radical Product Innovation: The Overlooked Role of Willingness to Cannibalize," *Journal of Market-ing Research* (November 1998): 474–487. We observe that managers within CoreCo are typically less willing to cannibalize than are senior corporate executives.

6. This recommendation is consistent with researchers' observations about the special challenges of managing *architectural* innovations, defined as those that may have only incremental advances in any one component but dramatically change the

configuration of the components. Architectural innovation is difficult for organizations because relationships in the product development function mirror relationships of the components within the product. If you change those relationships, the organization falters. The problem is similar in strategic innovation except that the relationships of interest are those between functions instead of within the product development function. To overcome the challenges of architectural innovation, researchers have recommended the use of *heavyweight teams*: groups guided by strong product development leaders, working separately from the rest of the organization, who are able to form new relationships. Analogously, NewCo must be managed by a strong leader who is able to create distinct relationships between functions, with substantial separation from CoreCo. See Kim B. Clark and Steven C. Wheelwright, "Organizing and Leading 'Heavyweight' Development Teams," *California Management Review* (Spring 1992): 9–28; William J. Abernathy and Kim B. Clark, "Innovation: Mapping the Winds of Creative Destruction," *Research Policy* 14 (1985): 3–22; and Rebecca M. Henderson and Kim B. Clark, "Architectural Innovation: The Reconfiguration of Existing Product Technologies and the Failure of Established Firms," *Administrative Science Quarterly* 35 (1990): 9–30.

7. Simultaneously trying to improve the efficiency of existing processes while creating entirely new processes can produce costly tensions. See Pankaj Ghemawat and Joan E. Ricart i Costa, "The Organizational Tension Between Static and Dynamic Efficiency," *Strategic Management Journal* 14 (1993): 59–73. Creating a separate division with a different basis for assessing individual performance minimizes these tensions. For example, Johnson & Johnson rewards managers based on "efforts" rather than "results" because their businesses are volatile. See Robert Simons, *Levers of Control* (Boston: Harvard Business School Press, 1995), 117–119.

8. Continuous process improvement has delivered such significant performance improvements that it is viewed as almost universally good. However, the essence of continuous process improvement is the elimination of variance. Innovation often requires seeking variance. Thus, NewCo needs some separation from CoreCo as well as a distinct culture. See Mary Benner and Michael L. Tushman, "Exploitation, Exploration, and Process Management: The Productivity Dilemma Revisited," *Academy of Management Review* 28 (2003): 238–256.

Chapter Four

1. A growing stream of research in the strategy literature, the *resource-based view*, argues that the presence of unique resources, and not positioning, is the strongest determinant of competitive advantage. This research highlights the importance of the borrowing challenge, to the extent that experimental new businesses can leverage existing firm resources. See, for example, Margaret A. Peteraf, "The Cornerstones of Competitive Advantage: A Resource-Based View," *Strategic Management Journal* 14 (1993): 179–191. Researchers have also observed that the inability to connect new businesses to existing organizational resources is a key barrier to innovation. See Deborah Dougherty and Cynthia Hardy, "Sustained Product Innovation in Large, Mature Organizations: Overcoming Innovation-to-Organization Problems," *Academy of Management Journal* 39 (1996): 1120–1153. Researchers have also shown that innovation is often dependent on combinations of new and existing knowledge bases. See Wesley M. Cohen and Daniel A. Levinthal, "Absorptive Capacity: A New Per-

spective on Learning and Innovation," *Administrative Science Quarterly* 35 (1990): 128–152; Riitta Katila, "New Product Search Over Time: Past Ideas in Their Prime?" *Academy of Management Journal* 45 (2002): 995–1010; and Riitta Katila and Gautam Ahuja, "Something Old, Something New: A Longitudinal Study of Search Behavior and New Product Introduction," *Academy of Management Journal* 45 (2002): 1183–1194. In the face of nonlinear shifts, incumbent firms' greatest protection from start-up firms is the presence of complementary downstream assets. But if incumbents cannot themselves connect innovative projects to these assets, they cannot commercialize innovations any better than start-ups can. See, for example, Charles W. L. Hill and Frank T. Rothaermel, "The Performance of Incumbent Firms in the Face of Radical Technological Innovation," *Academy of Management Review* 28 (2003): 257–274; David J. Teece, "Profiting from Technological Innovation: Implications for Integration, Collaboration, Licensing, and Public Policy," *Research Policy* 15 (1986): 285–305; and Mary Tripsas, "Unraveling the Process of Creative Destruction: Complementary Assets and Incumbent Survival in the Typesetter Industry," *Strategic Management Journal* 18 (1997): 119–142. Although this branch of study supports the need for borrowing, researchers have not examined how to foster optimal borrowing in the context of strategic innovation.

2. The story of Boston.com, another property of The New York Times Company, is as interesting as that of NYTimes.com. Boston.com was positioned primarily as a portal for local information for the Boston metro area, one that also included access to content of the *Boston Globe*. See Thomas Eisenmann and Jon K. Rust, "Boston.com," Case 9-800-165 (Boston: Harvard Business School, revised August 30, 2000).

Chapter Five

1. See Marco Iansiti, F. Warren McFarlan, and George Westerman, "Leveraging the Incumbent's Advantage," *MIT Sloan Management Review* 44 (Summer 2003): 58–64, for additional discussion of why integration becomes more difficult.

2. Clayton Christensen and Erik A. Roth, "OnStar: Not Your Father's General Motors (A and B)," Case N9-602-081 (Boston: Harvard Business School, 2001).

3. See Charles A. O'Reilly and Michael Tushman, "The Ambidextrous Organization," *Harvard Business Review* (April 2004): 74–81.

4. Researchers report that strong socialization of new organizational members makes it difficult for them to forget. In enabling borrowing, the dynamic coordinator must ensure that outsiders hired to work in NewCo, particularly the general manager, do not become exposed to excessive forces of socialization. See George P. Huber, "Organizational Learning: The Contributing Processes and the Literatures," *Organization Science* 2, no. 1 (February 1991): 88–115.

5. Researchers have noted that shifts in the underlying configuration of power are necessary to achieve innovation, a notion consistent with our observation that the DC must shift power to NewCo. See Deborah Dougherty and Cynthia Hardy, "Sustained Product Innovation in Large, Mature Organizations: Overcoming Innovation-to-Organization Problems," *Academy of Management Journal* 39 (1996): 1120–1153.

6. From Anil K. Gupta and Vijay Govindarajan, "Knowledge Management's Social Dimension: The Case of Nucor Steel," *MIT Sloan Management Review* (Fall 2000): 71–88.

Chapter Six

1. See Adrian Wooldridge, "A Survey of Telecommunications," *Economist*, October 9, 1999, 1; and "Cellphone Ownership Soars," *USA Today*, August 2, 2002.

2. Intelligence is built through one of two processes: rational calculation and learning from experience. See James G. March and Johan P. Olson, "Organizational Learning and the Ambiguity of the Past," in *Ambiguity and Choice in Organizations*, eds. J. G. March and J. P. Olsen (Bergen, Norway: Universitetsforlaget, 1976). Rational calculation proceeds by collecting data, analyzing alternatives, and forecasting results. See, for example, Howard Raiffa, *Decision Analysis* (Reading, MA: Addison-Wesley, 1961). Much of the apparatus of knowledge management in corporations is geared toward rational calculation. When data is limited and the future unknowable, as is the case with strategic experiments, however, there are limits to rational calculation. Managers must guide strategic experiments through experimentation and learning.

3. The literature on organizational learning describes two types of learning from experience. *First-order learning* is learning to bring performance in line with (presumably feasible) targets. *Second-order learning*, the type of learning relevant to strategic experiments, is learning what targets are feasible; targets are as yet unproven. In other words, first-order learning is learning to achieve, and second-order learning is learning what is achievable. First-order learning has been studied fairly closely, but little empirical data has been collected on second-order learning.

Models for first-order learning have three components. First, organizations set a target level of performance. Second, performance perceptions are defined by a comparison between actual performance and the target. Third, organizations change their behavior when they perceive failure (performance below target). Over time, changes bring performance in line with aspirations. The defining characteristic of first-order learning is that the target level of performance is presumed to be feasible. First-order learning is desirable in mature businesses. New managers learn to achieve the (demonstrably feasible) standards set by their predecessors.

In second-order learning, targets are unproven. Through experience, a theory is developed that allows reasonable targets to be established. See, for example, Teresa K. Lant and Stephen J. Mezias, "An Organizational Learning Model of Convergence and Reorientation," *Organization Science* 3, no. 1 (February 1992): 47–71; Pertti H. Lounamaa and James G. March, "Adaptive Coordination of a Learning Team," *Organization Science* 33, no. 1 (January 1987): 107–123; Barbara Levitt and James G. March, "Organizational Learning," *Annual Review of Sociology* 14 (1988): 319–340; and Richard M. Cyert and James G. March, *A Behavioral Theory of the Firm* (Englewood Cliffs, NJ: Prentice Hall, 1963).

4. There is little empirical data on learning from experience while managing strategic experiments. See George P. Huber, "Organizational Learning: The Contributing Processes and the Literatures," *Organization Science* 2, no. 1 (February 1991): 88–115. The work that does exist demonstrates pitfalls and not success models. See, for example, Andrew H. Van de Ven and Douglas Polley, "Learning While Innovating," *Organization Science* 3, no. 1 (February 1992): 92–116. Most of the research on learning from experience has tested the basic learning model in simpler contexts using simulation studies, laboratory experiments, mathematical analyses, and retrospective analyses of organizational events where feedback is clear and rapid. These approaches do not reflect the learning context in strategic experiments.

5. The practice of the scientific method is not natural even for scientists. It takes discipline and structure for everyone, because humans are genetically predisposed to interpret the world through narrative and gossip. For more, see Edward O. Wilson, "Life Is a Narrative," Introduction to *The Best American Science and Nature Writing 2001*, eds. Edward O. Wilson and Burkhard Bilger (Boston: Houghton-Mifflin, 2001).

6. Unfortunately, these two areas seem to be the only ones in which experimentation is viewed as a valid process. When experiments are attempted elsewhere, they are not truly viewed as experiments. Consequently, leaders are willing to openly discuss and analyze only positive outcomes, a practice that severely hinders learning. See George P. Huber, "Organizational Learning: The Contributing Processes and the Literatures," *Organization Science* 2, no. 1 (February 1999): 88–115.

7. See Steven Spear and H. Kent Brown, "Decoding the DNA of the Toyota Production System," *Harvard Business Review* (September–October 1999): 97–106.

8. Organizational knowledge is described as action-outcome predictions about transforming inputs into outputs. Therefore, organizational learning is the revision of these action-outcome predictions. See Robert Duncan and Andrew Weiss, "Organizational Learning: Implications for Organizational Design," *Research in Organizational Behavior* 1 (1979): 75–123. The theory underlying the predictions must be debated and discussed. Simply adjusting predictions so that they are more closely in line with actual experience can lead to false conclusions. See, for example, Daniel Levinthal and James G. March, "A Model of Adaptive Organizational Search," *Journal of Economic Behavior and Organization* 2 (1981): 307–333.

9. The confluence of planning and the scientific method is not the norm. It is characteristic only of strategic experiments. Companies that excel at the scientific method within specific functions, or excel at product or process innovation, can still stumble when it comes to learning from a strategic experiment. They may have no experience in testing entire business models.

10. This notion is consistent with James G. March and Johan P. Olson, "Organizational Learning and the Ambiguity of the Past," in *Ambiguity and Choice in Organizations*, eds. James G. March and Johan P. Olson (Bergen, Norway: Universitetsforlaget, 1976). "The elaboration of the meaning of experience is a claim (of time or energy) on a limited capacity system," the authors write. "Learning will be affected by the characteristics of other demands on the system."

11. For some people, the notion of "scientific management" brings visions of the ancient time-and-motion studies popularized by Taylor early in the twentieth century. This approach to management treated employees as parts of a large machine and sought to optimize the machine. It fell into disrepute when it became clear that it could go only so far in perfecting manufacturing operations; human behavior is complex and captured only partially by time-and-motion studies. This recognition, however, hardly invalidates the scientific method, which still has broad applicability in business.

12. Of course, interpretations of disparities between predictions and outcomes could include elements of both; that is, the disparity is due in part to management failure and in part to unrealistic predictions. In practice, however, interpretations of one type or the other predominate.

13. Researchers have investigated the extent to which target levels slowly adapt to changing conditions, even in businesses that are reasonably mature. See Theresa K. Lant, "Aspiration Level Adaptation: An Empirical Exploration," *Management Science* 38, no. 5 (May 1992): 623–644. For example, target levels may slowly rise as an

organization gains experience, or slowly drop as competition intensifies. Targets adapt to actual results, a process that is different from what is needed in strategic experiments. Targets (that is, predictions) should not simply adapt to actual outcomes; they should change only as critical unknowns are resolved. When targets change, the changes may be dramatic, as opposed to the incremental adaptation that characterizes mature businesses.

14. In fact, researchers have shown that while senior executives recognize the need to allow greater decentralization and autonomous action to compete effectively in complex and changing environments, they also *increase* demands for accountability. The logic seems to be this: "I'll let you do your own thing, but you'd better deliver the results." See, for example, Robert M. Grant, "Strategic Planning in a Turbulent Environment: Evidence from the Oil Majors," *Strategic Management Journal* 24 (2003): 491–517. As uncertainty increases, however, this approach can backfire because it disables learning.

15. Psychological safety is a critical input to the learning process. When a sense of failure takes root, learning stops. See Amy Edmondson, "Psychological Safety and Learning Behavior in Work Teams," *Administrative Science Quarterly* 44 (1999): 350–383.

16. What we are proposing is analogous to behavior control, which is an alternative to output control. See William Ouchi, "A Conceptual Framework for the Design of Organizational Control Mechanisms," *Management Science* 25 (1979): 833–848.

17. Other researchers have drawn connections between accountability and learning. For example, see Rita G. McGrath, "Exploratory Learning, Innovative Capacity, and Managerial Oversight," *Academy of Management Journal* 44 (2001): 116–131, which highlights the importance of reduced oversight, greater autonomy, and less formal, revisable goals set by the innovating teams. This logic, however, can be taken too far if senior managers disengage entirely. In our view, it is crucial for the senior management team to remain involved—by lending its experience and knowledge to the learning process and not by enforcing accountability for results.

18. Even when the predictions themselves are not altered by the learning disabilities we describe, interpretations of predictions versus outcomes are still subject to self-interest. Because of the ambiguity associated with strategic experiments, multiple interpretations of predictions and outcomes are possible. Ambiguity spawns politics. Individuals prefer interpretations that support their interests, so competition between interpretations is shaped more by social interaction and power structure than by evidence. See Barbara Levitt and James G. March, "Organizational Learning," *Annual Review of Sociology* 14 (1988): 319–340. Even when there is little ambiguity, individual insight must be converted into organizational knowledge, and this process itself can be difficult, especially when the new knowledge overturns an established paradigm backed by influential executives. See Robert Duncan and Andrew Weiss, "Organizational Learning: Implications for Organizational Design," *Research in Organizational Behavior* 1 (1979): 75–123.

19. See, for example, Bo L. T. Hedberg, "How Organizations Learn and Unlearn," in *Handbook of Organizational Design*, eds. Paul C. Nystrom and William H. Starbuck (Oxford: Oxford University Press, 1981). Hedberg describes substantial research supporting the notion that in any context, organizations respond only to some available information and use specific filters and theories to interpret it. In strategic experiments, the relevant perceptual filter is planning templates, through whose lenses managers analyze and interpret performance feedback.

20. These observations about analytical pitfalls encountered when trying to interpret experience are drawn from several sources. See especially Daniel A. Levinthal and James G. March, "The Myopia of Learning," *Strategic Management Journal* 14, Special Issue: Organizations, Decision Making, and Strategy (Winter 1993): 95–112; also see James G. March, Lee S. Sproull, and Michal Tamuz, "Learning from Samples of One or Fewer," *Organization Science* 2, no. 1 (February 1991): 1–13, and Barbara Levitt and James G. March, "Organizational Learning," *Annual Review of Sociology* 14 (1988): 319–340.

21. Other researchers have stressed the importance of merely gaining an awareness of barriers to learning. See J. Edward Russo and Paul J. H. Schoemaker, *Winning Decisions* (New York: Doubleday, 2002), chapters 8 and 9, for an explanation of how these and other learning barriers can arise during any effort to learn from experience.

Chapter Seven

1. See G. Wayne Miller, *Toy Wars* (New York: Times Books, 1998), 22–23.

2. As if to underscore the unpredictability inherent in experimental businesses, Hasbro ultimately did have a significant and unexpected success in interactive games. Hasbro purchased Wizards of the Coast, a company that had created an extremely popular fantasy and role-playing game called Magic: The Gathering, which involved creating characters with certain attributes who then fought battles. (Wizards of the Coast was never part of Hasbro Interactive and was not sold with that company.) What was surprising was the online success of Magic: The Gathering. Fans of the game wanted to interact, and the Internet was the ideal way to do so. Still, it was not clear how this success could be translated to traditional Hasbro properties.

3. One of the difficulties of learning from strategic experiments is that the sample size is only one. Many explanations of performance are possible. Humans naturally have a bias for first creating stories that they feel are favorable and then selecting data that supports those stories. See, for example, James G. March, Lee S. Sproull, and Michal Tamuz, "Learning from Samples of One or Fewer," *Organization Science* 2, no. 1 (February 1991): 1–13. Leaders of strategic experiments therefore may focus only on data that tends to support the long-term vision of the business, particularly when current results do not look promising.

4. Organizational learning theorists have noted that mental maps (theories) of how businesses are supposed to work tend to be socially constructed, implicit, and rigid. See Bo L. T. Hedberg, "How Organizations Learn and Unlearn," in *Handbook of Organizational Design*, eds. Paul C. Nystrom and William H. Starbuck (Oxford: Oxford University Press, 1981). This is consistent with our observation that in the social context of business performance reviews, measures and standard benchmarks for CoreCo are often applied to NewCo—without recognition of the implicit assumptions underlying the CoreCo business model (assumptions that may not apply to NewCo). Further, CoreCo leaders have succeeded on the basis of a certain set of rules and expectations and naturally want to stick to them and impose them on others. See Daniel A. Levinthal and James G. March, "The Myopia of Learning," *Strategic Management Journal* 14, Special Issue: Organizations, Decision Making, and Strategy (Winter 1993): 95–112. The DC must be alert to this process and prevent it.

5. We also observed that leaders within CoreCo may try to judge the performance of a strategic experiment by comparing it with a previous experimental business that turned out well. If NewCo doesn't show the potential to be as big and as

profitable, it is deemed not worthwhile. For example, Corning Microarray Technologies (chapters 2 and 3) was compared to Corning's highly successful fiber-optics business.

6. The phenomenon of rigid predictions is widespread. People are reluctant to give up on an established prediction, even when experience indicates that it needs to be altered. Simulation-based studies that eliminate the impact of organizational politics show that even in relatively rich feedback environments, ideal for trial-and-error learning, commitments to existing predictions persist. See Theresa K. Lant and Amy E. Hurley, "A Contingency Model of Response to Performance Feedback," *Group & Organization Management* 24, no. 4 (December 1999): 421–437, which showed that the phenomenon of remaining committed to existing predictions weakens as outcomes diverge further from predictions. However, our research showed that in strategic experiments, commitments to original predictions can endure even when outcomes are nowhere near predictions and even as evidence of failure becomes unambiguous.

7. Several researchers have documented the phenomenon of escalation of commitment, particularly in contexts similar to strategic experiments, in which large investments are made but feedback is infrequent. Decision makers redouble their commitments, even in the face of negative feedback, to prove their initial investment decision correct. See, for example, Barry M. Staw, "The Escalation of Commitment to a Course of Action," *Academy of Management Review* 6 (1981): 577–587.

8. See, for another example, Clayton Christensen and Gregory C. Rogers, "Hewlett Packard: The Flight of the Kitty Hawk," Case 9-697-060 (Boston: Harvard Business School, 1997). The case study details HP's introduction of a revolutionary disk drive in the early 1990s. HP's cofounder appeared at the press conference announcing its launch. A great deal of press coverage followed, and HP's CEO talked constantly about the upcoming new drive. The general manager recalled the attention: "The great news was that we were in a project with a lot of visibility. That was also the bad news . . . If it crashed, there was going to be one hell of an explosion." High-level attention makes it difficult to reduce expectations.

9. However, a long-term revenue goal alone is not a sufficient vision for the future. The vision should also give the organization direction and focus, without specifying exactly the path to the future. See, for example, C. K. Prahalad and Gary Hamel, "Strategic Intent," *Harvard Business Review* (May–June 1989): 63–76.

Chapter Eight

1. In fact, the pattern of expanding from products to services is common. Many companies attempt it as their product businesses mature. See Chris Zook and James Allen, "Growth Outside the Core," *Harvard Business Review* (December 2003): 66–73.

2. Organizations must shift between periods of execution and periods of reevaluation. They cannot be constantly reevaluating, but in strategic experiments two years is far too long between reevaluations. Researchers have studied how strategies of reevaluating at specific intervals of time or only at critical events or junctures affect innovation. See, for example, Connie J. G. Gersick, "Pacing Strategic Change: The Case of a New Venture," *Academy of Management Journal* 37 (1994): 9–45.

3. For more thorough observations about how organizations actually learn from their own experiences, see James G. March, Lee S. Sproull, and Michal Tamuz, "Learning from Samples of One or Fewer," *Organization Science* 2, no. 1 (February

1991): 1–13, and Bo L. T. Hedberg, "How Organizations Learn and Unlearn," in *Handbook of Organizational Design*, eds. Paul C. Nystrom and William H. Starbuck (Oxford: Oxford University Press, 1981).

4. For a much more thorough analysis of the limitations and pitfalls of organizational learning, see Daniel A. Levinthal and James G. March, "The Myopia of Learning," *Strategic Management Journal* 14, Special Issue: Organizations, Decision Making, and Strategy (Winter 1993): 95–112.

5. See Rita G. McGrath and Ian C. MacMillan, "Discovery Driven Planning," *Harvard Business Review* (July–August 1995): 44–54.

6. In fact, this is the example used in McMillan and McGrath, ibid.

Chapter Nine

1. Researchers have identified many reasons that planning is important even for entrepreneurial ventures, and many of them are related to learning. Plans can clarify assumptions, ensure that they are internally consistent, identify information gaps, set motivating goals, establish a logical sequence of actions that is cognizant of bottlenecks and the critical path, and establish a framework for interpreting feedback. See Frederic Delmar and Scott Shane, "Does Business Planning Facilitate the Development of New Ventures?" *Strategic Management Journal* 24 (2003): 1165–1185. See also Peter J. Brews and Michelle R. Hunt, "Learning to Plan and Planning to Learn: Resolving the Planning School/Learning School Debate," *Strategic Management Journal* 20 (1999): 889–913. The authors note that formal, specific planning is valuable in all environments, but it must be more flexible in uncertain environments. TFP is our design for ensuring that plans remain flexible and support learning.

2. Researchers have identified other characteristics of planning systems that support innovation: such systems heavily scan the environment, they are flexible, they offer opportunities for many people to get involved, and they deemphasize financial targets. See Bruce R. Barringer and Allen C. Bluedorn, "The Relationship Between Corporate Entrepreneurship and Strategic Management," *Strategic Management Journal* 20 (1999): 421–444. The authors note that these characteristics generate greater entrepreneurial intensity. TFP has a different purpose: it is designed to ensure that after new businesses are created, they are able to learn and adapt as they proceed.

3. Real strategic experiments can take several years. Thus, proving TFP in a real-world context would have been impractical. Simulation allowed us to compress time and to focus strictly on the planning process.

4. The scenario was created in 2000, near the peak of the run-up in the NAS-DAQ. Although it seems exaggerated in retrospect, the key themes are still relevant. In fact, the impact of advances in wireless Internet technologies is still hotly debated at New York Times Digital, and the range of possible outcomes is still extremely wide.

5. In these figures, we show only one trend graph for each function. However, as shown in the prior example, it is possible to sketch trend graphs for the initial outcome as well as each subsequent outcome. Again, the objective is to explain, as fully as possible, trends through the time periods associated with cause and effect. This often requires more than one graph.

6. For a thorough description of the utility of a holistic performance measurement approach that emphasizes similar groups of measures, see Robert S. Kaplan and David P. Norton, *The Balanced Scorecard* (Boston: Harvard Business School Press,

1996). Although TFP tools are similar to those used in the balanced scorecard, TFP is designed for a different purpose. Balanced scorecards provide improved performance information for established companies that are implementing strategies in relatively predictable environments. TFP emphasizes *testing* strategies in dynamic and unpredictable environments. Thus, TFP emphasizes predictions, trends, and critical unknowns.

7. Many references guide the assessment of the value of first-mover advantage. See, for example, William Boulding and Markus Christen, "First-Mover Disadvantage," *Harvard Business Review* (October 2001): 20–21; Marvin B. Lieberman and David B. Montgomery, "First Mover (Dis)advantages: Retrospective and Link with the Resource-Based View," *Strategic Management Journal* 19, no. 12 (December 1998): 1111–1125; and Richard Makadok, "Can First-Mover and Early-Mover Advantages Be Sustained in an Industry with Low Barriers to Entry/Imitation?" *Strategic Management Journal* 19, no. 7 (July 1, 1998): 683–686.

8. We have emphasized throughout the need to learn as quickly as possible. However, learning quickly does not mean jumping to conclusions. Strategic experiments are especially subject to noise—false signals of performance. Conclusions must sometimes be labeled tentative for some time before the evidence is sufficient to justify a change in direction. Researchers have demonstrated through mathematical modeling that learning that is "too fast" can be counterproductive. See, for example, Daniel Levinthal and James G. March, "A Model of Adaptive Organizational Search," *Journal of Economic Behavior and Organization* 2 (1981): 307–333, and Pertti H. Lounamaa and James G. March, "Adaptive Coordination of a Learning Team," *Management Science* 33, no. 1 (January 1987): 107–123.

9. We compare theory-focused planning to conventional planning in Vijay Govindarajan and Chris Trimble, "Strategic Innovation and the Science of Learning," *MIT Sloan Management Review* 45, no. 2 (Winter 2004): 67–75.

Chapter Ten

1. Ray Stata, interview with author Chris Trimble, August 14, 2002.

2. Today, almost all automobiles use MEMS devices to actuate air bags. The most sophisticated air bag systems take advantage of recent MEMS advances that allow for sensing rotational accelerations and linear accelerations in multiple dimensions. This enables deployment of air bags during rollovers and differentiated control of side air bags.

3. Ray Stata, interview with author Chris Trimble, August 14, 2002.

4. Ibid.

5. Jerry Fishman, interview with author Chris Trimble, August 15, 2002.

6. The intriguing list of possibilities included applications in video games, appliances, security devices, and even new interface mechanisms within personal digital assistants and cellular telephones that were based on the motion of the entire device.

7. Jerry Fishman, interview with author Chris Trimble, August 15, 2002.

8. Ira Moskowitz, interview with author Chris Trimble, August 14, 2002.

9. The semiconductor industry is highly cyclical. ADI's profitability in 1998 was low, but managers could reasonably guess that it would rebound the following year. MEMS would not take such a large bite out of earnings for a sustained period.

10. Although it is hard to put a dollar value on a capability such as MEMS, researchers have encouraged the inclusion of the value of new competencies as a mea-

sure of the performance of innovative activities, offsetting even failed ventur Erwin Danneels, "The Dynamics of Product Innovation and Firm Competere *Strategic Management Journal* 23 (2002): 1095–1121. Further, researchers have sl that strategic decisions made with a "real options" perspective improve innova capacity. MEMS knowledge gave ADI a unique real option on several future mark See Charles W. L. Hill and Frank T. Rothaermel, "The Performance of Incumbe Firms in the Face of Radical Technological Innovation," *Academy of Management Re view* 28 (2003): 257–274. Another perspective on the value of ADI's competence in MEMS is that it increased its absorptive capacity in this area. In other words, it was one of the few firms prepared to recognize new opportunities in this field. See Wesley M. Cohen and Daniel A. Levinthal, "Absorptive Capacity: A New Perspective on Learning and Innovation," *Administrative Science Quarterly* 35 (1990): 128–152, and Mary Tripsas, "Surviving Radical Technological Change through Dynamic Capability: Evidence from the Typesetter Industry," *Industrial and Corporate Change* 6 (1997): 341–377.

11. Jerry Fishman, interview with author Chris Trimble, August 15, 2002.

Index

About the Authors

Vijay Govindarajan and Chris Trimble are on the faculty at the Tuck School of Business at Dartmouth College. In 2000, they cofounded the William F. Achtmeyer Center for Global Leadership at Tuck (www.tuck.dartmouth.edu/cgl). Since then, they have focused on conducting the research that culminated in this book. Drawing on the research, the authors publish a monthly column on *Fast Company*'s Web site (www.fastcompany.com).

Vijay (known as "VG") is the Earl C. Daum 1924 Professor of International Business (www.vg-tuck.com). His area of expertise is strategy, particularly strategic innovation, industry transformation, and global strategy and organization. He has been recognized by *BusinessWeek*, *Forbes*, *Wall Street Journal Online*, and *Across the Board* as a top thought leader in the field of strategy.

VG's scholarly awards are numerous. He was ranked by *Management International Review* as one of the "Top 20 North American Superstars" for research in strategy and organization, and one of his papers was recognized as "one of the ten most-often cited articles" in the forty-year history of the prestigious *Academy of Management Journal*. His publication credits also include articles in *Strategic Management Journal*, *Academy of Management Journal*, *Academy of Management Review*, *Harvard Business Review*, *MIT Sloan Management Review*, and *California Management Review*. He has published six books, including *The Quest for Global Dominance* (San Francisco: Jossey-Bass, 2001).

Chief executive officers and top management teams often call on VG to discuss, challenge, and escalate their thinking about strategy. He regularly keynotes conferences, CEO forums, and leadership development programs. Representative clients include Boeing, British Telecom, Chubb, Colgate-Palmolive, Corning, Hewlett-Packard, IBM, International Paper, J.P. Morgan Chase & Co., Johnson & Johnson, The New York Times Company, PricewaterhouseCoopers, Sony, and UBS.

VG received his doctorate and his MBA (with distinction) from the Harvard Business School and his Chartered Accountancy degree in India, where he was awarded the President's Gold Medal for obtaining the first rank nationwide.

Chris (www.chris-trimble.com), in addition to his faculty position at Tuck, is a senior fellow at Katzenbach Partners LLC (www.katzenbach.com). Chris has worked with several corporations in executive education or as a consultant, including Boston Scientific, British Telecom, Colgate-Palmolive, Corning, Dreyer's Grand Ice Cream, Eaton, Ford, General Electric, Hitachi, John Deere, Johnson & Johnson, Motorola, The New York Times Company, Pitney Bowes, Staples, Sealy, and Xerox. Chris has been a discussion leader at the center's CEO leadership summits and has spoken at several conferences, including the *BusinessWeek* CEO Forum.

Publication credits include articles in *Harvard Business Review*, *MIT Sloan Management Review*, *California Management Review*, *Across the Board*, *Fast Company*, and *The Financial Times*. Chris holds an MBA degree (with distinction) from the Tuck School, and a bachelor of science degree (with highest distinction) in mechanical engineering from the University of Virginia.